Effective Communication

Communication

FIFTH EDITION

NICHOLAS HARVEY

BORU
PRESS

Boru Press Ltd.
The Farmyard
Birdhill
Co. Tipperary
www.borupress.ie

© 2022 Nicholas Harvey

ISBN 978-1-7396232-0-3

Print origination in Ireland by Carole Lynch
Illustrations in Ireland by Derry Dillon
Index by Eileen O'Neill
Printed by GraphyCems Ltd, Spain

All rights reserved. None of this publication may be copied, reproduced or transmitted in any form or by any means without written permission of the publishers or else under the terms of any licence permitting limited copying issued by the Irish Copyright Licensing Agency.

A catalogue record is available for this book from the British Library.

For permission to reproduce photographs and artworks, the author and publisher gratefully acknowledge the following:
© Alamy: 11, 25, 112, 113, 120, 121, 125, 126, 135. © Cartoonstock: 6, 9, 70, 104, 151, 185, 187, 235, 271. © IHREC: 23. © Isaac Cordal: 139. © iStock: 47, 62, 63, 77, 92, 100, 102, 106, 115, 120, 125, 134, 146, 237, 246, 268. © Shutterstock: 3, 17, 18, 20, 21, 22, 28, 36, 38, 39, 47, 48, 56, 74, 75, 76, 79, 95, 96, 116, 119, 120, 124, 125, 126, 130, 131, 138, 153, 181, 182, 183, 187, 219, 220, 227, 237, 239, 241, 242, 243, 244, 249, 250, 251, 253, 257, 258, 269, 274. © Wiseman, Richard: 115.

'Digging' by Seamus Heaney, from 100 Poems by Seamus Heaney, published by Faber and Faber Ltd, 2018

Contents

- Acknowledgements — iv
- Preface — v

Part 1: Introduction — 1
1. Introduction to Communication — 2
2. Perception and Culture — 17

Part 2: Listening and Speaking — 33
3. Listening Skills — 34
4. Speaking Skills — 46
5. The Interview — 61
6. Groups and Meetings — 73
7. Presentation Skills — 92

Part 3: Nonverbal and Visual Communication — 109
8. Nonverbal Communication — 110
9. Visual Communication — 133

Part 4: Reading and Writing — 149
10. Reading Skills — 150
11. Writing Skills — 162
12. Personal Writing — 180
13. Workplace Documents — 195
14. The Report — 214

Part 5: Communication Technology — 233
15. Communication Technology — 234
16. The Telephone — 253
17. Email — 261
18. Legislation — 267

- Appendices — 276
- Bibliography — 280
- Answers — 283

Acknowledgements

I would like to thank the following:

Jennifer Alford, Frances Gaynor, Anne Geraghty, Patrick Harvey, Niina Hepojoki, George Jacob and Thomas Riedmuller for their proofreading, useful tips and suggestions.

Staff and students at Kinsale College of Further Education and Sallynoggin College of Further Education for their support and encouragement.

Maria Raha for kind permission to reproduce her story 'Angel'.

Marion O'Brien and Anna Carroll at Boru Press for their support and assistance.

Preface

This new edition of *Effective Communication* has been thoroughly revised and updated to suit the needs of students in today's fast-changing world. It includes new developments in communication technology and legislation, as well as new sections in each chapter to take into account issues such as GDPR and COVID-19.

Some chapters and sections are specifically suited to QQI assessment requirements, and others offer support, information, preparation for assessments and/or material for class discussion. Points for discussion and activities are included in each chapter to help put some of the most essential skills into practice. This is to encourage active participation by students and provides opportunities for expressing views and for developing speaking skills.

Further education attracts such a wide range of students of differing ages and abilities that teachers and class groups can decide for themselves how to proceed with discussions and activities in a way they feel is appropriate to their individual requirements, e.g. division into smaller groups, pair work, etc.

The book need not be read or studied in the order in which it is presented. It is possible to select and dip into chapters that are of particular interest or relevance.

Communication is not something at which we can become experts in a year or two. It is a skill that can be refined over a lifetime, and at the end we still won't have mastered it all. This book serves as an introduction to the main topics and themes of communication. Oscar Wilde said, 'Nothing that is worth knowing can be taught.' Communication skills are best learned by doing, by practising and by experiencing. So, take the ideas in this book and try them out by putting them into practice yourself.

The personal pronouns 'he', 'she', 'they', 'him', 'her' and 'them' are used interchangeably throughout the book.

Part 1
Introduction

In brief:
- Introduction to Communication
- Perception and Culture

Chapter 1
Introduction to Communication

In this chapter, you will learn:
- To Communicate Is Human
- What Is Communication?
- Why Do We Communicate?
- How Do We Communicate?
- The Media of Communication
- Media Appropriateness
- A Guide to Effective Communication

Words transform both speaker and hearer; they feed energy back and forth and amplify it. They feed understanding or emotion back and forth and amplify it.

Ursula K. Le Guin

To Communicate Is Human

Communication is one of the things that makes us uniquely human. Between one and two million years ago, when early humans had separated from other primates, and walked upright on the grasslands of the African Savannah, they were more vulnerable to attack by large predators than their closest relatives, the chimpanzees and bonobos, who still lived in the relative safety of forests. They learned that survival depended on close co-operation, and that successful hunting also required working as a group. According to some anthropologists, this resulted in the evolution of our earliest form of language, nonverbal communication, using gestures and facial expressions to communicate how best to work as a team to kill or escape from a large animal. Gradually over the millennia, more complex verbal communication was added to this unique skill.

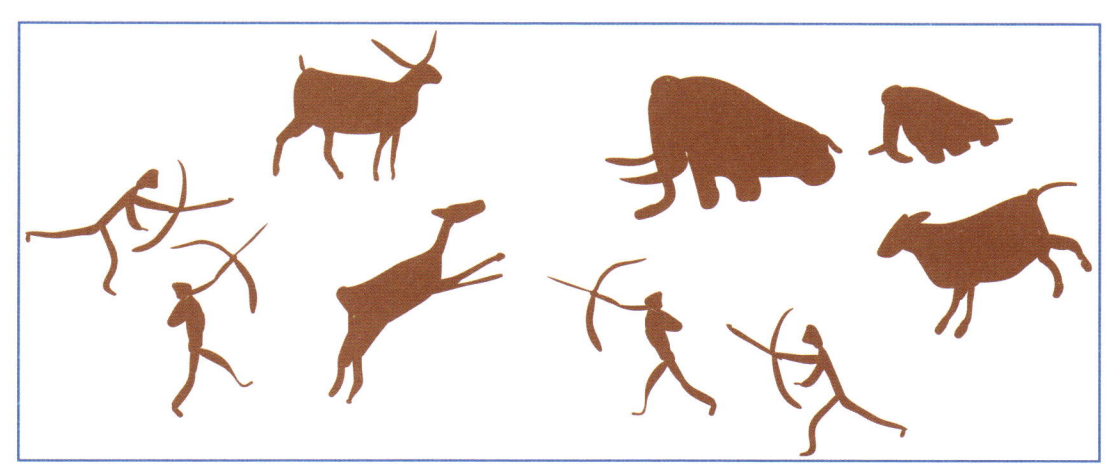

Fig. 1.1

We are physically better equipped to communicate than most other species. We have a large brain, which can process and produce complicated language, and a tongue, jaw and throat, which are shaped to produce a wider variety of sounds than other animals. We also have the urge to make contact with others. We are a social species, and we love to network. It is possible that these skills helped early *Homo Sapiens* survive while other human species, such as Neanderthals, became extinct. This ability allowed us to convey complicated messages such as 'Over that hill, down by the river, beneath a tree lives an animal that you can eat'. Compare that sentence with this one: 'Over that hill, down by the river, beneath a tree lives an animal that can eat you.' One small change in word order could have meant the difference between living and dying.

Our ancestors could communicate important and detailed information that helped them survive and thrive, while the ill-equipped Neanderthals, who kept to themselves in small, isolated groups, died out. Put simply, we were better social networkers. Fast forward to the twenty-first century and we find ourselves being bombarded by huge amounts of information coming at us from all over the world via a vast array of technologies.

The communications revolution has created an entirely new range of communication tools and techniques: the internet, email, social networking, mobile phones, texting, digital television, etc. These are all changing the ways we communicate with one another and in turn we need to learn new skills to master them.

Fig. 1.2

Just as communication helped our species survive in the past, it can still help us survive today's fast-paced technology-driven world. Information is key to this survival. In order to have access to the latest information, be it about jobs, health, education, business, shopping, entertainment or socialising, we need to have good communication skills. However, for all the marvels of technology that enable us to speak instantly to someone thousands of miles away, we are often still at a loss as to how to express ourselves. When it comes down to saying what we really want to say, we often find ourselves in a mess of muddled words and jumbled sentences. Words we use amongst our close friends won't necessarily impress a potential employer. We can't use words like 'cool' or 'crap' in an interview or a formal letter of complaint because we won't be taken seriously. The abbreviated language we use in emails and text messages is fine for informal situations, but we can't use emojis in a letter of application!

We can use the technologies available to us, but we also need the skills to know what to say, how to say it and when it is appropriate to say it. The more ways we can communicate, the better equipped we are to deal with the modern world.

Fig. 1.3

Communication and language are uniquely human traits. In a sense, learning how to communicate is about becoming more human. Some people have a natural flair for it and others don't. But no matter how good or bad we think we are as communicators, all communication skills can be learned and improved.

◗ What Is Communication?

The word 'communication' comes from the Latin word *communicare*, which means 'to share, impart or make common'. How well we communicate is often determined by how easily we can share or impart information or find common ground with other people.

Discussion

What other words in English derive from the Latin *communicare*? Make a list and discuss the various meanings of each word. These might give us a fuller understanding of the meaning of the word 'communication'.

> *'Communication'…is based on the Latin* commun *and the suffix 'ie' which is similar to 'fie,' in that it means 'to make or to do.' So one meaning of 'to communicate' is 'to make something common' i.e. to convey information or knowledge from one person to another in as accurate a way as possible.*
> (David Bohm, *On Dialogue*)

Communication is an active process that is forever changing. Language doesn't stay the same, it evolves. We don't use the same English today that Shakespeare did. Almost every time we speak, we somehow put together a collection of words that we have never used before. When two people are put together, eventually they are going to start communicating with each other, and neither has any idea where they will end up. A frightening thought, perhaps, but an exciting one as well.

We can define communication as an exchange of messages between two people or two groups of people.

▶ Why Do We Communicate?

In their book *More than Words*, Richard Dimbleby and Graeme Burton list 12 needs and purposes of communication.

Survival

We need to communicate to buy food and clothing; to rent or buy accommodation; to seek help from others if we are sick or in danger, all of which are necessary for survival.

Co-operation

We communicate for the purpose of trade; to exchange ideas and information; for the enjoyment of interaction or just to get on with other people.

Personal Needs

As humans we have a basic need for contact with others. Exchanging thoughts and feelings can help satisfy our personal needs.

Relationships

Relationships are formed and sustained by communication. Problems that occur within relationships are often a result of a lack of communication. One of the best ways to sort out problems is by talking about them.

Persuasion

In our everyday communication with others we may use persuasion more than we think. Whether we are trying to convince potential employers that we are the best person for the job, persuading a college teacher to give us a deadline extension or trying to borrow money, we are using persuasion to get what we want.

"It's like you haven't heard a single thing I've thought."

Fig. 1.4

Power

We communicate for power by winning arguments and by impressing others with our knowledge and skill as communicators. More negatively, we can misuse it by making others feel inferior by putting them down.

Societal Needs

Communication within and between all the different organisations in our society is crucial for it to function properly. Government departments, schools, colleges, hospitals and businesses would collapse without proper communication facilities to help run them.

Economy

Buying and selling cannot take place without some form of communication between the buyer and the seller. Advertising also plays a role in this process.

Information

Information is fundamental to human existence. It may be something as simple as reading a sell-by date on a food item or being told the time. Gossip is information, although it may not always be accurate! We send emails, texts and letters to let friends and relatives know how we are and what we're doing. The media inform us about people and events in the world and advertising informs us about products. What we learn at school and college – education – is all information.

Making Sense of the World

Children are naturally inquisitive. They often ask questions beginning with 'Why' in order to make sense of the world around them. As adults, we also ask similar questions when we need to understand something and to give events and situations meaning.

Decision-making

When a couple talk about what to do on a date, they are making a decision. When a company holds a board meeting to discuss the potential of a new product, it is making decisions.

Self-expression

When we are involved in the creative process, we communicate by tapping into the imagination and expressing ourselves in an artistic way:
- Visual – painting, drawing, sculpture, etc.
- Writing – poetry, stories, etc.
- Music
- Dance
- Body adornment – make-up, jewellery, etc.
- Drama

Activity

Which of the 12 needs and purposes are being used in the following messages?

1. You only got a merit in Communications? I got a distinction.
2. Of course she should have left him years ago. That's what I always said.
3. Here, I've made you a nice cup of tea. Sit down there and relax.
4. She won't be left behind. She's got the latest model.
5. You have the most beautiful eyes I've ever seen.
6. Please may I have a drink of water?
7. This is the third time you've been late for work this week.
8. How do you feel now?
9. 'Teachers to go on strike!'
10. Don't count your chickens before they hatch.
11. I will send you the goods as requested.

12. 'Strawberry Fields forever.'
13. No, let's not go to the cinema; let's just have a drink.
14. Someone left the milk out of the fridge again.
15. The telephone is ringing.
16. We'll make you an offer you can't refuse.
17. Can you spare some money for a sandwich?

Discussion

In groups of four or five, make a list of the specific communication skills you think you might need for your chosen vocation.

Now make a list of the communication skills you would like to improve for your own personal needs.

▶ How Do We Communicate?

Every time some form of communication occurs, there is a specific process that takes place. We can break this process down into its different parts so that we can see what exactly is happening and identify any problems that can occur. By doing this we can try to eliminate these problems and become better communicators. (Keywords are in italics in the following.)

> A *sender* (a person or persons) sends a *message* (information, thought, feeling, etc.) to a *receiver* (another person or persons).

The message is encoded, *code* being the language used by the sender. It may refer to the actual language that we speak, e.g. English, Irish, etc. or it can refer to verbal, e.g. spoken and written language, or nonverbal, e.g. body language, facial expression, signals, etc. It can also mean tone of voice.

The *message* is transmitted by a *medium*, e.g. face to face, telephone, email, letter, etc. and travels along a *channel*, e.g. telephone line, postal system, etc.

The *receiver* receives the message and decodes it, i.e. makes sense of it. Some messages are literal. Others can contain implied meanings that may be misinterpreted. In this case the receiver may also have to *interpret* the message for other meanings. For example, 'Do you want to come back to my place for coffee?' literally means an offer of coffee. What is its implied meaning?

The receiver gives *feedback* by sending another message back to the sender to reply or to acknowledge receipt of the first message. Feedback is vital in communication. Without it the sender has no idea if the message has been received, never mind if it has been met with agreement or not. Feedback can be either positive (supporting or agreeing with the message) or negative (criticising or disagreeing with the message).

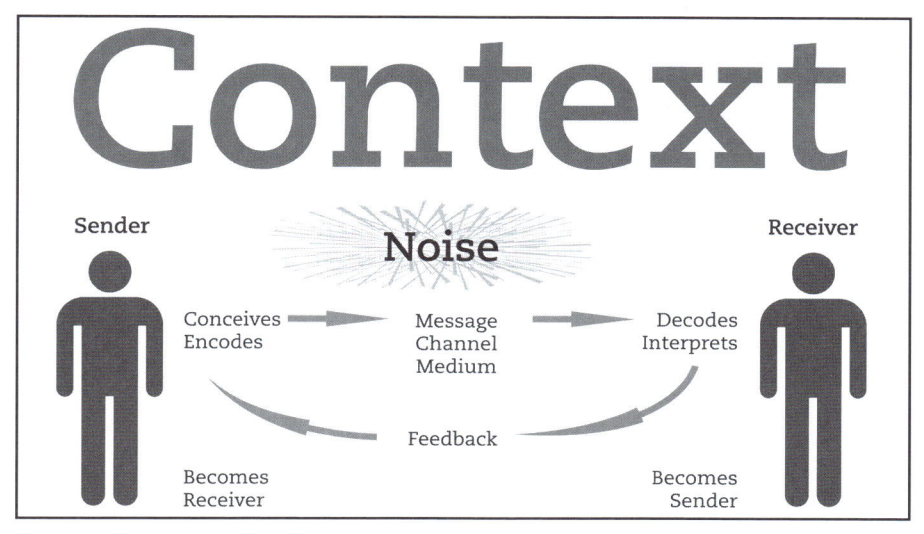

Fig. 1.5 The communication process

Once feedback has been given, the process may continue with another message from sender to receiver, and so on, and the roles may swap so that the receiver becomes the sender and the sender becomes the receiver.

Noise is any kind of interference that interrupts or prevents the successful transmission of the message. It can be:

- *Physical* – e.g. roadworks outside a building interrupting a conversation
- *Emotional* – e.g. mistrust between the sender and receiver interfering with the message
- *Psychological* – e.g. a receiver who is tired finding it difficult to take in a lengthy, complicated message
- *Technological* – e.g. fear of computers preventing some people using them to communicate

Fig. 1.6

The *context* is the situation in which the communication takes place. It usually refers to the time and place but may also include the people involved. The context can influence the way we communicate. Communication in a work context is likely to be more formal than it would be in a nightclub.

Now we have looked at the process of communication, try to think of some of the pitfalls that could occur at each stage of the process. For example, at the encoding stage a sender might use an inappropriate level of vocabulary, which the receiver might not understand.

Activities

1. One-way Communication

A volunteer from the group will be the sender of a message and the rest will be the receivers. The sender stands at the back of the room, chooses one of the shapes in Appendix 1 (p. 276), and tries to describe it using words only. The receivers, who are not allowed to speak, will try to draw the shape from the sender's description. The sender should not see what the receivers are drawing.

2. Two-way Communication

Do the same activity as above, except this time the sender stands at the front of the room, facing the receivers, who may speak and ask questions.

The purpose of this activity is to illustrate that in order for communication to be effective, it has to be a two-way process. In the first part (one-way), there was incomplete communicating going on as no feedback was permitted. The two-way communication probably took longer, but the message will have been more accurately transmitted. Discuss any problems and difficulties experienced by both senders and receivers during this activity. A sender often makes the mistake of assuming the receiver knows more than he actually does. Communicators sometimes fail to realise that a sent and a received message are not always the same. This is one common cause of communication breakdown.

The Media of Communication

We can put all types of communication into five media groups:
1. Written
2. Spoken
3. Visual
4. Technological
5. Mass media

Discussion

Divide into groups of four or five. Using flipchart sheets and markers, each group discusses one of the mediums of communication, makes a list of four or five examples of that medium, then makes a list of its pros and cons. Finally, each group presents their results to the class group.

▶ Media Appropriateness

Some of the worst mistakes in communication are made as a result of using an inappropriate medium. There is no point in a company informing all its shareholders about a new business venture by telephone. It would be too time-consuming. A famous TV and film star once finished his relationship with his girlfriend by sending her a text. Is this an appropriate medium for this type of communication?

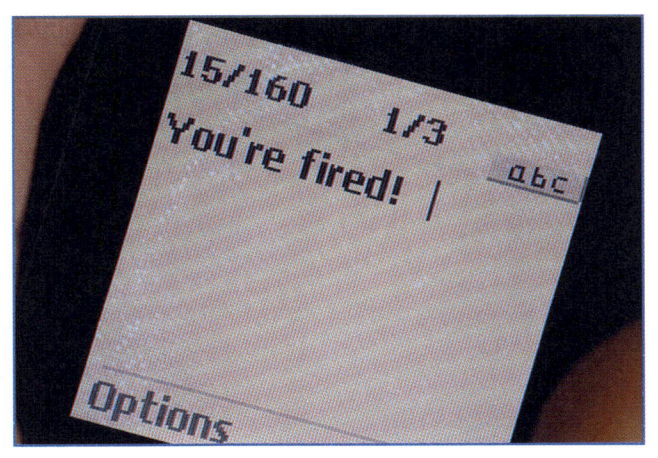

Fig. 1.7

Activity

What medium of communication would you choose for the following and why?

1. Applying for a job
2. Firing someone from a job
3. Complaining about a holiday to a travel agent
4. Offering sympathy to the family (living abroad) of a friend who has died
5. Explaining a personal problem to your boss
6. Requesting information about different types of bank account
7. Asking customers to switch off mobile phones as they enter a theatre

8. Advertising a new leisure complex in a hotel
9. Asking for a bank loan
10. Informing a colleague that you resent his/her offensive behaviour
11. Telling the board of directors of a company about your new marketing strategy
12. Informing your class teacher that you are sick on the day of an assignment deadline
13. Advertising a concert you've organised in your local community hall
14. Letting colleagues (10 or more) know about a meeting to be held the following week
15. Sending a list of costs and rates of the hotel where you work to a potential customer arriving in Ireland from Italy in two days
16. Asking someone out to dinner
17. Seeking a quote for paper and ink for your printers
18. Giving your students important information about an assignment – explanation, number of words required, deadline, etc.
19. Complaining to a neighbour about persistent noise late at night
20. Supplying a quote for work as an electrician
21. Letting students in college know about the Christmas Social
22. Resigning from your job
23. Informing a client that their payment for goods received is overdue
24. Finding information on the latest cinema releases
25. Complaining to your boss about the extra hours that you've been asked to do
26. Finding out the latest football results
27. Relaying a detailed phone message to your employer

▶ A Guide to Effective Communication

Here are some tips for improving communication skills in general.

As Sender

Conceive the Message Carefully
- Decide what your communication objectives are. Do you want to inform, entertain, impress, persuade or get information? Aim for clarity and avoid vagueness, ambiguity and unnecessary jargon.

Have Empathy
- This means understanding where the receiver is coming from, her beliefs, feelings, values and interests. Put yourself in the receiver's shoes. She may not see things the way you do.

Choose an Appropriate Code and Medium
- Choose a code that the receiver understands and a tone that is appropriate. We wouldn't use the same tone talking to our employer as we would to a child. For the medium, see the activity above.

Consider the Context (Time and Place)
- An attempt to communicate with someone who is too busy to listen to us will inevitably fail. Reprimanding someone for a misdemeanour should take place somewhere private and not in a public place in front of others.

Check for Feedback
- As a sender, it is vital to know that the message has been received and understood. Ask if it's OK.

As Receiver

Pay Attention
- Many messages are lost due to poor listening or lack of concentration.

Decode Correctly
- Make sure you understand the message and if not, seek clarification. Be aware of implied meanings in messages.
- Ask yourself these questions:
  — Does this make sense?
  — Does this person have an agenda?
  — What do I think of this person?

Give Feedback
- Always let the sender know you've received and understood the message. A simple nod or 'Yes' is often enough to show the sender you've got the message.

Activity

Think of two examples of communication you took part in during the past week. In each case write down the following:

1. The purpose of each communication
2. If you were the sender or receiver
3. If the message was well conceived
4. The choice of code, medium and channel
5. The context in which each took place
6. The feedback given
7. Whether there was any noise
8. Whether each communication was successful
9. Whether there was room for improvement

Discussion

In groups of four or five, answer the following questions.

1. When do we not communicate?
2. Are we better or worse communicators than our parents?
3. One of the biggest communication problems is that we don't communicate enough. Discuss how a lack of communication might be harmful to the following:
   - Personal relationships/marriages
   - Between employers and employees
   - Amongst employees
   - In the home
   - Between a food company and the public
   - Between staff and students at school/college
   - Between the Government and the public
   - Between a doctor and patient
4. Is there ever a danger of too much communication?

Chapter Review

1. What makes communication a uniquely human experience?
2. What are the chief purposes of communication?
3. Outline the main stages in the communication process.
4. Explain the importance of feedback.
5. Why is it important to choose the appropriate medium for communication?
6. Explain the following:
   - Code
   - Channel
   - Noise
   - Context

Chapter 2
Perception and Culture

> **In this chapter, you will learn about:**
> - Perception
> - Stereotyping
> - Prejudice
> - Culture
> - Social Communities
> - Xenophobia
> - Ethnocentrism
> - Race and Ethnicity
> - Sectarianism
> - Gender
> - Sexism
> - Improving Intercultural Communication

▶ Perception

Before children can speak or even understand words, they begin to make sense of the world around them by means of perception. They perceive the world through the fives senses of sight, hearing, smell, taste and touch. As adults, we continue to make sense of the world by perception. We can say that perception is the way in which we select, organise and interpret information about the world around us.

Perception and Culture 17

Activity

Look at Fig 2.1. Describe what you see. Do you see a young woman or an old woman? There are two possible ways of seeing the picture. The chin of the young woman becomes the nose of an old woman.

Fig. 2.1

Sensory Variation

The problem with perception is, first, that our senses are not 100 per cent reliable. Railway tracks appear to get narrower as they get further away; a straight stick appears to bend in water; an ambulance siren changes tone as it moves past us. Second, we all perceive things slightly differently from one another. Some people have better sight than others; a ferociously hot curry to one person may be mild to another; deafening music may be too quiet to another. This is called sensory variation.

Fig. 2.2

Discussion

Our perception influences how we communicate. If we perceive things differently from others, we may run into communication problems. Discuss how you think this might occur.

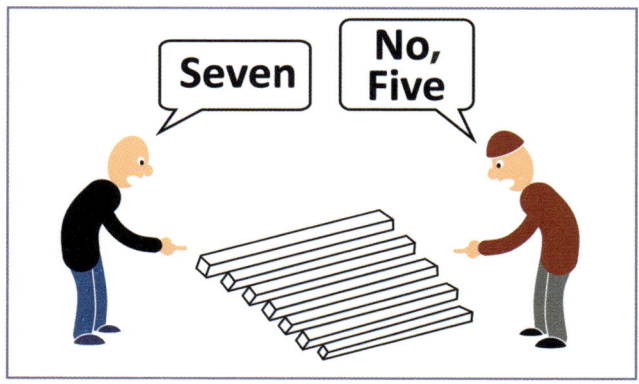

Fig. 2.3

Selection

We don't perceive everything that is going on around us, otherwise we would be bombarded by unnecessary information. So we only select what we need at a particular moment and the rest we filter out. Think of things you notice on the way to college or work. Now consider the amount of information you don't notice. What do you perceive where you are sitting right now? Why do we select some things and fail to notice others?

Once we've perceived and selected something, we organise it to make sense of it, matching it with what we already know, understand or believe. This depends on our experience of life. If, as a child, we had the experience of being bitten by a dog, the next time we see a dog we might perceive it as being a threat. If, however, our experience of dogs is that they are friendly animals, whenever we see one we will probably perceive it in a more positive way. Since we all have different experiences, we won't always agree on what something *means*, and this can naturally lead to communication difficulties.

Fig. 2.4

Discussion

Take two or three advertisements or photographs from a magazine or newspaper and discuss what they mean to you.

Activity

It is possible to train the senses to become more effective. Visually impaired people may develop better hearing, smell and sense of touch than people who can see. Certain occupations need well-trained senses. Can you think of a few?

People Perception

The most important type of perception for a course in Communications is people perception.

Discussion

We perceive people initially through their appearance: size, shape, hair, clothes, skin, etc. What is the problem with this?

When we meet people initially, we perceive them based on their appearance and the role they are playing, and we match it to our own expectations and experience. We begin to weigh them up and make assumptions about them. We categorise them and put them in a 'box' based on our perception. Categorising is a useful tool, as it enables us to label things and make sense of the world. Unfortunately, people are far more complex than things and we cannot use such a simple system of classification for perceiving them. The worst kind of categorising is stereotyping.

▶ Stereotyping

As a simple and convenient way of trying to understand the world, stereotyping can be useful. We stereotype objects, situations and people based on how we think they will live up to our expectations of them. Sometimes our expectations are accurate and sometimes they aren't. Stereotypes are generalisations, sometimes based on facts that are generally true about a group. They can also be based upon assumptions instead of facts.

Activity

Make a list of common stereotypes. They may be based on physical appearance, occupation, gender, age, nationality/ethnicity or religious beliefs. In groups of three or four, make a list of characteristics of one stereotype group. Which characteristics are based on fact, and which are based on perception? Which are stereotypes? Share your results with the class group.

Iceberg Analogy

People perception is problematic because it is based on only a fraction of the whole person. Just as we can only see approximately 10 per cent of an iceberg, so when we initially perceive someone, we only see 10 per cent of them.

Fig. 2.5

▶ Prejudice

Prejudice is our attitude towards a group or individual without having adequate knowledge of them and stemming from a stereotype, preconceived opinion or inaccurate perception (misperception). As the old saying goes, we can't judge a book by its cover.

Perception and communication are very much intertwined. On the one hand, perception influences how we communicate. For example, if we perceive someone as being authoritative and we admire them, we'll probably communicate with them in a respectful way. If we perceive someone as being stupid or worthless, we will probably communicate with them less than respectfully! On the other hand, communication influences our perception of others. The way someone talks, their accent, their articulation, their pitch and tone of voice can often shape our opinion and our perception of them.

Reflection

Next time you meet someone, pay attention to the way you perceive him. Do you perceive him as a potential friend or not, based on his appearance? Do you focus purely on his appearance or do you try to get to know the other 90 per cent? If you don't like his appearance, will this prevent you from trying to get to know him? Do you stereotype based on appearance/accent?

Discussion

1. Describe an occasion when your initial perceptions of someone were totally wrong. Explain why.
2. What are your first impressions of the people in Figs 2.6 a–h?

Fig. 2.6a

Fig. 2.6b

Fig. 2.6c

Fig. 2.6d

Fig. 2.6e

Fig. 2.6f

Fig. 2.6g

Fig. 2.6h

Culture

Culture is the set of beliefs, values, understandings, practices and ways of making sense of the world that are shared by a group of people. Culture is not static or fixed. It is constantly changing and evolving, losing old practices and customs and adopting new ones. The culture in which we are brought up determines our thinking, our behaviour, our perceptions and how we communicate.

Discussion

1. Make a list of Irish cultural characteristics. How many of them are stereotypes? What other Irish stereotypes are there? How do non-Irish members of the class perceive Irish cultural values and norms? In what ways do you think Irish culture has changed over the past 20 years?
2. Individually, write down three ways you think you fit your cultural stereotype and three ways you don't. Discuss as a class group.

When we speak about Irish culture we often think of Celtic influences, because the Irish language is a Celtic language. However, Irish culture is a mixture of pre-Celtic, Celtic, Viking, Norman, English, Scottish and American cultural influences. Today, many people from all over Europe, Africa and Asia have come to live in Ireland, adding to the already interesting mixture.

Ireland is a multicultural society, and this cultural diversity is a source of richness for society. In such a culturally diverse world, we come into contact with people with hugely different experiences and backgrounds from our own in terms of their ethnic group, religious beliefs, skin colour, sexual orientation, etc. To avoid misunderstandings, we need to be aware of the differences in how they communicate.

Discussion

In what ways do people from different cultural backgrounds communicate differently?

Fig. 2.7

How we communicate with each other defines the culture to which we belong and in turn, our culture determines how we communicate. The language and expressions we use every day reveal our cultural origins. For example, 'I'm after eating my tea' is English but is also a direct translation of an Irish idiom and would not be found in other English-speaking countries. This is sometimes called Hiberno-English.

Discussion

1. What other expressions and words are peculiar to Ireland? Would a visitor from another culture find it easy to understand these expressions even if she spoke English?
2. Proverbs, sayings and clichés illustrate how communication can define culture. Think of some Irish proverbs, sayings or clichés that underpin aspects of Irish culture. What do they say about the values and beliefs of Irish culture? For example, 'May you be in heaven half an hour before the devil knows you're dead' shows the traditional Irish belief in heaven and the devil and perhaps the value of trickery. Non-Irish students in the class group could share their own proverbs.

▶ Social Communities

A minority culture can also exist within a larger dominant culture. Such groups of people are called social communities. Social communities may be defined by countries of origin, for example the Polish community in Ireland, but also by their different ways of communicating and behaving.

Discussion

Make a list of social communities that exist in Ireland today. They may be based on:
- Ethnicity
- Religious beliefs
- Skin colour
- Sexual orientation
- Social class
- Age
- Special needs
- Gender

Consider your own identity. Write down a list of the social communities you belong to based on the above criteria.

Have you ever experienced prejudice because of your particular culture or social community? Discuss your experience with your class group.

In recent years a number of movements such as Black Lives Matter and #MeToo have started to protest against not just discrimination but harassment and violence against social communities. The former emerged following the shooting of a young black man in Florida in 2012 and grew in the wake of more killings of black people and is a racial justice movement. #MeToo arose when actor Alyssa Milano went on Twitter and asked anyone who had experienced sexual harassment or assault to reply 'me too' to her tweet.

Fig. 2.8

What is the purpose of the advertisement in Fig. 2.8? Do you think it works? Why?

Activity

Our language is full of words and phrases that can be hurtful and offensive to minority social communities. If it feels appropriate and if students feel comfortable discussing it, think of examples of such words that could cause offence to the following groups of people:

- Travellers
- LGBTQ community
- Black and Asian people
- Elderly people
- Jews
- Muslims
- Protestants
- Catholics

Consider the origins and meanings of these words, why they are offensive and why they should not be used.

Fig. 2.9 Chain Prejudice cartoon

Xenophobia

Xenophobia is the fear and dislike of strangers. In primitive times this fear might have been useful because it lessened the likelihood of being captured or killed by rival tribes. In most modern societies xenophobia is unacceptable and, in some forms, such as incitement to violence or hatred against a group of people, it is prohibited by law.

Ethnocentrism

Ethnocentrism is the application of one's own culture or ethnicity as the frame of reference to judge other cultures, practices, behaviors, beliefs, and people, instead of using the standards of the particular culture involved.

Race and Ethnicity

The term 'race' has now become discredited as a word used to describe groups of people based on physical, biological or ideological differences. The acceptance of the term 'race' has been used to justify racism, in which one group believes it is superior to others and tries to dominate, suppress or even destroy them. The word 'ethnicity' has replaced 'race', so we talk about an ethnic group as being one that has a common identity based on a shared culture, history, ancestry and geographical origin.

Fig. 2.10 *Two politicians from either side of the political and religious divide overcame their differences when forced to share power in the Northern Ireland Assembly. The Rev. Ian Paisley and Martin McGuinness were frequently seen laughing heartily together during their public appearances, which earned them the nickname 'The Chuckle Brothers'.*

Sectarianism

Sectarianism is prejudice against people who belong to a different sect or religious denomination. In Ireland this has particular resonance, because intolerance has for many years been displayed between some individuals belonging to the Roman Catholic Church and some from the Protestant Church. To many observers, it is ironic because both belong to the same Christian religion.

Sectarianism occurs in many parts of the world where groups with different religious beliefs live next to each other.

We can reduce ethnocentrism, racism and sectarianism by understanding that cultures vary in their beliefs, values and behaviour, and no one culture is the normal or right one. For example, we might find it strange that Jewish people don't eat pork or that Hindus don't eat beef. But the French might find it odd that we don't eat horse meat. Some might find it peculiar that there are people who don't eat any meat at all.

▶ Gender

The words 'gender' and 'sex' are often used interchangeably, but whereas sex relates to biological differences, gender refers to the different social characteristics that may include a range of identities in the broad spectrum from feminine to masculine. Most cultures have traditionally had a gender binary – a division into two distinct genders, masculine and feminine. Some cultures have recognised a third gender, such as the Hijra in South Asia, while some North American indigenous cultures have names for a third gendered person. Today gender has become more fluid with some choosing to be identified as non-binary, in other words not fitting into the traditional masculine or feminine groupings, having a variety of sexual orientations and in some cases completely rejecting gender identities.

▶ Sexism

Sexism is discrimination of a person on the ground of her/his sex.

> ### Discussion
> Discuss examples of communication that you consider to be discriminatory based on any of the above terms.

Socialisation

Socialisation is the process by which we learn to fit into our society and culture and the rules and expectations that govern each of those. We learn through relationships and experience how to behave appropriately in a variety of situations and communication is a vital part of that process.

Studies have shown that in Western society boys and girls are socialised differently in the games they play. Girls tend to play games that involve co-operation and talk such as house and school. Boys usually are more competitive and action-orientated and play at war and team sports.

These rules of play often continue later in life and women tend to communicate more expressively, talk about feelings and relationships and tend to see talking as vital in making and sustaining relationships. Men are usually more competitive in their communication, focusing on tasks and activities, preferring to do things with their friends and partners.

It must be stressed that the following differences between feminine and masculine communication traits don't apply solely to women and men respectively. Most people have a mixture from each list, and this is perfectly normal and sometimes preferable. Some men might display more feminine ways of communication than women and some women may communicate more masculine traits than men. It is important here not to fall into the trap of stereotyping.

Feminine communication **in general:**
- Includes and shows interest in others
- Is co-operative
- Observes turn-taking in speech
- Is responsive to what others say
- Uses talk expressively – talk deals with feelings, personal ideas and problems, and is used to build relationships with others
- Seeks approval in an attempt to be liked by others
- Is better in private conversations and dialogue
- Asks questions to make connections, to lessen the potential for disagreement and to seek information that shows respect for another's knowledge

Masculine communication **in general:**
- Is self-assertive and competitive
- Uses talk to establish identity, expertise and knowledge, to prove oneself, to seek status and maintain independence
- Uses talk to gain and hold attention, to take the talk stage from others, interrupt and reroute topics to keep the focus on themselves and their ideas
- Uses talk instrumentally – talk accomplishes something such as solving a problem, giving advice or taking a stand on issues
- Involves stories and jokes in an attempt to be the funniest, cleverest, etc.
- Is better in public situations and monologue
- Doesn't like to ask questions as it shows a lack of self-sufficiency and independence and a loss of face
- Asks questions as a way of arguing

(Adapted from Julia Wood, *Communication in Our Lives*, p. 91)

In positions of leadership, women tend to downplay their authority by seeking feedback, asking questions and expressing more doubt than men. They are unlikely to draw attention to their achievements or to their trappings of success as much as men. Compared with men, they will praise others more, apologise and accept blame more. As leaders, men generally downplay their faults and weaknesses, and see how another's position of power might affect their power.

Both feminine and masculine ways of communicating are equally valid, and neither is right or wrong. By being aware of these differences, and by practising some of the styles of communication of the opposite gender, we can avoid many misunderstandings.

We often experience pressure to conform to standards of masculinity and femininity, so that men are sometimes afraid of appearing effeminate and women of being 'macho'. However, the most effective communicators are equally comfortable using both ways of communicating.

Discussion

Discuss the statements in Figs 2.11a and 2.11b. How do they affect gender stereotypes? What effect can they have on people and society? How would you feel if they were spoken to you?

Fig. 2.11a

Fig. 2.11b

Reflection

Observe yourself in social and vocational situations and how you interact with different groups of people. Do you exhibit predominantly masculine or feminine ways of communicating?

▶ Improving Intercultural Communication

The majority of us spend most of the time with people from our own culture and social community. We can communicate easily in these groups because we have shared understandings about appropriate language and behaviour. When we encounter people from other social and cultural groups, we don't have the same guidelines. Researchers have come up with a process that consists of five levels of response to cultural diversity. It can help develop an awareness of other cultures and minimise misunderstandings. It can take time to go from one stage to the next and some people will take to it more quickly and easily than others. Ultimately, it should reduce our ethnocentrism and improve our intercultural communication skills.

1. Resistance

This occurs when we regard other cultures' practices as being inferior to our own. Level one is recognising our own ethnocentrism. We might believe our culture is the best, but that is merely an opinion, not a fact.

2. Tolerance

This is when we accept and tolerate the differences of other groups, even though we might not understand or approve of them. We may still assume our ways are the standard and that others are somehow inferior. Level two is avoiding criticism of other cultures.

3. Understanding

At this stage we attempt to understand the values and beliefs of other cultures because we realise that there are various reasons why some social communities have different practices from our own.

4. Respect

At this level we begin to see others for what they are and appreciate their differences. If we show respect for people from other cultures, they will do the same to us.

5. Participation

The final level in this process is when we actively participate in some activity of another culture. We become 'multilingual' in that we can communicate with a variety of social communities without losing our own identity. Many immigrants in Ireland are already bilingual in that they can speak their own language but in order to fit into the dominant culture they have learned English. At this stage we can focus on individual people, not cultures. Each culture is made up of individuals who all think and behave differently from one another. They won't all conform to stereotypes!

Reflection

Consider at which level you operate and try to progress to the next level.

By remaining stuck in our own culture's way of living we not only miss out on the richness of life, but we also maintain a very narrow way of communicating. At some point we are going to meet people very different from ourselves and we need to be able to communicate with them comfortably and effectively.

Due to the power that language can have, some say it can be misused to legitimise dominant cultures and to label other cultures as inferior. Political correctness refers to language and behaviour that avoids causing offence to social communities and disadvantaged people. Members of a group have a right to be called by a collective name with which they are comfortable. For example, in Ireland 'Travellers' has replaced 'itinerants' and 'tinkers'. Whereas many of these terms succeed and are appropriate, many are over the top and even bizarre. Many people find `male nurse' and `lady doctor' unnecessary and even offensive.

Discussion

What groups do you think the following terms apply to?
- African American
- Visually impaired
- Follicly challenged
- Outdoor urban dweller
- Socially misaligned
- Senior citizen
- Native American
- Vocally challenged
- Utensil sanitiser
- Non-human companions

Can you explain the reason for the above words? Which do you find appropriate, and which are over the top? What about the use of 'person' instead of 'man' as a suffix, e.g. chairperson, postperson, fireperson? Think of other examples and discuss whether you find them appropriate or unnecessary.

Chapter Review

1. Explain how misperception can lead to communication problems.
2. Explain the role of sensory variation in the process of perception.
3. What does selection mean?
4. What is the significance of stereotyping in relation to perception?
5. What is culture? How does it affect the way we perceive and communicate?
6. Explain the concept of socialisation.
7. What is a social community?
8. What are the main differences between the way men and women communicate?
9. Explain the following:
    - Cultural diversity
    - Xenophobia
    - Ethnocentrism
    - Racism
10. Outline the five stages for reducing ethnocentrism and improving intercultural skills.

Part 2
Listening and Speaking

Some Examples
- Conversations
- Discussions
- Debates
- Interviews
- Meetings
- Classes
- Presentations
- Speeches
- Announcements

Advantages
- Direct
- Personal
- Expression of tone and feeling
- Easier to convince/persuade
- Good for negotiations
- Inexpensive

Disadvantages
- No written record
- Possibility of dispute
- Difficult to control
- Preparation required

Chapter 3
Listening Skills

In this chapter, you will learn about:
- Listening and Hearing
- Types of Listening
- Barriers to Listening
- Selective Listening
- Active Listening
- Paraphrasing
- Interrupting
- Note-Taking
- Control of Response

Most people do not listen with the intent to understand; they listen with the intent to reply.

Stephen R. Covey

We should not underestimate the importance of listening as a communication skill. Most people listen to about 25 per cent capacity. In other words, they lose or misinterpret 75 per cent of the information they receive. Poor listening can result in anything from the loss of business or falling out with a friend or partner to industrial or international disputes.

Fig. 3.1

All this is in spite of the fact that listening is the first communication skill we practise as infants.

Activity

Listening Self-assessment

Look at the following statements and tick the box that applies to you.

	Statement	Usually	Sometimes	Seldom
1	I keep eye contact with the speaker when I am listening.			
2	When I am listening, I just listen to the facts.			
3	I am easily distracted by other stimuli (e.g. mobile phone) when I am listening.			
4	I interrupt the speaker.			
5	When I am listening, I think about what I am going to say next.			
6	I ask questions for clarification.			
7	I stop listening when put off by the speaker's voice, accent or appearance.			
8	I listen to part of the speaker's story and then interrupt with my own.			
9	I listen out for the feelings behind the words.			
10	I daydream easily when I am listening.			
11	I just pretend I am listening.			
12	I only listen to what interests me.			
13	I listen to the full message before giving my response.			

Discuss as a class group which of the statements are positive and which are negative listening habits.

Listening and Hearing

Listening is a skill of perception that helps us make sense of the world. Like perception, we select what we want to listen to.

Activity

From where you are sitting now, close your eyes and concentrate for a few moments on all of the sounds you can hear. Make a mental note of them. How many of them were you actually aware of before you started concentrating on them? Probably very few. How many of them could you make sense of? All of them? This illustrates the difference between listening and hearing. We can hear many things going on around us, but it is only when we make sense of them and understand them that we are listening to them. It isn't practical to listen to everything we can hear. It would also be exhausting. But listening is an active skill, which requires a certain amount of concentration, whereas hearing is passive. Effective listening isn't always easy, but it is a skill that can be learned.

Types of Listening

Informational Listening

This involves listening for information, for facts, times, names, places, etc. It is the most common type of listening that we do most of the time.

Critical Listening

Critical listening entails making judgements, evaluations and forming opinions of a speaker's ideas. A teacher evaluates a student's oral presentation by listening critically for signs of careful preparation, structure, accurate information and good expression.

Fig. 3.2

Relational Listening

Relational listening refers to the empathising we do when, for example, we are listening to a friend discuss his problems or worries. Relational listening often involves trying to understand another's feelings and interpreting signs that are hidden behind the information we hear.

Listening for Pleasure

Listening for pleasure is what we do when we listen to music, go to a concert, poetry reading or comedy show. This normally doesn't need too much concentration unless we want to focus on specifics like a lyric or a drum beat in a song.

Listening to Discriminate

This is what a mechanic does when fine-tuning an engine, detecting the subtle difference in sounds, or when parents decide if a child's crying is due to hunger, discomfort, a need for attention or a nappy change.

Listening to Interpret

This means we can make sense of the words we hear and really understand what the speaker is saying. Interpreting also means we can summarise the message and rephrase it in another way.

> ### Activity
>
> This is a good activity for breaking the ice when a class has first met. Students stand in a circle and the first one says his/her name and answers one of these questions:
>
> - What was your favourite subject at school?
> - Where would you like to go on your next holiday?
> - What are your goals for the future?
>
> He/she then throws a soft ball to another student who says his/her name and answers one of the three questions. Continue until everyone has introduced themselves and answered a question. Sit down again and try to write the names of all your classmates and the information they provided. How easy/difficult was it to focus/listen/remember names and information?

▶ Barriers to Listening

To try to improve our listening techniques, we must first isolate the problems that prevent us from listening. Here are some of the most common ones:

- Poor physical or mental state, e.g. if we are hungry, cold, tired or anxious
- Lack of interest in the speaker or subject
- Prejudice about the speaker's appearance, accent or command of the language
- Prejudice about the subject, e.g. 'I disagree with her views so why should I bother paying attention?'

- Noise and distractions from the surrounding environment
- Internal distractions such as daydreaming and thinking of things from the recent past or immediate future, e.g. 'She shouldn't have said that to me at break' or 'I'm going to have pasta for lunch'
- Inability to understand what the speaker is saying
- The speaker's speed, e.g. too slow and we may get bored; too fast and we may not be able to follow what is being said
- The message is too complex or unclear
- Attention span. With increasing use of the internet and smartphones our attention spans are decreasing. While the average person can comfortably concentrate for up to 20 minutes, the average time spent on a website is less than one minute. There are also particular times of the day when we may find it harder or easier to concentrate – some people are morning people, while others are more alert at night.
- Impatience

Fig. 3.3

Activities

1. Look at the list below. Imagine you have to listen to each of the people on the list and try to honestly assess your listening ability using a scale of 0 (very poor) to 10 (excellent) in each case:
   - Your boss giving you instructions
   - Someone you're trying to impress telling you about herself
   - A teacher you like (in class)
   - A teacher you don't like (in class)
   - A reprimanding parent
   - A child telling you about his day at school
   - A friend telling you about a personal problem
   - A tourist asking for directions
   - A very funny comedian
   - Someone you are arguing with

- Someone complimenting you
- Someone explaining the current political/economic situation to you
- Someone giving you directions

Discuss the results. Why did you give greater scores to some than others?

2. **'Talking Stick'**
   Brainstorm a few conversation topics on the board/flipchart. Sit in circles of seven to ten people. Place an item such as a stick in the centre of the circle. Participants can only speak when holding the stick and the rest must remain silent and listen. While holding the stick, the student must talk on one of the conversation topics for one minute and then place the stick back in the centre of the circle. The next student may respond on the same topic or start a new one. Continue until everyone has spoken.
   - What was it like to listen to the others without interrupting?
   - What was it like to speak and be listened to?
   - Was it easy to tune in or did you occasionally tune out?
   - How much information do you remember?

Selective Listening

We tend to pick and choose to whom and to what we want to listen. For the most part, we give our attention to people and subjects that we are interested in. Or we focus on individuals and things that can benefit us, and the rest we frequently ignore. However when we're listening to important messages that need to be passed on to someone else, we have to select the important information and omit the rest.

Active Listening

By giving the speaker feedback verbally, e.g. 'Yes', 'OK' or nonverbally, e.g. eye contact, 'Mmm', 'Uh-huh', we are not only helping ourselves to focus and listen better, but we are also encouraging the speaker to speak better. This is active listening.

Fig. 3.4

> ## Activity
>
> Divide the class into pairs of A and B.
>
> A tells B what he did last weekend and B listens actively. Next A tells B what he will do next weekend and B gives no verbal or nonverbal feedback. Then swap roles and do the same. Compare the different situations. Was it easier to speak to someone who is paying you attention? How does it feel to talk to someone who appears not to be listening? Did you struggle to keep talking? How does it feel to ignore someone who is speaking to you?
>
> Finally, A tells B what she did last summer and both A and B make constant eye contact. Discuss how it feels.
>
> In normal interaction who makes more eye contact, the speaker or the listener?

Paraphrasing

By repeating phrases back to the speaker we are showing them not only that they have been listened to but also understood. Their feelings have been acknowledged. We do not have to agree with what they say, leaving us with the option of saying either yes or no to a request. This type of listening gives us the possibility of further communication and helps avoid conflict because it makes a distinction between acknowledgement and agreement.

> **Sample paraphrase openings:**
> - 'So what you're saying is...'
> - 'Am I right in assuming that you think/feel...'
> - 'In other words...'

In each of these examples we are acknowledging what has been said, even though we might not agree with it. Such statements from the listener must be kept to a minimum. We should avoid taking over the conversation, but at the same time we want to keep it going. We also need to find the correct tone, using our own style, so that we do not sound insincere. Paraphrasing not only encourages the speaker but also helps the listener focus on the message, and whole communication is improved.

> **Asking questions is another way of actively listening:**
> - 'Do you mean to say...?'
> - 'Can you elaborate on that...?'
> - 'Would you like to explain that idea further...?'

Other simple phrases we can use are:
- 'I hear you.'
- 'I understand what you're saying…'
- 'I see your point.'

In a conflict situation we could use phrases such as:
- 'I understand what you're saying. The way I see it is this…'

Interrupting

Interrupting a speaker is often considered bad manners and can cause conflict. It can indicate that we have not been listening, are not interested or believe what we have to say is more important. However, there are occasions when interrupting is just about the cut and thrust of conversation. During political debates on television or radio, we hear members of a panel say, 'If I can be allowed to finish…' We should always let someone finish her point before making our own contribution.

If someone is dominating a conversation or going on too long, we can gently interrupt by using phrases such as:
- 'Sorry for interrupting but…'
- 'I hate to interrupt but…'

Activities

Divide the class into pairs of A and B.

1. A gives B detailed directions on how to get from his house to college/work, including how to get to bus stops, stations, etc. and B listens without interrupting (unless for clarification), then repeats back what she has heard. Then swap roles and repeat the activity.

2. A tells B how the first few weeks/months of term have been for her, including any challenges. B listens without interrupting (unless for clarification) and paraphrases back to A. Avoid giving advice or offering solutions as this can show you're not really listening. Swap roles and repeat the activity.

Note-taking

When we are faced with an hour-long talk or lecture on a new subject, hearing shouldn't be a problem, but understanding may be a challenge and retaining information will be extremely difficult unless we take notes. Our memories are not capable of holding all the information given during the course of an hour, so a written record, to which we can refer later on, will help jog our memory.

Here are some suggestions:
- Always head the page with the date and subject.
- Never try to copy entire sentences.
- Listen for a few minutes and then summarise what has been said.
- Shorten everything – words by using abbreviations, sentences into keywords, phrases and headings.
- Leave out examples, anecdotes and irrelevant information.
- Stick to the facts.

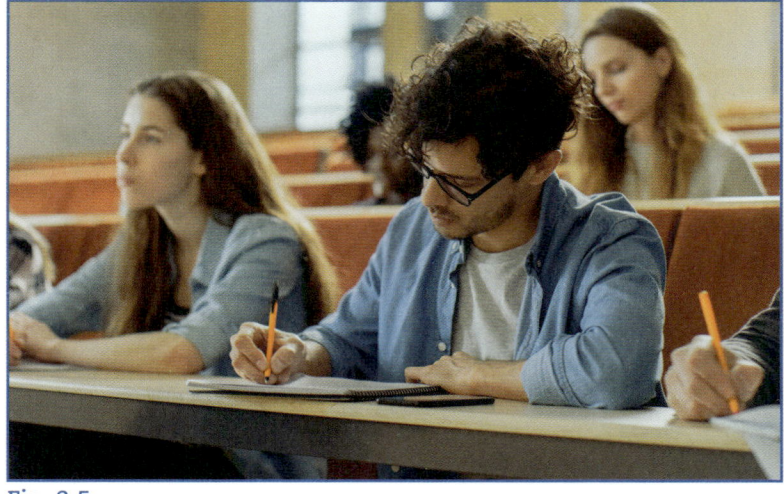

Fig. 3.5

These will be rough notes and they need to be read and rewritten later in the same day. If they are left too late the memory wears thin and they will make less sense than on the day they were taken. Note-taking challenges us to use both our listening and writing skills. As we listen, we distil the information and jot down what immediately seems important and relevant.

Activities

1. In pairs, take it in turns to read each other a detailed message (see samples below). In each case the listener should listen carefully to all the relevant information, and then relay the message back to the speaker to check for accuracy.

    As an alternative, try a game of Chinese Whispers. If possible, sit in a circle and relay a message around each member of the class, one at a time, quietly, so that no one else can hear. At the end, the last person to hear the message should relay it to the class group, to compare it with the original message, and to see how much detail was lost in transmission.

Sample Messages
A. Ms Williams, a company manager at Drumlinn Clothing Ltd, is returning from a trip to England on the 7.50 flight from Heathrow, which is due to arrive in Dublin airport at 8.45 am. She was due to give a report to staff at a meeting on the company's end of year progress, scheduled for 11 am. However, the flight has been delayed and will not arrive now until 10.30 am. It will take at least two hours for her to get to the Drumlinn Clothing office, so the meeting has been rescheduled for 1 pm. She wants Sheila to pick her up at the airport.

B. Class starts at 10 o'clock each morning. You have a break for 10 minutes at 11.15, and lunch is from 12.30 till 1.30. The secretary is in her office all day except during her lunch hour, which is from 1 to 2 pm. The principal is available from 10 till 11 am each day and the student council meet on Tuesdays at 9 am in the performance space. The computer room is open for students' use from 4 till 5 pm and the caretaker is around all day every day.

C. There was an interesting group doing the course in 2020. There were 12 students altogether: eight came straight from school, Angela and Dermot both had already completed degrees and Margaret and Alex had spent most of their adult lives working. There was also a good multicultural mix with Christian and Helena from Germany and Dan from the USA. The age profile was also diverse, ranging from the eldest, Frank (52), to the youngest, Elaine (19).

2. Look up and watch one or more of the following videos and afterwards see how many key points you can remember. Do you understand the content of the video(s)? Do you agree with it?
    - '5 Ways to Listen Better' – Julian Treasure, TED Talk
    - 'Being a Good Listener' – The School of Life/Alain de Botton (personal relationships)
    - 'The Power of Listening' – William Ury, TEDx San Diego (business/negotiation/conflict resolution)

Control of Response

There is a difference between responding and reacting to information. Sometimes when we hear someone say something we don't like or disagree with we can react too quickly without thinking it through. This can lead to conflict. Responding, on the other hand, is when we take some time to consider the message we have received and think carefully about how we will reply. Having a controlled response often leads to a better outcome than reacting.

Activities

1. Each student should write down two or three controversial statements. In pairs, take turns to read them to each other and see if you react or respond. Here are some examples:
   - Women should stay at home and do the housework.
   - Most men are potential rapists.
   - The Irish are a nation of poets and drunks.
   - COVID-19 was a hoax perpetrated by the pharmaceutical industry to make profits.
   - Climate change is going to wipe out all humans in 100 years.
   - Your work is awful. A monkey could do a better job.
   - Donald Trump was a fine president.
   - You're always late for class (or work). You must be really disorganised or just lazy.

2. In pairs, write a message related to your own vocational area and read it to other members of the class group for listening, retaining and relaying information. For example, it could be about the closure of a business due to a storm or COVID-19 and alternative arrangements that need to be made.

Tips for Effective Listening

- Make eye contact
- Remove and resist distractions (internal and external)
- Make sure you can hear properly
- Focus on areas of interest and ask yourself, 'What am I getting out of this message?'
- Be patient and hear the full message before judging
- Give appropriate feedback
- Keep an open mind – be objective
- Look for feeling/intention behind the words
- Avoid interrupting the speaker with your own story
- Help to keep conversations going
- Ask questions if necessary

Avoid:
- Fidgeting
- Frowning
- Looking at your phone/watch

It is also important not to be too exaggerated or artificial in our listening responses. Inane nodding, staring or grinning can put the speaker off so a balance should be found. The skills here should be tried and practised and will depend on the speaker and the situation.

Chapter Review

1. Give a brief explanation of the importance of listening.
2. What is the difference between hearing and listening?
3. List six barriers to effective listening.
4. Explain the meaning of active listening and selective listening.
5. How can paraphrasing help listening?
6. List six points for effective listening.
7. Name four things that can help us to take notes.

Chapter 4
Speaking Skills

> **In this chapter, you will learn about:**
> - The Voice
> - Language of Speech
> - Conversation
> - Formal and Informal Speaking
> - Intent and Consent
> - Negotiation Skills
> - Presenting a Point of View
> - Persuasion and Advocacy

> *Mankind's greatest achievements have come about by talking, and its greatest failures by not talking.*
>
> Stephen Hawking

> *Before you speak, let your words pass through three gates.*
> *At the first gate ask yourself,*
> *'Is it true?'*
> *At the second ask,*
> *'Is it necessary?'*
> *At the third gate ask,*
> *'Is it kind?'*
>
> Rumi, *The Gates of Speech*

Speaking face to face is the most direct, personal and open type of communication because it involves verbal, nonverbal and visual contact. We can hear the speaker's voice and its tone and see their facial expressions and body movements, giving a very complete, healthy and satisfying form of communication (see also Chapter 8: Nonverbal Communication). It satisfies a basic human need for social contact with other people. During the COVID-19 lockdowns, in spite of all the chats, conversations and meetings we could have online, we were still disconnected and found the experience far less appealing than sitting in the same room in the presence of another person.

Fig. 4.1

Other benefits of spoken communication are the instant feedback from the receiver and the quick flow and exchange of thoughts, ideas and feelings. We can support what we say and add expression and colour to our speech by using nonverbal signs. These signs can reveal our emotions and personalities, which may be a good or bad thing depending on the context. Our accents can show our cultural origins and our choice of words can reveal our level of education. So we cannot conceal ourselves easily in a face-to-face situation.

Fig. 4.2

The Voice

> *Words mean more than what is set down on paper. It takes the human voice to infuse them with deeper meaning.*
>
> Maya Angelou

'It's the way I tell 'em!' This statement about telling jokes may seem trivial, but it rings true. Why is it that one person can tell a joke and it has the audience in fits of laughter, and then when we try to tell the same joke, word for word, it is met with stony silence? The reason probably lies in the way we use our voice. Many professionals take speech lessons to change the tone of their voice because they believe it will help their career. A powerful deep voice can sound more convincing when giving a speech at a business conference than one that is high-pitched or squeaky. The way we speak at an interview or during a speech can be more relevant to our success than what we actually say, so using the voice effectively is important in the study of speaking skills.

Discussion

Consider what types of voice make people switch off. Think about what actors, media presenters and politicians you enjoy listening to. Which teachers did and didn't you enjoy listening to at school? Why?

Unlike writing, speech has a wonderful array of subtle variations that we can use to alter the meaning of our messages. Of course these variations can lead to problems if we don't know how to use them properly, but they enable us to liven up a word or phrase to give it depth, colour and meaning that is harder to create in writing. This is called paralanguage.

Pitch and Tone

Younger people have higher-pitched voices than older people. Sometimes when we are nervous, our pitch becomes higher due to constriction of the throat. We can reduce this by relaxing the muscles in the stomach, chest, shoulders and neck. A monotonous voice is one that speaks in monotone – one tone – and is boring to listen to. Inflection is the changing of the vocal pitch, something we do naturally in

Fig. 4.3

speech, often depending on our mood. If we are interested in or excited by the topic, we inflect more and we will sound more interesting.

Volume

It is important that people can hear us when we speak. Some voices are naturally louder than others. A loud voice can be commanding and demands to be heard, but in some contexts a quiet, firm voice can be more effective than a loud one.

Emphasis

We can illustrate the importance of specific words or phrases by placing emphasis on them. We do this by changing the pitch and volume. Which words would you emphasise in the following sentences:
1. The next train for Dublin leaves at 11 am from platform number four.
2. Don't you ever do that again!
3. Football is the most popular sport in the world today.
4. I will not tolerate this kind of behaviour.

Pace/Speed

We tend to speed up if we are excited, nervous or angry and we slow down when relaxed and comfortable or if we want to give emphasis. If we talk too quickly, we can lose our listeners; if we are too slow, we may bore them.

Articulation

When speaking, we tend to contract words and sentences. 'What do you think?' becomes 'Whatcha think?', 'How are you?', becomes 'Howya?', 'Do not' becomes 'Don't', etc. It is easy to be lazy when speaking, especially in informal situations, and sometimes we just mumble and slur. We shouldn't be afraid to use our mouth, lips and tongue to full effect but without sounding forced or unnatural.

Activities

1. **Tongue-twisters**

   Try repeating some of these tongue-twisters, focusing on articulation and pronunciation:
   - A big blue badly bleeding blister
   - Rubber baby buggy bumpers
   - A shifty snake selling snakeskin slippers
   - Eleven benevolent elephants

- Teaching ghosts to sing
- Selfish shellfish
- Really rural
- Unique New York
- The tip of the tongue, the lips, the teeth
- To titillate your tastebuds, we've got these tasty titbits
- I'm not the pheasant plucker, I'm the pheasant plucker's son, I'm only plucking pheasant till the pheasant plucker comes!

2. Give the Voice Expression

Sit in circles of five or six people. Take some of the phrases below. Each person says the phrase using a different expression from the previous speaker. Try to express some of the following expressions: neutral, asking a question (pitch goes up at the end), bored, angry, excited, scared, surprised, shy, happy, sad, whispering, shouting, crying, laughing, rapping, Gregorian chant, opera, sarcastic, proud, tired, suspicious, seductive.

Suggested phrases:

- I want to go home.
- It's my turn.
- What are you doing tonight?
- We have to do an assignment.
- The new computer's broken.
- Hello, how are you?
- No one here gets out alive.
- Drop it or else.
- Just do as I say, will you?
- My helicopter is full of eels.
- We've missed the bus.
- This is getting ridiculous.

Alternatively, each student writes a line from a song/poem/film/play/book, says it aloud and it goes around the circle in the same way.

3. **Newscaster**

   Read aloud a short newspaper article and try to make it sound as interesting as you can. Depending on the nature of the news item, you will have to adopt an appropriate tone of voice, e.g. serious, sympathetic, funny, quirky, etc.

   Newsreaders and comedians are helpful to listen to as they use vocal techniques to keep their audience's attention.

4. **Appropriate Expression**

   Choose one of the following passages and read it aloud, using appropriate voice expression:

   A. Sorry? You're sorry? Is that all you can say? I've been waiting here for 45 minutes in the freezing rain and all you can say is sorry. Why didn't you call me? You've got a phone, haven't you? Or did you forget that too? You know, sometimes I wonder why I bother with you at all.

   B. Now there is a breakfast cereal to really get you going – 'Eat and Go'! If you're feeling slow and sluggish, flush away those early morning blues with 'Eat and Go'! Full of natural goodness, iron and vitamins, 'Eat and Go' is made from organic oats and wheat, grown especially on our own farms and scientifically tested in our laboratories. Get yourself up and out with 'Eat and Go'!

   C. An evil has been unleashed upon the world, an evil older than history. In a race against time, a struggle against the odds, a battle with forces too great for mere mortals, only one man knows how to stop the destruction of the entire planet. Power beyond imagination, terror beyond belief. A film that will chill you to the bone.

   D. Once upon a time, in a land far, far away, there lived a princess who was the most beautiful princess in all the land. She lived with her evil stepmother and two ugly sisters in a great big castle. One day, news went out across the land that a magnificent ball was to be given by the handsome Prince Charming to find a suitable princess for him to marry.

▶ Language of Speech

The language of speech is very different to that of writing. It is far less formal and structured, and grammar and punctuation often seem non-existent. We do, however, punctuate our speech with fillers such as 'well', 'you know', 'like' and 'em'. We hesitate, stammer, stop, restart, repeat and use redundant words. If we wrote down, word for word, what we said, it would look very inelegant compared with the written word.

Not all speech needs to be so chaotic. It depends on the context in which we are speaking. A conversation between friends would be very different from a prepared speech to a company board of directors. A well-prepared speech can be very close in structure and use of language to the written word.

Conversation

Whether formal or casual, conversation forms an important social function in our daily lives and yet many people still feel they lack the confidence to carry on a good conversation. Good conversation can establish and improve personal and professional relationships. Like all forms of communication, it should be a two-way process and not dominated by one speaker.

There are a number of distinct stages in a conversation:
- Greetings
- Introductions
- Small talk
- Core conversation
- Summary of decisions
- Small talk/exit

At the outset, a smile, eye contact and a greeting opens the door for the conversation to start. After the introductions comes the small talk. Here it's not what is said that is important but what it implies, i.e. that both speakers are on friendly and equal terms. It could be a comment about:
- The weather
- The immediate vicinity, e.g. 'What an amazing view of the sea!'
- Something both speakers have knowledge of, e.g. 'That was a great game last night.'

Small talk can also include:
- Open questions, e.g. 'How far have you come today?'
- Neutral topics, e.g. 'Traffic's not too bad this morning.'
- Icebreakers/humour. This is down to personal taste but be careful: a joke that fails can be very embarrassing, especially if you're trying to make an impression on someone.

Such small talk should elicit agreement, so avoid anything too controversial or threatening.

Keeping a conversation going is often a challenge. Asking questions of the other speaker(s) is useful as well as speaking about your own topics, stories and interests. Respond and react by giving appropriate feedback.

Activities

1. In the following conversation, fill in the blanks with appropriate feedback responses:

    A: I'm going to France for my next holiday.

    B: _____.

    A: Yes, I'm going with some friends to celebrate our graduation.

    B: _____. And what are you going to do there?

    A: We're going to go kayaking down a gorge.

    B: _____.

    A: But I also want to spend some time just lying on a beach reading my book.

    B: _____.

2. In pairs, conduct a role-play in which you meet a friend/acquaintance outside a cinema or waiting at a bus stop and arrange to meet up for lunch. Include greetings and small talk. Enact another role-play in which one person is the other's employer/teacher.

3. Each student writes down a statement about something he did recently. Students take it in turns to sit in a chair at the front of the classroom, read their statement and the rest of the group asks three or more questions about the statement to which the student has to reply quickly.

4. Consider the following typical spoken routines and insert appropriate formal and informal words, phrases or sentences.

	Formal	Informal
Greeting		
Leave-taking		
Asking the time		
Offering a drink		
Asking directions		
Asking someone to be quiet		

Formal and Informal Speaking

Informal speaking with friends and family is usually easy. We aren't under pressure to 'perform'. They will understand if we make mistakes, though we may occasionally feel a little foolish. Small talk, chit-chat and conversation are informal speaking activities we engage in every day.

Formal speaking is more difficult. It needs to be more structured and grammatically correct and usually requires some planning and preparation. We use it in work situations, at interviews, giving talks and holding debates. Even giving someone instructions or directions needs to be clearly structured to avoid misunderstandings, which may lead to mistakes.

The following activities can prepare us for speaking assignments.

Activities

1. **Narration**

    Tell a story to the class group. Here are some suggested topics:

    - Your day up to the present moment. Begin: 'I woke up this morning...'
    - A film/television programme/book you enjoyed
    - What you did at the weekend
    - A memorable holiday you went on
    - A simple story (we all know fairy tales – better still, make one up!)
    - A narrative-style joke

    Try to make it personal and include details to make it as interesting as possible. Use your voice effectively.

2. **Description**

    A. Spend three minutes preparing a one-minute talk describing an activity with which you are familiar. Topics could range from your own pastimes, your work, sport, preparing a meal, etc. Your teacher could give assistance in preparation. Your talk should result in your audience knowing roughly how to do the activity themselves.

    B. Think of an everyday object/mechanical device/mode of transport, etc. Describe it to the class group without revealing what it is. They should be able to work it out if your description is good enough.

Intent and Consent

Sometimes if we need to have a discussion with someone it is helpful to:
- State our intent
- Ask for consent

By stating our intent, we are preparing the receiver for our discussion; if he is prepared, he will be in a better position to partake in and contribute to it.

By asking for someone's consent to have a discussion, he is more likely to oblige than if we dump him straight into the middle of it. We are also showing him respect by allowing him to decline our request if he wants. We shouldn't assume a person wants to or has time to talk to us. Stating intent and asking consent invites co-operation and reduces the potential for misunderstandings.

Sometimes a simple phrase such as 'I need to talk to you, do you have a couple of minutes?' is a sufficient statement of intent and request for consent.

Activities

1. Compare the following statements:

   - 'My assignment is giving me a lot of trouble. For starters, I can't find any information on...'
   - 'I would like to talk to you about my assignment. Have you got a few minutes?'

   - 'This new job I have is really bothering me. You see, I have to stay behind an hour later every day...'
   - 'I'm not sure about my new job. Do you have a minute to talk about it?'

   Which statement is likely to get a better response?

2. Try the following role-plays. Each can be adapted to suit the group's vocational area.
   - An employer has given an employee a job to do, for which the employee feels she is not qualified, and/or it is not part of her normal duties. Employer and employee discuss the situation.
   - A client is complaining about poor service/shoddy goods. Client and company/organisation representative discuss the problem.
   - An employee has been making comments that a colleague feels constitute sexually harassment/racism/discrimination. The two employees discuss the problem.
   - Two colleagues were supposed to meet to discuss an important issue at work. One colleague didn't turn up. The next day, the other colleague confronts him.

Negotiation Skills

Nelson Mandela once said, 'No problem is so intractable that it cannot be resolved through talk and negotiation rather than force and violence.' He went on to say that, in negotiations, neither side is right or wrong, but all sides need to compromise.

We might think that negotiation is about business, but it is a discussion between two people or groups of people when each wants something that the other might be unwilling to give. It is a process of finding compromise with each side gaining but also giving something.

Fig. 4.4

Negotiation takes place when:
- An employee wants a wage increase
- A child wants to eat sweets and the parent wants her to eat vegetables
- A customer bargains for a better deal with a salesperson
- A couple has to decide who will drink and who will drive
- A band wants €10,000 to make a record and the record company offers €5,000

Each side is usually out to get what it wants, and this can result in distrust, suspicion, even anger and confrontation. We negotiate because the alternative might be worse, e.g. a workers' strike, the break-up of a relationship, a court case, even war. These alternatives are often used as negotiating tactics, e.g. 'If you don't give me what I want, I'll sue you.'

Guidelines for Negotiation

Pre-negotiation

1. Know your opposition's situation, skills, assets, strengths, weaknesses, etc.
2. Be clear about your goals:
    (a) What are your initial demands?
    (b) What would you settle for?
    (c) What's your bottom line?
    (d) What do you both agree on?
3. If possible, choose a neutral space within which the negotiations can take place, where neither side feels at an advantage or disadvantage.
4. Timing – if it's late in the day, some people may be tired or irritable.

Discussion

> The negotiations for the 1921 Anglo-Irish Treaty between Britain and Ireland led by Michael Collins were held in Downing Street. How do you think this location affected those involved?

During Negotiations
1. Aim for a win-win situation, where both sides leave reasonably satisfied.
2. Begin by asking for more than you think you will get.
3. Be prepared to compromise.
4. Never give ground without gaining something in return.
5. Don't put all your cards on the table at the outset; keep some in reserve.

Communication in Negotiation
1. Be clear and use plain language.
2. Clarify any possible ambiguities.
3. Keep a record of all proceedings, especially any agreements.
4. Make sure both sides clearly understand the outcome.

Nonverbal Signs
Be aware of nonverbal signs:
1. Direct eye contact shows a firm positive attitude and willingness to communicate.
2. A warm facial expression shows interest and willingness to be persuaded.
3. A cold, steely-eyed, hard-faced expression can mean an inflexible attitude.

Lack of confidence is shown by:
1. Excessive smiling
2. Fidgeting
3. Hesitation
4. Speaking very quickly

Confidence is shown by:
1. Direct eye contact
2. Upright posture
3. Leaning forward slightly
4. Speaking slowly and deliberately

Negotiators should be flexible, firm, courteous, reasonable, persuasive, self-controlled, realistic and prepared to listen.

Breakdown

If a deal cannot be reached, one side might walk out. If there is a walkout, contact should be made immediately afterwards to prevent the proceedings from turning sour and to arrange another meeting.

Activities

1. Divide into groups of six. Conduct negotiations between management (three) and staff (three) of a company/organisation of your choice about proposed working hours and conditions over the Christmas period.
2. In groups of six, negotiate between those in favour of the construction of a wind farm in a local area and those against.

The following activities are for one-to-one negotiations:

3. Two people, A and B, are at a market and both see something they want to buy. A has enough money; B doesn't. B reminds A that she owes him money, the exact amount of the item for sale. They negotiate a deal.
4. You arrive at the station to catch the last train home, which is due to leave in five minutes. You suddenly realise you've lost your ticket and have no more money. Negotiate with the ticket collector to let you onto the train.
5. A rock star and her manager are arguing about how to leave the airport after a successful world tour. The fans are screaming outside, and the manager wants them both to leave by a back exit, but the star wants to meet the fans.
6. Granny is coming to stay. You have to give up your room but don't want to. Negotiate with your mother.
7. You want to buy a rare vinyl record by one of your favourite bands at a market stall, but it costs just a little bit more than the money you have on you. Negotiate with the stallholder.
8. The landlady wants to raise the rent. You cannot afford to pay what she is asking for. You'll only be there till the summer holidays and there are odd jobs you could do in the house. Negotiate a deal.
9. A famous TV presenter has missed his flight to London. He has to be there in time for the show later that evening. He tries to persuade a businessman, who wants to do some sightseeing in London before a meeting the following day, to give him his seat.

Presenting a Point of View

Many of us shy away from giving our opinion on some specific 'hot' topic. We may feel we cannot argue our point effectively enough to do so. Or we may simply not have any strong opinions about anything. Is this a good or a bad thing?

To present a point of view or opinion effectively, it is important to back it up with good reasons. If you can list your reasons by numbering them, so much the better. Another good technique is to give other points of view, comment on them and reach your own point of view, having explored the other ones. You can reach a better conclusion this way. This is useful in situations such as interviews, group discussions or when giving a presentation.

Activities

1. Make a list of controversial discussion topics on the board. Divide into groups of four to five people. Each group chooses a topic to discuss for 20 minutes. Try to present your point of view as clearly and convincingly as possible and to back it up with reasons.

2. Here is a list of topics you might use either for a class debate or for practising solo speaking. They may be adapted as required.

   - If I ran the country…
   - What I like/dislike about college
   - Social media
   - Legalise cannabis
   - Climate change
   - Veganism
   - Advertising
   - Discrimination (of any kind)
   - Religion
   - Biodiversity loss
   - Gender
   - Smartphones
   - Television
   - The housing crisis

   Think up your own topics. There may be something specific to your own vocational area that you'd like to speak about.

   Consider the following before speaking:

   - Decide if you want to do some research on the topic beforehand.
   - Decide on how you will approach the subject, e.g. an argument for or against, an informative or a persuasive speech, etc.
   - What tone of delivery will you use? Angry, passionate, calm, reasonable, etc.

Persuasion and Advocacy

Speaking to persuade or speaking in support of a cause needs certain skills in order to get the message across effectively. Here are a few guidelines:

- Present the facts about your subject. Use statistics and evidence to support your argument.
- Try to tailor it to your listeners' needs or interests. Try to connect with them. Is there any reason why they should listen to you/believe you?
- Structure your argument well. If you sound disorganised, it will be harder to convince your listener.

Here is a sequence of topics to follow:
1. Present information that grabs the listener's attention.
2. Explain why there is a need or a problem that needs solving.
3. Present your solution to the problem.
4. Visualise the future when the problem has been solved.
5. Suggest a course of action for the listener to take in order to reach the solution.

In this type of speaking you need to be both persuasive and informative. It might be a useful technique for an oral presentation.

Activities

1. As a group, brainstorm the subject of climate change using the guidelines above. Students could volunteer to stand up and be the advocate for a more sustainable lifestyle.
2. Make a list of causes you feel strongly about and in pairs take it in turns to try to persuade each other to take up one of the causes. Alternatively, try to persuade each other to take up a sport, hobby or activity you feel strongly about.

Chapter Review

1. In what ways can we use our voice to improve our speaking skills?
2. What are the main differences between formal and informal speaking?
3. Explain the importance of intent and consent.
4. How do you effectively present a point of view?
5. What is advocacy and what are its key components?
6. What is negotiation?

Chapter 5
The Interview

In this chapter, you will learn about:
- Preparation
- Structure
- Formal and Informal Interviews
- Types of Question
- STAR Method

The purpose of an interview is to get information about someone by asking questions. There are many types of interviews, which we may experience in our college, working and social lives, such as a counselling or medical interview, or a progress interview in which an employer or tutor will assess our work and performance. This section will focus on the employment interview.

The main reason for an employment interview is for the employer to assess the potential employee. It also provides the candidate with an opportunity to learn about the position and the prospective employer and to see whether or not they might fit in.

What is important about an employment interview is that the employer gets to meet the potential employee face to face, to see and hear them first-hand. It illustrates the benefits of this kind of communication over all others. A letter, email or CV can only impart so much information. The interview fills in the gaps that they have left.

An employment interview is not always simply a one-to-one question-and-answer session. Nowadays, candidates may have to do a psychometric test (a series of rapid written questions, which determines a candidate's personality and ability), a role-play and may even find themselves at a group interview with a panel of up to five interviewers and a number of other candidates. It is good to find out beforehand what type of interview you will have so that you can prepare appropriately.

▶ Preparation

(This could be done as a brainstorm with the whole class.)

Pre-interview

An interview for a job is likely to be a formal type of communication and, as such, we must be prepared for it. Here is some guidance for interview preparation:
- Be familiar with details in your CV and application letter.
- Research the job/company/organisation, e.g. employer's name, number of employees, products and services offered.
- Research the job requirements (what qualifications are needed) and job specification (what duties and responsibilities it entails).
- Be aware of any recent developments in the job sector for which you are applying.
- Prepare any relevant documents you might want to take with you.
- Dress appropriately, avoiding bright colours, strong perfume or aftershave, or excessive jewellery.
- Be neat and tidy.
- Prepare a list of your USPs (unique selling points), e.g. strengths, skills, experiences, qualifications, achievements, interests. These must be relevant to the job.
- Think of ways to turn weaknesses into strengths.
- Do a mock interview using the questions at the end of this section (pp. 68–9).

Fig. 5.1

At the Interview

The impression that you make on your interviewer can be as important as your credentials and achievements. Your social skills, attitude and ability to communicate are evaluated with your experience and education. Here are some essential instructions to help you prepare for a successful interview.
- Be on time! Aim to arrive 15 minutes before the time of the interview.
- First impressions last, and it only takes 30 seconds to make your first impression. Try to appear friendly, polite and sincere.
- Use appropriate nonverbal communication:
  — Shake hands firmly at the start and finish – the interviewer will usually offer their hand first.

- Don't be afraid to smile.
- Sit when asked. You may not be asked, so sit when it feels comfortable after the handshake, or just ask, 'May I sit down? Thank you.'
- Keep a straight but not rigid posture and lean forward slightly.
- Don't fold your arms, cross your legs, slouch or fidget.
- Try to appear relaxed.
- Maintain appropriate eye contact when speaking with the interviewer.

▶ Speak formally, avoiding slang and fillers such as 'like', 'um', 'you know what I mean'.
▶ Try to elaborate on 'Yes' and 'No' answers.
▶ Give full answers, stick to the point and avoid waffle.
▶ Be honest. If you don't know an answer, say, 'I'm sorry. I don't know the answer to that.'
▶ If you don't understand a question, ask to have it explained.
▶ If you 'freeze', or your mind goes blank, just say, 'Sorry, could you repeat the question, please?'
▶ If the interviewer discovers any mistakes you've made or weaknesses you have, don't deny them.

Fig. 5.2

▶ Try to turn any weaknesses into strengths, e.g. 'I've never done spreadsheets before, but I'm good at basic word processing and I am quick to learn computer skills.'
▶ Listen carefully to the questions and don't rush your answers. Take a second to pause and gather your thoughts.
▶ Be positive and enthusiastic. You want this job, so try to show it!
▶ Don't relax too much. Some interviewers use an over-friendly tactic to catch candidates off guard.
▶ Don't become defensive or argumentative if questioning becomes too rigorous.
▶ Don't be afraid to sell yourself. Be confident but not cocky.
▶ Never criticise a previous employer. It shows a lack of loyalty.
▶ Have your own questions prepared in case you are asked if you have any.
▶ At the end, thank the interviewer for seeing you and shake hands again.
▶ The interview isn't over until you've left the room, so as you leave be polite, smile and don't slam the door.

After the Interview

An assessment and analysis of your performance afterwards is useful as preparation for future interviews.

List the questions you were asked and evaluate the following:
- Your appearance
- Your entrance
- Your nonverbal communication
- Your good answers
- Your bad answers
- Your listening ability
- Your own questions
- Details you forgot
- Your exit

An interview, no matter what type it is, should be structured in a particular way so as to create a positive communication climate. This is largely up to the interviewers since they are the ones leading the way, so to speak. However, interviewers can get tired, bored and nervous during long days of interviewing, so if you can create a positive climate by smiling and appearing warm and enthusiastic, it can be beneficial.

▶ Structure

In very structured interviews there are often three stages: the opening, the main section and the closing stage.

The Opening Stage

In this stage an effective climate is briefly created by means of small talk or some sort of preview of what will be discussed. For example:
- 'I see you come from Galway. Do you like living there?'
- 'Since the last time you were with us, are there any changes that have occurred in your life?' (If being interviewed for a job in the same organisation/company)
- 'I see you went to Drumlinn College. Is Mr Maguire still teaching there?'

Jobs can be gained or lost based on the first three minutes of an interview.

Main Body of Interview

This is where the main questions are asked and an interviewer often uses the funnel sequence of questioning, i.e. moving from broad topics to specific ones.
- 'Tell me about yourself.'
- 'So, you're a good team worker?'
- 'Have you held any positions of responsibility?'

- 'How would you deal with someone with whom you didn't get on?'
- 'Tell me about a situation in which this happened.'

The Closing Stage

This stage is also brief. You could be asked if you have any questions, there may be a short summary of the content of the interview, statement of a follow-up, e.g. 'We'll let you know...' and a friendly parting.

If there is an interview panel, each interviewer may take a different stage, or a different set of topics to ask, depending on the job. Be careful not to be lulled into a false sense of security if the first or second interviewer comes across as friendly. You may find the next one is more rigorous!

Formal and Informal Interviews

In very formal interviews, both parties remain in their social and professional roles. So in an employment interview, the interviewer is the potential employer and the interviewee, the prospective employee. The interview will follow a standard format, which the interviewer may have prepared and written out. Nonverbal signs from the interviewer like a firm handshake, formal dress, a formally decorated room and straight postures all communicate a formal style.

Informal interviews tend to be more relaxed, are less likely to follow a rigid structure, and the roles of the participants will be less clearly defined. Informal surroundings, casual dress and more in the way of chat and smiling can signify an informal interview style but are no less serious for that.

Types of Question

Open Questions

These allow the interviewee to expand and elaborate on certain topics. Examples:
- 'Tell me about yourself.'
- 'What sort of work experience do you have?'

As an interviewee, you have the opportunity to steer the communication towards topics that will interest you or show yourself in a positive light. Answers could contain 'sticky information' that an interviewer will remember about you, e.g. stories about yourself working or studying in certain situations that they can visualise. Try to add as much detail as possible.

Closed Questions

These call for a specific response, usually either 'yes' or 'no', but try to elaborate on such answers.
- 'Did you enjoy your time at Drumlinn College?'
  'Yes, it was a great experience. I met some really interesting people, and I learned a lot about...'

- 'How many modules did you take?'
'I did eight modules in the first year, including Communications, Work Experience...'
They may be followed by open questions, e.g. 'What did you enjoy about it?'

Probing Questions

A probing question is one that tries to get beneath the surface to gain more information from an interviewee on a topic.
Interviewer: 'What did you enjoy about college?'
Interviewee: 'There was a good mixture of people there and it had a friendly atmosphere.'
Interviewer: 'What do you mean by a good mixture of people?'
Interviewee: 'There were people from different backgrounds, different nationalities, different ages and cultures.'
Interviewer: 'Why do you think that is a good thing?'
Interviewee: 'It helps to broaden your mind when you meet people from different walks of life. It makes it more interesting and stimulating. You begin to see that there is more to the world than simply your own way of looking at things.'

Hypothetical Questions

These kinds of questions give the candidate a hypothetical situation to see how he would deal with it. For example: 'Suppose you have a colleague who always arrives late and leaves early so that you are often left to cover for him/her. What would you do in this situation?'

Mirror Questions

Mirror questions reflect or bounce off the previous response. For example:
Interviewer: 'Tell me about yourself.'
Interviewee: 'I'm very interested in working with other people.'
Interviewer: 'So you enjoy being part of a team?'
Interviewee: 'Yes. I was involved in the student council at college.'
Interviewer: 'Then you're interested in organising things with a group?'
Interviewee: 'Yes. I think working as part of a group improved my communication skills.'
In this way, interviewees have a degree of power over the direction of the interview.

Summary Questions

These generally cover topics that have already been discussed, or are intended to allow the interviewee to add anything of relevance that has been left out, e.g. 'Is there anything else you'd like to discuss?'

Leading and Discriminatory Questions

The following two types of questions are undesirable in an interview:

Leading Questions

These usually suggest a desired response and don't get an honest reply from the candidate. For example, 'You wouldn't mind travelling as part of this job, would you?'

Discriminatory Questions

These are based on any of the nine grounds for discrimination under the Employment Equality Acts – gender, civil status, family status, sexual orientation, religion, age, disability, race and membership of the Traveller community – and are illegal as they may unfairly disadvantage the candidate. If asked such a question, the interviewee may politely refuse to answer, e.g. 'I'm sorry. I would rather not answer that, if you don't mind.'

▶ STAR Method

STAR INTERVIEW METHOD

S – Situation: Describe the context
T – Task: Provide details on your responsibilities
A – Action: Demonstrate how you responded or took charge
R – Result: Explain the impact you made or the lessons you learned

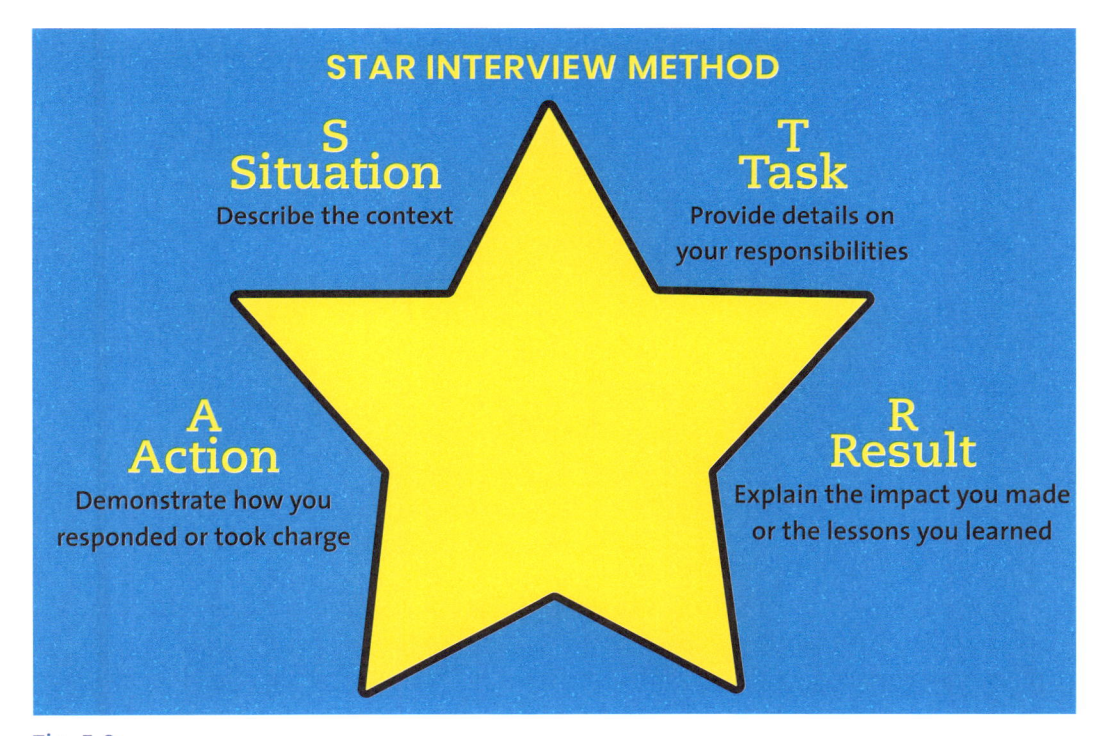

Fig. 5.3

The STAR Method for interview questions is helpful for creating a detailed story-like answer that will show how you dealt with a challenging situation, solved a problem or resolved a conflict.

S = Situation

Describe the context of your story. Be specific about where and when it took place. Describe the challenge/problem you faced.

T = Task
Describe your role or responsibility regarding the situation.

A = Action
This should be the most in-depth section of your answer. Give a detailed description of what action(s) you took to resolve the issue.

R = Result
What was the outcome of the action(s) you took to deal with the situation? Explain what the most positive effects of your action(s) were. As an extra you could describe what you learned from the situation and that you feel you are now more capable and confident as a result.

Typical Interview Questions

Here is a list of typical interview questions with a few suggestions for answering.

General
- Tell me about yourself.
  Give a brief overview of your life since leaving school or college. Finish your answer with something like: '…and now I'm ready and looking forward to working in this sector.' Don't tell your life story or give personal information.
- What are your best qualities?
  Mention some of your USPs and, if possible, describe a situation that illustrates them.
- Do you have any weaknesses?
  Mention a non-essential skill that you are working to improve. Turn a negative into a positive.
- What is your greatest achievement?
- What have you done that shows initiative?
- How do you cope with stress?
- Can you work under pressure?
  Use the STAR method.
- What do you do in your spare time?
  Ideally describe three activities to show: you are physically active and reasonably fit, you are involved with groups of people, you have a brain and you use it.
- Do you read?
- Do you play any sports?

Education
- What did you like about college?
- What did you dislike about college?
  Try to turn this into a solution, e.g. 'It would have been great if the library had late opening hours.'
- Tell me about your course at college.
  Describe some of the modules you studied (your favourite ones), something about your work experience and what you enjoyed learning.

- Why did you go to college?
- How did you find the course?
- Why did you choose to study…?
- Are you satisfied with your results?
- Was there anyone you didn't get on with?
- Describe a problem you had to deal with at college.

Current Application

- What experience do you have for this particular job?
- Give me some reasons why I should employ you.
- Why would you like to work for this company/organisation?
- What attracted you to this job?
- What could you bring to this company/organisation?
- What skills or qualities do you have that would be useful for this job?
- What do you know about this company?
- Do you have any creative ideas that could benefit the workplace?
- How did you find out about this position?
- What are you looking for in a job?
- Where would you see yourself in five years' time?
- What kind of salary do you expect? (See next page for questions about salary.)

Previous Experience

- Tell me about your previous employment experience.
- Have you held any positions of responsibility?
- What have you learned from any positions of responsibility?
- Have you ever worked as part of a team?
  Show that you understand the importance of teamwork and what it involves, e.g. collaboration, supporting each other, listening skills, etc.
- How well did you fit into the team?
- Did you have to work with anyone who let the team down?
- How would you cope with a colleague you might find difficult to work with?
- Describe a problem you had to deal with in your last job.
- What were your main responsibilities in your last job?
- Why did you leave your last job?
- What did you like/dislike about your last position?
- What skills did you learn in your last job?

Do You Have Any Questions?

It is good to have prepared a question or two of your own as it shows you are interested in the job. Here are some suggested questions you may ask at an interview:

- Do you provide training?
- Are there opportunities for promotion?
- What sort of hours would I be working?
- Do the employees get together socially?

- Do you have any plans to expand the company?
- Are there opportunities for working overtime?
- What qualities are you looking for in an employee?

Questions on the Salary

Questions, either from the interviewer or interviewee, about salary always cause a little consternation. Many job advertisements include information about the salary, in which case there is no reason for the interviewee to ask, unless they feel the work is excessive for the amount being paid. An interviewee could ask, 'If offered this position, what would the rate of pay be?' Many people feel embarrassed asking this, so only ask if you feel comfortable doing so. It is useful to find out the rate of pay for the job for which you are applying.

"WHEN I ASKED IF YOU WERE FLEXIBLE, MRS. HARKNESS, I WAS TALKING ABOUT YOUR HOURS!"

Fig. 5.4

Activities

1. In pairs, interview each other as if for a job using questions from the list above. Don't prepare what questions you will ask each other. At an interview we don't know exactly what we will be asked, so keep it as authentic as possible. If possible, have your CV with you so that questions might be relevant to the interviewee.

2. For a more involved activity, put together an interview panel of three students. The panel should prepare what kinds of questions each member will ask, e.g. one can introduce, another can focus on education, another on work experience, etc. Conduct interviews with volunteers from the class and the rest of the group can assess the performance of each candidate.

Reflection

It is useful to reflect on your performance after an interview so you can improve for your next one.

Here are some questions you could ask yourself:

1. How did you feel before the interview?
2. How did you feel during the interview?
3. How did you feel after the interview?
4. How well prepared were you?
5. How well did you answer the questions?
6. How was your appearance/dress?
7. How was your nonverbal communication (eye contact, posture, facial expression, gestures)?
8. What did you find challenging?
9. What went well/what were you happy with?
10. What needs improvement?
11. What have you learned for the future?
12. What will you do differently next time?

For a more thorough reflection, use Gibbs' Reflective Cycle in Appendix 2.

Tips for Effective Interviews

- Prepare well beforehand.
- Dress appropriately.
- Arrive early.
- Check your nonverbal communication.
- Show interest and enthusiasm.
- Give full, complete answers.
- Don't give out personal information.
- Check your social media platforms to make sure there is nothing that will undermine your chances of getting the job.

Chapter Review

1. Outline the importance of nonverbal communication in an interview.
2. List five things you should do to prepare for an interview.
3. List five things you should not do during an interview.
4. List five things to assess after the interview. Why are these important?
5. Describe the STAR Method.
6. What are leading and discriminatory questions and what is wrong with them?

Chapter 6
Groups and Meetings

In this chapter, you will learn about:
- Reasons for Joining Groups
- Group Influence
- Effective Communication in Groups
- Synergy
- Group Discussion
- Meetings
- Formal Roles
- Documents for Meetings
- Communication at Meetings
- Conflict
- Decision-Making

If you want to go fast, go alone. If you want to go far, go together.
(African proverb)

We all belong to a variety of groups. From our families, through our colleagues at work or classmates at college, to our friends and peers at clubs or societies, we are constantly involved with some form of group. Belonging to a group can have a positive effect on our wellbeing. We are, after all, highly social beings, and regular interaction with others makes us feel socially 'connected', which can contribute enormously in terms of life satisfaction. Being a member of a variety of groups helps us relate, interact and communicate with others and this interaction can improve our sense of social belonging as well as our self-confidence.

Fig. 6.1

Interaction in a group is also a vital part of our working lives. Many employers look for people who can get along with their colleagues and work effectively as part of their team. If we can communicate well in group situations, we will enhance our opportunities for employment and promotion.

> ## Activity
> Make a list of all the groups to which you belong. Notice that there are some you chose to join and some you didn't, such as your ethnic group, family or school. Select one that you chose to join and write down your reason(s) for joining it.

Reasons for Joining Groups

- Security – we feel safe in the company of others who have the same interests and share our views
- Identity – being a member of a particular group gives us a sense of who we are
- Common goal or cause
- Information/education
- Social reasons

> ### Lessons from Flying Geese
>
> Read the following facts in relation to the science behind the flight habits of geese and the lessons we can learn from them:
>
> **Fact 1:** As each goose flaps its wings, it creates an uplift for the birds that follow. By flying in a V formation, the whole flock adds 71 per cent greater flying range than if each bird flew alone.
>
> *Lesson:* People who share a common direction and sense of community can get where they are going quicker and easier because they are travelling on the thrust of one another.

Fact 2: When a goose falls out of formation, it suddenly feels the drag and resistance of flying alone. It quickly moves back into formation to take advantage of the lifting power of the bird immediately in front of it.
Lesson: If we have as much sense as a goose, we stay in formation with those headed where we want to go. We are willing to accept their help and give our help to others.

Fact 3: When the lead goose tires, it rotates back into the formation and another goose flies to the point position.
Lesson: It pays to take turns doing the hard tasks and sharing leadership. As with geese, people are interdependent on each other's skills, capabilities and unique arrangements of gifts, talents or resources.

Fact 4: The geese flying in formation honk to encourage those up front to keep their speed.
Lesson: We need to make sure our honking is encouraging. In groups where there is encouragement, the production is much greater. The power of encouragement (to stand by one's heart or core of values and encourage the heart and core of others) is the quality of honking we need.

Fact 5: When a goose gets sick, wounded or shot down, two geese drop out of formation and follow it down to help and protect it. They stay with it until it dies or is able to fly again. Then, they launch out with another formation or catch up with the flock.
Lesson: If we have as much sense as geese, we will stand by each other in difficult times as well as when we are strong.

(Taken from a speech by Angeles Arrien at the 1991 Organizational Development Network and based on the work of Milton Olson)

Fig. 6.2

Group Influence

The groups to which we belong have a strong influence on how we think and behave. We are usually obliged to conform to the group's norms, i.e. patterns of thought and behaviour that are considered to be normal within a particular group. This may involve what we can and cannot speak about, the toleration of humour, a set of rules to which we must adhere or even wearing a specific type of clothing. These group norms are common to all members of the group and help develop and build trust between members. Other groups who think and behave differently may be perceived as a challenge or threat. Our peer group often exerts peer pressure upon us to do things with which we may not always feel comfortable.

Fig. 6.3

Effective Communication in Groups

To make the most of our group situations, we need to know how to interact with others successfully, how to make our groups effective in their tasks and how to foster group cohesion. Dialogue and negotiation skills come into play in group situations, but there are a number of specific communication skills that can help us contribute to the groups to which we belong and maximise the benefits we receive from them:

- Acceptance of other members and their ideas
- Offering support and praise to group members for their contributions, e.g. 'Well done', 'That's a good idea'
- Taking turns so that everyone can contribute
- Listening to others
- Positive body language – facing and making eye contact with other members
- Keeping focused on the group's objectives
- Creating a relaxed atmosphere, using humour perhaps, without it becoming a distraction from the main purpose

- Showing agreement with other members
- Offering contributions, either by suggesting ideas or volunteering to take action
- Evaluating others' ideas positively, e.g. 'That's a good idea, and it might work better if we...'
- Inviting the views and opinions of others, e.g. 'What do you think?'
- Bringing ideas together, e.g. 'Are we all agreed on that?'
- Suggesting actions, e.g. 'Why don't we...?

Negative Group Communication

- Never contributing
- Speaking out of turn
- Being distracted from the group's objectives
- Insulting remarks about/to other members and their ideas
- Negative comments about the group's goals/purpose
- Regular disagreement with other members
- Behaviour that goes against what is acceptable to the group
- Self-centred communication
- Aggression
- Dominating behaviour

Such attitudes and behaviour within a group can lead to problems such as a bad atmosphere, resentment or hostility between members. This in turn can result in a lack of progress and productivity.

Synergy

Synergy, which comes from the Greek word *sunergos* for 'working together', means that the combined effect of the whole group is more than the sum of its parts. In other words, a group works to its maximum effect if each member puts aside his/her individual interests in favour of the interests of the group. If we find our interests constantly clash with those of the group, maybe it's time for us to leave. If we don't actively contribute to the group, remain passive and silent, we become like a limb that has no purpose. The worst we can do is constantly be at odds with the group, in which case we may be asked to leave.

Fig. 6.4

Group Discussion

Discussion in groups usually focuses on one or several specific aims or goals. It is important to keep the purpose of the discussion in mind so as to avoid straying from the group's task. Discussions often get bogged down when one or two members concentrate or dwell for too long on minor and unimportant details. Discussions should move forward in the direction of a satisfactory outcome. Contributions to the discussion should:

- Be relevant to the task at hand
- Focus on the goal
- Be constructive
- Move the discussion forward

Activity

Divide into groups of four or five. Each group is a band in search of a manager. There are five candidates for the job and each group has 20 minutes to select the one they think is best suited to the job.

The candidates are:

- **Mick.** Early twenties. Mediocre Leaving Cert results. Great charm and very popular. Could talk his way out of anything. Bit of a chancer. No musical talent of his own. Daytime job as salesperson. Never lets things get on top of him. Close friend of band since schooldays together.
- **Alan.** Late twenties. Boyfriend of band's lead singer. Accountant. Rather reserved – perhaps shy. Extremely efficient and clear-headed. Dresses conservatively. A perfectionist, he's interested in the business possibilities.
- **Sheila.** Mid-twenties. Degree in theatre studies. Some experience working in an arts centre. Vivacious with a sympathetic personality. Level-headed and sensible, she relates easily to others. No particular knowledge of the music scene but she knows what she likes.
- **Don.** Mid-thirties. Has extensive experience of DJ work and local radio. Encyclopaedic knowledge of music world. Thinks that at last he has spotted a winner. Tends to boss, and keen on doing things his way. Superficial jollity but quite a cold personality. Ambitious to make it, but time is running out.
- **Lucilla.** Has done a further education course in journalism and, at 20, is looking for openings in the media. Very energetic and bright. Good organiser but makes no secret of the fact that she doesn't suffer fools gladly. Sarcastic and funny. Quick to learn. Comes from a wealthy background.

Give an honest assessment of your own and your group's performance by answering the following questions without consulting the rest of the group:

- Did the group reach a consensus, i.e. agreement?
- Did the group go about the task in an organised way or not?
- How?
- Did anyone take charge/dominate?
- Did everyone contribute to the discussion?
- Were your contributions positive or negative?
- Did you put your views across clearly?
- Did you listen to others' contributions?
- Did you enjoy working as part of a team?
- What improvements would you make next time?

Compare your answers with the other members of your group.

(From Stephen Daunt, *Communication Skills*)

Meetings

Meetings are crucial to the smooth running of most organisations. Important decisions are made at every level of social and working life at meetings. A large company may hold a meeting to decide on new product development; trade union meetings take place to discuss the welfare of the employees; a student council meeting may be held to arrange a social; even at home when a family sits down to make plans for a holiday, it is a kind of meeting.

Fig. 6.5

Many people dislike having to attend meetings, as they are often badly planned and poorly run. Meetings should be positive, constructive, stimulating and well organised. They can have many advantages. Within an organisation they can promote a sense of belonging, identity and involvement amongst members, as each person is allowed to have an input. They can encourage a wide range of ideas and suggestions from the different participants. In short, they are democratic in that everyone can and should have an equal say.

Purpose of Meetings

- Problem-solving
- Decision-making
- Negotiation
- Generating ideas
- Giving and receiving information

Types of Meetings

- *Formal meeting* – held according to specific rules and procedures, perhaps contained within a constitution
- *Informal meeting* – no specific rules
- *Ordinary general meeting* – regularly held (monthly or weekly) to conduct routine discussion or business
- *Extraordinary general meeting* – held outside the regular times to deal with a specific issue, often a crisis
- *Annual general meeting (AGM)* – held annually so members of a company can ask questions and get information about the company
- *Committee meeting* – a sub-group of the parent organisation
- *Public meeting* – any member of the public may attend, held in a public place, often dealing with political or community issues
- *Private meeting* – only members of the organisation may attend

Formal Roles

Chairperson

The phrase 'Through the chair' often precedes comments made at formal meetings. This means the chairperson is the 'channel' through which all comments and discussion are directed. This ensures that a certain degree of order is maintained and that any potential conflict is avoided as participants do not communicate directly with each other. The most important person at a meeting is the chairperson. A meeting's success or otherwise can depend on how effectively it is chaired.

An *effective* chairperson:
- Draws up the agenda with the secretary before the meeting
- Sticks to the agenda
- Keeps control without being dictatorial
- Encourages participation from everyone
- Is impartial
- Steers the discussion towards decision-making
- Seeks consensus on decisions, by a vote if necessary
- Sums up main decisions/points, making sure that everyone clearly understands them

A chairperson should also have excellent communication skills: listening to the members, keeping the discussion relevant, having qualities of tact, empathy, warmth, humour and good judgement and summarising the main points discussed.

An *ineffective* chairperson:
- Dominates the proceedings
- Loses control
- Allows private conversations and interruptions among the participants

The Secretary

The secretary is in charge of all written documentation connected with meetings.
Before the meeting, the secretary:
- Sends out notice of the meeting
- Draws up the agenda with the chairperson
- Prepares any relevant documents, e.g. correspondence such as emails or letters
- Prepares a suitable venue/room

During the meeting, the secretary:
- Records attendance
- Reads minutes of the previous meeting
- Reads any correspondence
- Gives a secretary's report, if required
- Takes notes for the minutes
- Supports and assist the chairperson

After the meeting, the secretary:
- Writes up the minutes
- Deals with correspondence
- Acts on decisions that have been made

The Treasurer

The treasurer manages all the finances and funds of the organisation and gives a treasurer's report if required, usually at an AGM.

Documents for Meetings

The Notice

Some meetings are held regularly on a specific day each month, and as members will be aware of this, no notice is required, though a reminder might be sent to them. However, if meetings are less regular the secretary should give notice, at least one week beforehand. It may be sent as a letter, memo or email, or simply as a typed or handwritten notice on a noticeboard, although each member should also receive an individual copy.

Sample Notice for Individual Member

Dear Member,
The next meeting of the Student Council will take place on Wednesday, 21 October at 1.15 pm in room 20.
Yours faithfully
Caroline Stevens
Secretary

Sample Notice for Noticeboard

Drumlinn College of Further Education
Student Council

The next meeting of the Student Council will take place on Wednesday, 21 October at 1.15 pm in room 20.

Caroline Stevens
Secretary

The Agenda

This is a numbered list of all the items to be discussed at the meeting, letting participants know in advance so that they can prepare. The secretary and chairperson draw up the agenda, though participants may request to have specific items included. It is often included with the notice.

Sample Agenda

Drumlinn College of Further Education
Student Council

Agenda
1. Apologies for absence
2. Minutes of previous meeting
3. Matters arising from the minutes
4. Correspondence
5. Use of computer rooms
6. Next social
7. Any other business
8. Date of next meeting

Items 1 to 4, 7 and 8 above are almost always included. After the minutes are read (item 2), they should be approved (proposed and seconded) and accepted by the chairperson signing them. Item 3 is to allow members to discuss anything relating to the minutes, for example to find out what action was taken since the previous meeting. Item 4 consists of any letters, memos or emails that the secretary has sent and received since the previous meeting. In order to save time these won't actually be read out in full unless the secretary is requested to do so. Item 7, often abbreviated to AOB, gives members the chance to bring up any other topics for brief discussion.

Minutes

The minutes are a brief record of what was discussed and decided at a meeting, written up by the secretary. They should be accurate and impartial. They should contain only the relevant points, but all motions and resolutions (see 'Decision-making' on page 86) should be recorded word for word. They should be written in the past tense and record the name of the organisation, the date, time, venue and attendance.

Types of Minutes

- Resolution minutes record only the decisions or resolutions. All discussion prior to this is omitted.
- Narrative minutes record both discussion and resolutions. This requires good summarising skills, including only relevant discussion and leaving out unimportant details.
- Action minutes record a brief summary of the meeting and a column listing the names or initials of those responsible for implementing decisions made. These columns are important for recording who is responsible for what.

Sometimes the minutes will consist of a combination of all three. The important items to be recorded are all the decisions and actions.

Sample Minutes

**Drumlinn College of Further Education
Student Council**

Minutes of the meeting held on Wednesday, 21 October at 1.15 pm in room 20.

Present:

Tadhg Pallone (Chairperson)	Fran Cochrane
Caroline Chambers (Secretary)	Deirdre O'Connor
Jane Smith (Treasurer)	Linda Farrell
Julia Flood (Staff)	Toki Tanaka
Helena McCarthy	Donal O'Callaghan
Joseph Onyesoh	Thomas Carney

Apologies: Ian Fitzgerald, Alayne Wild, Belinda Foley, Liz Riedmuller, Valerie O'Leary.

Minutes of previous meeting

The minutes of the meeting on Wednesday, 14 October were read, approved and signed.

Matters arising

The chairperson reported that he had met with the principal and that a quotation for new lockers had been sought and that the lockers would be purchased in the new year.

Correspondence

The secretary read an email from The Bayview Hotel offering student rates for the end-of-year social, and a letter from the Simon Community thanking the students for their fundraising activities. It was decided that a similar fundraiser will take place this year.

Use of computer rooms

Fran Cochrane expressed concern that students on her course did not have sufficient time in the computer rooms to work on assignments and that more hours should be made available to them from the computer department.
Toki Tanaka agreed and suggested that an extra hour each evening between 5 and 6 o'clock should be requested.

Next social

Helena McCarthy reported that she had confirmed the booking of Frankie's Nightclub for the next social, and that it was free of charge. Ticket prices were agreed at €10, and Joseph Onyesoh volunteered to design and print tickets.

AOB

Thomas Carney said that a number of his classmates had complained about the canteen facilities. He said that the sandwiches were unsatisfactory, and that hot food would be welcomed. There was broad agreement with his comments and Deirdre O'Connor suggested that a canteen committee consisting of students, teaching staff and canteen staff be set up to discuss improvements. Julia Flood said that she would raise the issue at the next staff meeting.

The meeting closed at 1.50 and the next meeting was set for 28 October.

The timing and environment of meetings can often be factors that determine their success or failure. Most people are at their best around mid-morning, and slightly tired immediately after lunch. Many people with families may find the hours between 5 and 7 pm difficult to accommodate. The size and arrangement of the meeting room is an important consideration, and it is the secretary's job to ensure that it is suitable for the size of the group and that the layout will encourage rather than inhibit communication. Here are some possible seating arrangements:

MEETING SEATING ARRANGEMENTS

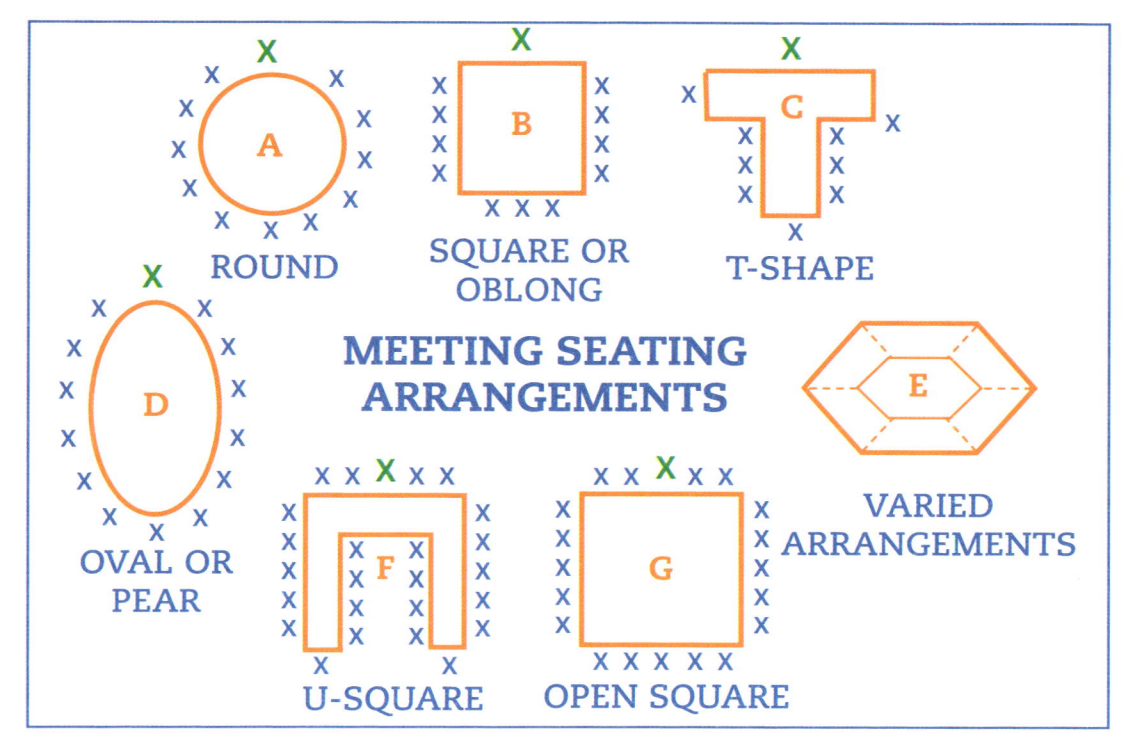

- A: ROUND
- B: SQUARE OR OBLONG
- C: T-SHAPE
- D: OVAL OR PEAR
- E: VARIED ARRANGEMENTS
- F: U-SQUARE
- G: OPEN SQUARE

Fig. 6.6

Discussion

What are the pros and cons of each of these different seating arrangements?

Communication at Meetings

As soon as everyone has arrived and is seated, the chairperson will open the meeting with, 'I will now call the meeting to order...' or a similar phrase. The chairperson has the ability to set the tone by being firm but friendly. A word of greeting or welcome can often help in this regard. Once the routine items have been quickly dealt with, the first item should be introduced and the chairperson should address the whole group with a question like, 'What does anyone think about...' or 'Does anyone have any suggestions for...'

Discussion is often dominated by a small number of participants who may intimidate new or shy members, and the chairperson should encourage everyone to contribute. A direct question here is useful, for example, 'What is your view on this matter, Linda?'

Be aware of nonverbal communication at meetings such as eye contact, facial expression, posture and gestures and avoid sending out ambiguous or negative signals. Try to use a tone of voice that is positive, decisive and firm and doesn't become angry or aggressive.

To contribute at a meeting, we should begin by clearly signalling to the chairperson our intention to speak by raising our hand before the previous speaker has finished or by saying, 'Through the chair'. If we hesitate, the moment may be lost, as the chairperson moves topics along quite quickly. We can start our contribution with a simple question: 'May I just ask what the previous speaker meant by...' or a simple comment: 'Through the chair, I agree with the previous speaker...' Only speak when it is relevant. We cannot know it is relevant unless we listen carefully to the discussion. As with other forms of communication, we should be clear, concise and courteous.

The chairperson must determine that all aspects of a topic have been fully discussed before moving to a decision and that time is not wasted by spending too long on any one item.

▶ Conflict

Conflict can be useful at meetings as it stimulates ideas and discussion, ensures that all perspectives are examined and increases members' understanding of opposing viewpoints. Displaying effective and empathic listening techniques such as, 'I understand you feel strongly about this, but...' can help alleviate conflict. If a member becomes so unruly that the meeting cannot continue, a last resort may be to ask the member to leave or to abandon the meeting. When there is no conflict at all, it could mean that not all aspects of a particular subject have been explored, and as a result there may be a lack of thorough analysis.

Two types of group conflict have been identified: disruptive conflict and constructive conflict. Disruptive conflict is when members are competitive, self-interested, adopt a win-lose approach, ignore opposing views, create an unhealthy communication climate that intimidates others, communicate defensively and resort to personal attacks. Constructive conflict occurs when participants are co-operative, focus on the interests of the group, adopt a win-win approach, listen to opposing views, create an open and positive atmosphere and communicate supportively. From the outset, it is again up to the chairperson to set the tone for the meeting and if conflict does occur, she must remain impartial and calm.

▶ Decision-making

Group decision-making can range from informal agreements to formal voting. Once a discussion has taken place and the chairperson thinks it has been covered sufficiently, she may suggest an action to be taken and ask if everyone agrees. If no one objects, a decision has been made. If there is no overall agreement, a vote may be taken and the majority wins.

Motion

A motion is a formal proposal to make a decision or take action about something. A motion must be proposed, seconded and start with the word 'that'. For example, 'I propose that the next social will take place in Coast Nightclub.' It is then followed by a vote, and if passed, becomes a resolution.

Consensus

Today more and more groups and organisations are using consensus as a means of decision-making because it can transform a gathering of diverse individuals into a strong and healthy group. In consensus, every group member's opinion is valid and is heard. It is different to majority rule by virtue of its more co-operative approach and the idea that decisions by vote might leave a minority feeling less committed to the decision and/or the group.

Groups that use consensus have similar roles but use different names such as facilitator instead of chairperson and note/minute-taker instead of secretary. A timekeeper is employed to ensure the group sticks to the agenda and a 'vibes watcher' might be employed to observe nonverbal cues of the general mood of participants. He will let the facilitator know if there are any signs of impending conflict or fatigue, for example.

The Process of Consensus

An idea is discussed, and the group arrives at a point where a decision is ready to be made. Someone will formulate a proposal, e.g. 'I propose that we use consensus as a decision-making tool.' The facilitator will ask, 'Do we have consensus?' (i.e. 'Are we all agreed?') In making the decision, a participant can take one of three actions:
1. *Give consent* – agree to the decision, even if she has some reservations about it or disagrees with it.
2. *Stand aside* – when she cannot agree to support the decision but thinks it is fine for the rest of the group to support it. This action absolves the individual from any responsibility for the decision.
3. *Block* – this is when someone cannot support the decision and believes it would be bad for the whole group, so the decision cannot be made. It is a serious action and should not be taken lightly. As a rule of thumb, a member should use blocking only three to four times while on a committee.

Stand asides and blocks are recorded in the minutes. If consensus is not reached, then those who don't agree raise their concerns, which are discussed and an amendment to the proposal is made. The cycle is repeated until consensus is achieved.

Open Space Technology and World Café

Two cutting-edge methods of group facilitation, Open Space Technology and World Café, which adopt a less formal and hierarchical approach, are being used more and more by organisations. Both are powerful tools for groups of any size wanting to explore specific important questions or issues.

Open Space Technology is a complicated-sounding term for a simple process and can seem a bit chaotic if you are a person who likes to be in control. It has four rules and one law. The four rules are:
1. Whoever come are the right people.
2. Whatever happens is the only thing that could have.
3. Whenever it starts is the right time.
4. When it's over, it's over.

The one law is the law of two feet: 'If you find yourself in a situation or discussion where you are neither learning nor contributing, feel free to use your feet to go to a more productive place.'

A facilitator explains the process at the start. The group sits in a circle, or concentric circles if there are too many. In the centre is a pile of A4 sheets and pens, and the title of the event, which is the question or issue being discussed, should be displayed on a wall or board so that everyone can see it. Also on the wall is an empty timetable, with session times on one axis and breakout spaces on the other, as in the table below. Each of the blank spaces on the timetable should be A4 in size.

	1 Library	2 Computer Room	3 Main Office	4 Table in Hallway
10 am–11 am				
11 am–12 pm				
12 pm–1 pm				

Then the facilitator asks people to come up with ideas for discussion related to the main topic and people write these on the A4 sheets. Whoever writes a suggestion has to lead that particular discussion. The topics are then slotted into the timetable, and if there are too many, they can be combined into similar themed topics.

When the timetable is full, participants look at it for a few minutes, and the facilitator announces the first session. Each breakout space should have lots of flipchart paper and pens.

At the end of the sessions, someone from each group gives feedback on their discussion to the whole group. The ideas can then be written/typed up and sent/mailed out to each participant later. This is a great way to draw people out who are passionate about a subject.

World Café was developed when someone realised that the best discussions at conferences took place during the tea break, so why not have one big tea break instead?

Seven principles of World Café have been devised:

1. Set the context. Prepare the event well, i.e.
   - Topic for discussion
   - Venue
   - Invite participants
   - Time
   - Hoped-for outcomes
2. Prepare the venue. Make it comfortable, with enough chairs and tables (big enough to seat up to five people), a supply of flipchart paper, pens and plenty of tea, coffee and snacks.
3. Carefully frame the question for discussion.
4. Encourage everyone to contribute. The more people who discuss, the more ideas and the more collective intelligence is unlocked.

5. Connect diverse perspectives. Every participant moves to another table every 15 minutes, bringing with them the ideas from their previous conversation. One person at each table remains. This is the table host, who writes down the ideas of that table. This means that over the space of a couple of hours, everyone will get to meet almost everyone else. At each changeover the table host shares the discussion from that table with the new group of participants.
6. Listen together and notice patterns. Listening is crucial for World Café so:
   - Listen to every speaker with the assumption that they have something important and wise to say.
   - Listen with a willingness to be influenced.
   - Listen with an open mind to a speaker even though he may have a different perspective and opinions to you.
   - When speaking, be clear and succinct – don't hog the discussion.
7. Share collective discoveries. Each table host can give feedback on his table's discussion points; the sheets of paper can be put up on the walls of the room for all to see; information can be typed up and emailed out to all participants.

Other Meeting Terms

- *Quorum* – the minimum number of members required to attend a meeting in order for it to be valid
- *Standing Orders* – the written rules that an organisation uses to run its meetings
- *Point of Order* – when a member checks to see if the proper procedure is being followed
- *Amendment* – a proposal to change a motion

Activities

1. Warmer

Divide into groups of five to ten and sit in a circle. One person starts by saying 'Brenda is going on holiday, and in her suitcase she packs...' adding one item. The next person repeats this and adds another item and so on around the group. Anyone who changes the order of items, or forgets any item, is out. If this takes too long, just do two rounds.

2. Preparation for Meeting Assessment

The group should elect participants to the key roles required, decide on a topic for discussion (see suggestions below), make a list of items to be discussed at the meeting and draw up a notice and an agenda.

Suggested scenarios:
- Class meeting to discuss a forthcoming social event
- Class meeting to discuss any issues or problems you are experiencing at college
- A residents' association meeting to discuss the problem of loud concerts being held at a venue in your community
- A residents' association meeting to discuss the problem of drugs and dealing in the community
- A small rural community meeting to discuss how to incorporate a group of 30 immigrants who have recently arrived
- A small rural community meeting to discuss the proposal to set up a wind farm in the locality
- A union meeting to discuss pay and working conditions
- A meeting at work to discuss the promotion and sale of a new product
- A meeting at work to plan a social event

Alternatively, make up your own scenario.

Hold the meeting in class and, if possible, record it on audio or video. Afterwards listen or watch the recording. Each member writes up the minutes of the meeting acting as if secretary.

Take note of your own communication skills at the meeting. Could you improve them in any way?

Use Gibbs' Reflective Cycle in Appendix 2 for a more thorough reflection on the group's and your own performance.

This may take a number of class sessions.

Tips for Effective Group Discussions and Meetings

- Listen to other members.
- Don't interrupt.
- Raise your hand to indicate that you wish to speak.
- Avoid sarcastic or offensive comments.
- Keep the discussion relevant.
- Keep comments clear and concise.
- Move the discussion towards a decision.
- Switch phones off or to silent.

Chapter Review

1. What are the advantages and disadvantages of group interaction?
2. List four ways of improving group communication.
3. What is synergy?
4. What are the purposes of meetings?
5. What are the duties and functions of a chairperson and a secretary?
6. Give explanations of notice, agenda and minutes.
7. Explain the two types of conflict.
8. What is consensus?
9. Outline the consensus decision-making process.

Chapter 7
Presentation Skills

> In this chapter, you will learn about:
> - Fear of Public Speaking
> - Extended Conversation
> - Preparation
> - Structure and Organisation
> - Delivery
> - Venue
> - Support Material
> - Dealing with Questions

There are a number of situations in which, at some stage in our lives, we may be asked to give a talk:
- Weddings and other celebrations
- Acceptance of an award/qualification
- Presentation of a new idea or product
- Introducing a guest speaker or new colleague at work
- Giving instructions/speech to new colleagues, clients or students about our job
- Giving a workshop
- Television or radio presentation

Fig. 7.1

These range from very brief, informal chatty-type talks, which require little preparation, to extensive, detailed and formal presentations that need careful planning and organisation. The latter is what is normally required of students for the purpose of a communications course.

▸ Fear of Public Speaking

Few of us like the idea of standing up and giving a talk in front of a group of people. This is known as communication apprehension or stage fright, and it is perfectly normal. Most professional speakers, be they actors, politicians, media presenters or teachers, suffer from nerves at some stage during their career, and they all know that the first time is the worst. For many students, this will be the first time they have given a presentation, and many reluctant students learn that they are in fact better speakers than they initially thought and surprise themselves with their good results. Having completed the task, they gain confidence, knowing that they have cleared the first hurdle of public speaking.

An oral presentation is one form of speaking for which you can and must be well prepared. The better prepared you are, the more confidence you have, and the more confident you are, the better the presentation.

First, it is important to remember that almost everyone gets nervous when giving a talk, so you are not alone. Second, even though the attention is on you when you are speaking, you should focus on the subject matter, not on yourself. Concentrate on getting the message across. This can take some pressure off.

Here are some techniques for relaxing and reducing nerves before giving a speech.

- Progressive muscle relaxation: Find a quiet place to sit or lie down and start with the feet – flex the muscles in your feet, then relax them. Slowly work your way through each muscle group in your body, tensing, then relaxing each group.
- Deep breathing: Breathe slowly into your stomach, feel it expand, then move the breath into your midriff and feel your ribs expand, and finally breathe into your chest and feel it and your shoulders expand. Hold your breath for several counts, then exhale slowly through the mouth. Do this three times.
- Breathe in for three seconds and out for six seconds.
- Hydrate: 'Dry mouth' often occurs when we are nervous, so make sure to drink plenty of water beforehand or suck a mint or lozenge.
- Coughing not only helps clear the throat but also helps relax the diaphragm, which in turn can reduce anxiety.
- Pressure point: You need to locate a point on your inner arm two and a half fingers width from your wrist crease. Use your thumb to repeatedly press firmly but gently on this pressure point for one to three minutes.
- Swinging the arms, rolling the head and shoulders and rubbing the earlobes may all help to reduce stress and anxiety before a presentation.
- Realise that you cannot give the perfect speech. You will tend to notice your mistakes more than the audience will, so don't be afraid of minor errors. Remember that the main thing is to get your message across. Conversation is full of minor errors, and we tolerate those. A speech is like an extended conversation.

It is virtually impossible to completely eliminate nerves before public speaking and it is also undesirable. A little anxiety is good, as it sharpens our concentration, but using some or all of the above exercises can help reduce nerves.

> ## Activity
>
> Make a list of the reasons you get nervous at the idea of giving a presentation. Here's what the experts would say are the causes of this type of anxiety:
>
> - The fear of communicating with people you don't know
> - A new or unusual situation
> - Being the centre of attention, which makes you self-conscious and embarrassed if you appear awkward or say something foolish
> - Evaluation – when being watched by a teacher or a video camera, you feel you are being examined
> - Past failures in similar situations
> - A learned anxiety from seeing others who are worried or afraid of giving a presentation

Extended Conversation

Most of us have no problem sitting with a group of friends, telling them what we did at the weekend. But moving from this situation to standing up in front of a group is quite a big shift. The main differences are:

- Everyone's attention is focused on you (and it's probably a bigger group).
- You are standing and they are sitting.
- There is a greater expectation on you to 'perform'.
- There is no turn taking or instant feedback.

Another important difference between a conversation and a speech is that a speech has been planned, prepared and organised.

Public speaking is a bit like an enlarged conversation, so we should try to speak as if in a conversation. A good speech does not need to use overly formal language. Often an audience will respond better to an informal, personal style, which helps them feel they are partaking in a conversation rather than being lectured to. Don't try to use language that wouldn't come naturally but avoid using excessive slang as well. Most listeners will tolerate minor errors and stumbles, as they would in normal conversation.

Preparation

An effective presentation is the result of careful planning, preparation and rehearsing. Without adequate preparation, the presentation will be ineffective and you will disappoint both yourself and your audience. It is a good opportunity to try something new, even if it is a daunting task, and many students of communications surprise themselves at the excellent results they achieve in this skill.

Choosing a Topic

If you have the option of choosing your own subject, then choose a topic that:
- You are interested in
- You already know something about
- You can get information on

If you are interested in the subject, it is more likely that you can make it interesting for others. You might choose some aspect of your course or a pastime or hobby.

Ask yourself:
- Is it suitable material for an oral presentation?
- Is it appropriate for the audience? (Will they understand it/find it interesting?)
- Is it appropriate for the occasion?
- Am I sufficiently interested in the topic?
- Where can I get information on it?
- Can I get some visual aids to make it more interesting?

Brainstorming

When you have chosen your topic, begin by brainstorming all the relevant themes associated with it, and create a mind map. This will give you an idea of how large the subject matter is, and you may need to narrow it down to one or two subtopics.

Fig. 7.2

Communication Objective

There are three main speaking purposes:
1. Entertainment
2. Information
3. Persuasion

Decide what your objective is. Do you want the audience to take up a hobby or join an organisation? Do you want to teach them a new skill? Or do you want to have them rolling in the aisles with laughter? Perhaps you will use a combination of all three.

You should be able to summarise the main idea of the talk in one concise sentence. This can be used as an opening statement and should be memorable even if the listeners don't remember the details of your speech.

Audience

It is important to know who your audience is going to be. Are they already interested in the subject? Do they have any prior knowledge of the topic? Will they share your sense of humour? Are they captive, i.e. will they listen to your every word, or will it be a struggle to force them to pay attention? A good understanding of your audience beforehand will assist you in knowing what kind of talk you will give, and what sort of language and tone of voice you will use.

Fig. 7.3

▶ Structure and Organisation

A well-organised speech can be a stimulating and inspiring piece of communication that can stay in our mind for some time afterwards. A disorganised presentation will be ineffective and even embarrassing. We have all experienced sitting in a class or listening to a speaker who rambles from one topic to the next, but do we remember what the main thrust of the speech was or any of the details? Probably not.

A well-organised speech works for the following reasons:
▶ It is easier to understand and digest.
▶ It is easier to remember.

- It has more impact and is more persuasive.
- It increases the speaker's credibility.

A well-organised speaker:
- Uses short sentences which are easy to follow
- Introduces the listeners to forthcoming information, e.g. 'The results of global warming are twofold...'
- Gives information in a clear and logical way, e.g. 'First... second... third...'
- Uses detailed statistical evidence to support information given
- Avoids vague and ambiguous information

Structure

There are three basic elements of an oral presentation:
1. *Introduction* – tell the audience what you are going to say.
2. *Body* – say it.
3. *Conclusion* – tell them what you've said.

Introduction

The opening of your speech is vital in that it can win or lose the audience. Remember that first impressions last, so try to get the listeners' attention from the start and explain briefly what the talk will be about. The introduction should have three sections:

1. An opening statement that will get the audience's attention. Consider using one of the following:
   - A controversial statement, e.g. 'Ireland is the worst greenhouse gas emitter in Europe'
   - A quotation
   - An interesting statistic
   - A visual aid with impact
   - A rhetorical question (a question that doesn't expect an answer) e.g. 'Have you ever wondered what it is like to swim in a crocodile-infested river?'
   - A personal experience
   - An anecdote
   - Humour (though be wary of telling a joke – it could spoil your talk!)

2. A statement of the main idea, which should give the audience a good understanding of what it will be about. For example:
   - 'Today I'm going to tell you about the causes and effects of climate change.'
   - 'This presentation is to try to illustrate the dangers of alcohol abuse.'
   - 'I want to inform you about rock climbing.'
   - 'This morning I'm going to show you how to grow your own tomatoes.'

3. A rough outline of the main points to be covered. This gives the audience an idea of what it is you are going to say – a bit like a table of contents. An audience likes to know where it is being taken.

Body of Presentation

In a five- to ten-minute speech aim for three to four main points selected from your mind map. They should be logically organised and should flow smoothly from one topic to the next. It is important to try to link topics together, and signposts can be used for this purpose. These can be single words, phrases or whole sentences. It is crucial to let the audience know when you are moving on to a new point. If you jump from one topic to the next too abruptly, the audience may get confused and lose interest.

Typical signposts might include the following examples:
- First/second/third...
- Due to this/because of this/as a result of this/consequently...
- Therefore/and so...
- Finally...
- Now that we've seen how the internal combustion engine works...
- I've looked at the causes of insomnia, now let's have a look at the effects...

Nonverbal signposts can also be used:
- The fingers can indicate first, second and third points.
- Silence or a pause can let the audience know that you are moving on to a new topic.
- Visual aids can be used to introduce a new point.
- Intonation is a good way of showing that you have reached the end of one section of your talk.

Conclusion

An effective conclusion is vital so as to finish on a strong note that will leave a lasting impression on the audience. At all costs avoid trailing off limply at the end. A conclusion is often like the introduction in reverse. Use it to summarise the main points and to leave the audience with a final thought on the subject that they will hopefully remember. Don't be afraid to repeat information at the end of the talk. The audience cannot rewind to go back over the topics already stated, so it is useful to restate some of the key ones, especially the main idea. As with the introduction, it should be brief, and no new themes should be introduced at this stage. Try to keep it positive and upbeat.

Typical concluding statements include:
- 'I hope you now have a better grasp of...'
- 'Let me leave you with one final thought...'
- 'Today I've given you a brief outline of...'
- 'I hope I have succeeded in informing you about...'

Finally

You need to let the audience know that you have finished your talk, to encourage questions and/or applause. To do this, you could follow your concluding statement with, 'Thank you for listening. Are there any questions?'

Timeline of Presentation

Break your talk into sections using the topics from your brainstorm. Along with the introduction and conclusion, it might look something like this:

- **Introduction – 30 seconds**
- **Subtopic 1 – two minutes**
- **Subtopic 2 – three minutes**
- **Subtopic 3 – two minutes**
- **Conclusion – 30 seconds**
- **Total – eight minutes**

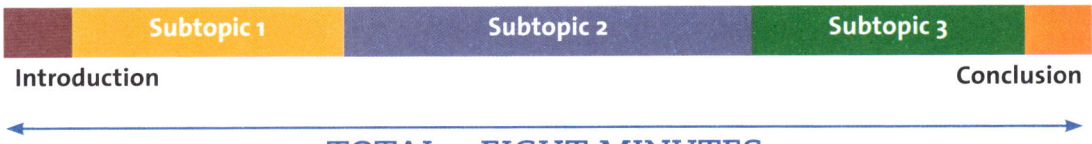

| Introduction | Subtopic 1 | Subtopic 2 | Subtopic 3 | Conclusion |

TOTAL – EIGHT MINUTES

Fig. 7.4

Now it seems quite manageable, because you only have to talk for a couple of minutes on each subtopic.

Practising Your Presentation

Next you should write out your speech in full. This gives you the opportunity to go through each point carefully, and to make sure that it is properly structured. Give each topic a heading. Practise by reading through it a few times to get used to the flow of it.

If you need to use notes, select keywords and phrases to write on cue cards. Write three or four points on each one, on one side only, and number each cue card so you don't mix them up.

Don't read from a written speech. It sounds boring, you have little opportunity to make eye contact with the audience and your voice can be lost as it disappears into the page.

Don't learn it off by heart. It can be very time-consuming, hard work and it may end up like a recital and not a talk. Unless you have a great memory and are a natural performer, this should be avoided.

▶ Delivery

Nonverbal Communication

An audience responds to a speaker's body language. If your body language shows interest and enthusiasm for the subject, the audience will respond in the same way. If you show that you aren't interested or that you're bored, the audience will feel the same.

Fig. 7.5

The Voice

The voice is obviously crucial in an oral presentation. The following are the main points to consider:

1. *Volume:* You must be audible and loud enough so that the people at the back can hear. Practise projecting your voice to someone at the opposite end of the classroom.
2. *Tone and pitch:* You should aim to make it sound interesting by sounding interested. Otherwise it may sound flat and monotonous. Inflection, changing the pitch of the voice so that is goes up and down, adds interest to a speech. We do this naturally when we speak about something that interests us. When we are nervous, unfortunately, we tend to remain at one level. Practise changing the pitch of your voice at different parts of your presentation.
3. *Emphasis:* Try to put stress on words that need emphasising.
4. *Pause:* Pausing is effective and useful to let the audience take in an important point, to signal a change of topic and to give yourself a break to check your notes. Don't be afraid to pause briefly every now and again.
5. *Speed:* We speed up when nervous. If you're too fast, you may lose the audience; too slow and you'll bore them.

In all of the above, aim for variety, as this will make the presentation sound interesting and hold the audience's attention.

Posture

Listeners pay more attention to a speaker who has a straight posture than someone with a crooked or slouched one. Stand with a comfortably straight spine and neck. When not operating a laptop or gesturing, a good default posture is holding your hands down in front of you with fingers interlocked.

Avoid:
- Shifting from one foot to the other
- Putting your back or shoulder to the audience
- Folding your arms
- Hands in pockets
- Hands behind your back

Gestures

Appropriate and controlled hand gestures can help support a speech. Unanimated speakers can be boring to watch, but don't use exaggerated gestures that will distract the audience.

Avoid:
- Wringing hands
- Rattling keys/coins in pockets
- Fiddling with hair, pens, glasses, etc.

Facial Expression

Introducing yourself with a smile can win over an audience from the start, and an occasional and appropriate smile during the talk can keep them on your side. If wearing a mask, a smile can be communicated with the eyes. The eyebrows are a very expressive part of the face and we can emphasise a point by raising them.

Eye Contact

Ideally, we should make eye contact at least once with everyone in the audience. But by staring at one person we can make them feel uncomfortable. However, by looking at the back wall, out of the window or at the floor, it appears that we are communicating with these things and not with the audience. In a very large venue with a big audience looking at the back wall can work but not in an average sized classroom where the audience is small. Aim to pass your gaze over the audience throughout your speech.

▶ Venue

You should find out about the venue beforehand. Consider the following:
- What sort of equipment is available?
- Is the room big or small? (Will your voice reach those sitting at the back?)
- Will there be a desk or podium on which to put your laptop, cue cards or visual aids?

If you don't know the venue beforehand, you might be surprised to find yourself somewhere totally unsuited to your needs.

▶ Support Material

A presentation that involves just speaking can be quite dull, so support material can help to make it more stimulating. Any of the following will add evidence, interest and credibility:
- Statistics
- Comparisons
- Quotations
- Visual aids
- Anecdotes/stories
- Examples
- Handouts

Visual Aids

Visual aids support and enhance an oral presentation in the following ways:
1. They make a talk interesting and stimulating.
2. They have a strong and lasting impact.
3. They can help an audience understand the topic by:
    - Illustrating with examples
    - Simplifying and supporting verbal information with charts or graphs

Types of Visual Aid
- Models and objects
- Maps
- Diagrams
- Charts and graphs
- Drawings, paintings, sketches
- Photographs
- Posters
- Whiteboard, blackboard and flip chart (not usually prepared beforehand, but you need to have clear handwriting or drawing skills)
- Slide projector and overhead projector (becoming obsolete with newer technologies becoming more widely available)

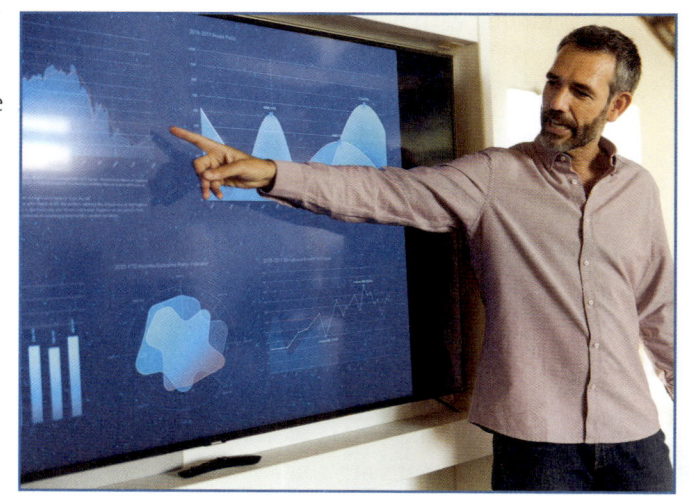

Fig. 7.6

Means of Display

- Software such as Microsoft PowerPoint or Apple Keynote are designed for presentations and are relatively easy and enjoyable to use. You will need a computer/laptop linked to a data projector and a screen. Slides that use a combination of images and a few bullet points of text will keep the audience interested. Avoid overdoing slide transition effects.
- Video – a relevant clip can also add interest to your speech. Keep it brief and don't talk over it.
- Always prepare your equipment beforehand to make sure everything is working properly.

Font Sizes

If using written text, make sure you use an appropriate font size. Here are some guidelines:

	PowerPoint	Handouts
Headings	36 point	18 point
Subheadings	24 point	14 point
Main Body of Text	18 point	12 point

Flip Charts/Blackboards/Whiteboards	
Headings	8 cm
Subheadings	5 cm

General Points to Remember about Visual Aids

- Keep them simple – simple language, simple images and limit the amount of text you use. An audience doesn't like to read too much.
- Make them big – they should be visible at the back of the room.
- Make them relevant – use visuals only if they support and enhance the speech. Don't let them dominate.
- They should look well – no one likes to look at unattractive or messy images.
- Colour is more attractive than black and white.
- For a five- to ten-minute talk, four or five visuals are sufficient. If using PowerPoint, you could use up to 10 slides.

Effective Use

- Prepare them well in advance of the presentation.
- Plan exactly when to use them during the talk. Don't have them all at the beginning or all at the end.
- Practise using them.
- Check that any equipment is working.
- Don't block the audience's view of them.
- When finished using them, switch them off or remove them.
- Remember, technology can always let you down at the last moment, and you may have to speak without it.

Handouts

Don't make your audience read too much. They will forget about you! It is best to use these at the end of the presentation. They should be headed with the title pf your presentation and your name.

▶ Dealing with Questions

When you've finished speaking, thank the audience for listening and ask if there are any questions. Here are some hints:

- Listen to the question carefully.
- Repeat the whole question in case not everyone has heard it.
- When answering, address the whole audience, not just the questioner.
- Give answers that are complete, concise and to the point.
- When finished answering, ask the questioner if your reply was sufficiently clear.
- If you don't know the answer, don't 'wing it'. Be honest and say you'll have to look into it.
- Stay alert.
- Bring the question session to an *effective* conclusion, e.g. 'If there are no further questions...'
- Say thank you at the end.

Fig. 7.7

Finally

Preparation for an oral presentation requires sufficient practice. This means spending time rehearsing either in front of a class group, at home with friends or family or on your own in front of a mirror. Without practice, you will be ineffective. Each time you practise, you improve.

Practice is vital for the following reasons:
- To time the speech to ensure you won't go too much over or under the allotted time
- To get used to the layout and flow of words in the speech
- To get comfortable with using the cue cards, and elaborating on the keywords and phrases
- To get comfortable with your visual aids, and to know when to use them
- To improve your overall performance: voice, body language, eye contact, etc.
- To get completely acquainted with and confident of your subject matter

Activities

1. **Viral speeches**

    Watch and analyse the following two speeches, which went viral.
    - Greta Thunberg's speech at the UN Climate Summit, 2019
    - Panti Bliss' Noble Call speech at the Abbey Theatre, 2014

    What do you think of them? What techniques are being used to good effect? Consider the communication used, verbal and nonverbal, posture, tone of voice, repetition and structure.

    Here are a few more examples of speeches to read, watch or listen to:
    - President John F. Kennedy's inaugural speech, 1961
    - Martin Luther King's 'I Have a Dream' speech, 1963
    - President Mary Robinson's inaugural speech, 1990
    - President Barack Obama's inaugural speech, 2009
    - Neil Gaiman's commencement speech at the University of the Arts, Philadelphia, 2012
    - The final speech from the Charlie Chaplin film *The Great Dictator*

2. **Vocal Warmup**

    It's useful to warm up your vocal cords before giving a speech. Stand comfortably straight, feet hip width apart and imagine you are drawing the number eight in the air with your nose for about a minute. This loosens up the neck muscles. Then 'draw' a number eight on its side. Next start making 'blah blah blah' sounds, really sticking your tongue out as you do it. Then change that into the noise children sometimes make by flapping your tongue in and out of your mouth and loudly vocalising. Next, make a continual 'ng' sound such as at the end of the word 'sing' but using your voice to go up and down making a sound like a siren, getting higher and lower each time. Then purse your lips to make an 'ooh' sound followed immediately by an 'ee' sound and alternate quickly between the two, really stretching your lips. Do this to the tune of 'Twinkle Twinkle Little Star'. By now your vocal cords should be warmed up nicely.

3. **Tongue-Twisters**

   Sit or stand in a circle and do a go-round, each student repeating the tongue-twisters on pages 49–50 (Chapter 4: Speaking Skills).

Fig. 7.8

4. **Three-Word Speech**

   Each student writes three words on three separate pieces of paper and puts them in a bowl/box/bucket.
   Students take turns to pick three pieces of paper and make up a story/speech on the spot containing the three words.

Tips for an Effective Presentation

- Prepare well.
- Keep it simple.
- Practise.
- Use good visual aids.

After you have given a presentation, use Gibbs' Reflective Cycle in Appendix 2 to consider your performance, what you did well and how you could improve it.

Chapter Review

1. Explain the main causes of fear of public speaking.
2. How can you get over your fear of public speaking?
3. What are the similarities and differences between an oral presentation and a conversation?
4. How can you organise a speech to make it easy for an audience to understand?
5. Why is it important to structure a speech?
6. What are the advantages of using visual aids?
7. Describe effective ways of opening a speech.
8. How can you make effective use of visual aids?
9. Explain the importance of nonverbal communication in an oral presentation.
10. Outline how to deal with questions from the audience.

Part 3

Nonverbal and Visual Communication

Some Examples of Nonverbal Communication
- Body Language
- Facial Expression
- Eye Contact
- Gestures
- Posture

Some Examples of Visual Communication
- Pictures
- Photographs
- Drawings
- Paintings
- Posters
- Diagrams
- Charts
- Maps
- Flags

Advantages of Nonverbal Communication
- Supports and reinforces verbal messages
- Adds interest
- Personalises messages
- Can give a more complete picture

Advantages of Visual Communication
- Reinforces spoken word
- Interesting
- Attractive
- Can simplify written and spoken word
- Has impact
- Easy to remember

Disadvantages of Nonverbal Communication
- May be vague or ambiguous
- May need verbal explanation
- Body language is mostly unconscious
- Cultural differences

Disadvantages of Visual Communication
- Can be vague
- Open to misunderstandings
- May need written/spoken support
- May be time-consuming to produce
- May be expensive

Chapter 8
Nonverbal Communication

> In this chapter, you will learn about:
> - Appearance
> - Facial Expression
> - Eye Contact
> - Gesture
> - Posture
> - Territory
> - Orientation
> - Physical Contact
> - Paralanguage
> - Silence
> - The Environment
> - Time
> - Music
> - Sounds
> - Smell
> - Dance
> - Art
> - Other Nonverbal Signs and Codes

Nonverbal communication (NVC) means communicating without words. It probably accounts for around 80 per cent of what we communicate, whereas the spoken word may be as little as 7 per cent. A look can often reveal more accurately what we are thinking than words can. We are constantly communicating nonverbally, by the way we look, gesture, stand, sit, smile, frown, dress ourselves, wear our hair, etc. This is why NVC is so important in any study of communication.

Let's look at a few general points about NVC before we examine the specific types.

1. NVC is ambiguous. There are always at least two potential meanings to any NVC, that of the sender and that of the receiver. It is not always possible to interpret the exact meaning of NVC, as it depends on both the context and the people involved. We should not attempt to attach fixed meaning to any one form of NVC in isolation from the other verbal and nonverbal messages that may be communicated with it.

2. NVC varies from culture to culture. What might be a friendly gesture in our culture may be a serious insult in another, so be careful! The circle sign made with the thumb and forefinger means 'OK' to Irish, British, Americans and most Northern Europeans. In France it signifies 'zero' or 'worthless', in Japan, 'money', and in parts of the Mediterranean it is an obscene insult.

3. Most of our NVC is unconscious. We wave our hands about and gesticulate when talking excitedly; our face changes shape depending on our emotional state; we twitch, fidget, scratch, stretch, shift our posture hundreds of times every day without even noticing it.

4. We are much less aware of our NVC than our speech. If we become more conscious of how we communicate nonverbally, we can learn to control it and become better communicators.

5. NVC:
   - *Supports speech* – hand gestures reinforce, elaborate and emphasise what we say, e.g. 'I caught a fish *this* big!' 'He went *that* way.'
   - *Modifies speech* – we can say 'Don't *do* that' in an angry, pleading, firm or light-hearted way.
   - *Replaces speech* – as in sign language.
   - *Contradicts speech* – as in, for example, '"Yes of course I'm fine!" she snapped, avoiding his gaze, and sighing heavily.'

6. First impressions count. When we walk through that door for an interview, we are immediately being judged on our appearance, how we walk, shake hands and sit down. Jobs are often disproportionately offered on this basis.

7. Actions speak louder than words. If someone says he has time to talk to you, yet continues what he is doing – gathering his books, erasing the board and checking the register, for example – do you believe his verbal or his nonverbal message? Most people, when confronted by such contradictory signs, believe the nonverbal communication. Since we are more in control of our words than our body language, most of us find it easier to lie verbally than nonverbally.

8. Baby signing, i.e. using hand signs to support verbal communication with babies, is believed to improve communication skills, behaviour, parent–child relationships and mental development in children.

Activities

1. Compare these two photographs of Donald Trump shaking hands, one with Barack Obama and the other with Vladimir Putin. Discuss the differences in facial expression, eye contact, orientation, posture and physical proximity.

Fig. 8.1   Fig. 8.2

2. Compare the body language of the two couples in the photographs.

Fig. 8.3

▶ Appearance

Appearance says a lot about the type of person we are. Even if we are the kind of person who dresses 'down' so as not to attract unwanted attention, we are still communicating something about ourselves. We can change how we present ourselves by making alterations to our hair, facial hair, make-up, clothes, accessories, and by using jewellery, tattoos and body piercing. By doing this we can communicate messages about our:

▶ *Personality* – conservative, rebellious, artistic, individual, extrovert, introvert
▶ *Occupation* – some jobs have specific uniforms

Nonverbal Communication 113

- *Role* – think of a few different roles you fulfil, e.g. at work, socialising (formal/informal, single/attached), at home, at an interview
- *Status* – in some occupations higher status is illustrated by different clothing, e.g. the army, nursing, the Church (different uniforms), the corporate world (expensive designer suits), etc.
- *Nationality*
- *Gender*
- *Sexual orientation*
- *Interests and tastes*
- *Club membership*

Activity

Compare the appearances of the men in these two photographs. What messages might they be consciously or unconsciously communicating?

Fig. 8.4

Fig. 8.5

Go to the end of the chapter to find out who they are.

It is important to consider how we present ourselves in different situations. For example, for job interviews it is recommended that we dress formally. However, if we dress too formally for an occasion that is casual, we may look and feel out of place. Our appearance projects a certain image of ourselves, and other people will respond to that image. At work and in formal situations we tend to respond more positively to those who are well dressed, but not overdressed.

Activities

1. In pairs, discuss your own appearance and consider the following:
   - Clothing
   - Hair
   - Facial hair
   - Body adornment (piercings, tattoos, etc.)
   - Jewellery
   - Shoes

2. Consider the clothes you wear. Have you ever thought about the signals that you might be sending out with them? Do you wear them:
   - For comfort/practical reasons
   - Because they are fashionable
   - To attract attention
   - To blend in with the crowd
   - To look 'cool'
   - To express your sexuality
   - Because they are long-lasting
   - To look rebellious/different
   - To be part of a clique
   - Because they have a certain logo

Facial Expression

The face is probably the main source of nonverbal communication, and the most important, authentic communication takes place face to face. The face is the best indicator of our feelings, and it is only when we are face to face with someone that we really connect with them. Even though expressions like smiling and frowning are inborn, we learn how to respond facially to others through interaction with our parents, families and friends, so for example, we smile as a response to another's smile. There is a concern today that many children who don't receive enough parental interaction due to busy lifestyles, and spend much of their time using electronic games, lose out on healthy face-to-face contact. As a result, they don't learn facial expression responses, and this can cause relationship problems in later life.

There are over 10,000 facial expressions caused by 44 facial muscles and two bones, the skull and the jaw. There are, however, seven primary expressions that promote a deep response in us – happiness, sadness, surprise, anger, fear, disgust and contempt.

The eyes and the mouth are the main communicators, and they are the features we focus on mostly when we are looking at someone. It has been said that the eyes are the windows of the soul, and we can usually tell how someone really feels by looking at the eyes.

The mouth smiles, sneers, pouts, purses, grins, opens wide, shuts tightly, etc. The ultimate facial expression, which seems to mean the same in every part of the world, is the smile. A true smile is never misunderstood and, as believed by some scientists, releases endorphins into the body that make us feel good. It also uses fewer muscles than a frown and therefore requires less energy!

Nonverbal Communication 115

Activity

Can you tell the real smile from the fake smile? Go to the end of the chapter to see if you were right.

Fig. 8.6a 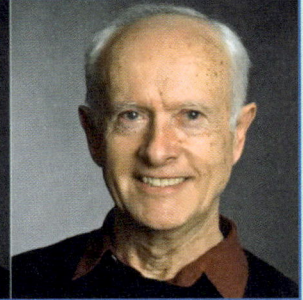   Fig 8.6b

Facial expression is so important that in order to avoid misunderstandings when sending texts and emails, we add digitally produced facial expressions – emojis. 🙂

Activity

Can you match the seven primary expressions of happiness, sadness, surprise, anger, fear, disgust and contempt with the pictures below? Go to the end of the chapter to see if your matches are correct.

Fig. 8.7a    Fig. 8.7b    Fig. 8.7c

Fig. 8.7d    Fig. 8.7e    Fig. 8.7f    Fig. 8.7g

Eye Contact

In Western society, when we speak with someone face to face, it is natural to look them in the eye. It is considered to show directness and integrity. Avoidance of eye contact shows lack of confidence and may indicate dishonesty. In the Czech Republic, avoiding eye contact when clinking beer glasses is interpreted as an indication that the person has something to hide and may not be trustworthy. In some Asian cultures, however, eye contact can be considered rude.

Eye contact is also a way of communicating that we are listening. It lets the speaker know we are interested. It is also used as an initial means of contact. Prior to speaking to someone we usually make eye contact with them.

Eye contact communicates:

- *Attitudes* – intense gazing into another's eyes shows trust and closeness between two people. Is there a difference between gazing and staring into another's eyes?
- *Attraction* – our pupils involuntarily dilate when we are attracted to or interested in someone or something.
- *Personality* – assertive, confident and extrovert types make more direct eye contact than those who are less confident.
- *Emotions* – avoiding or breaking eye contact can show annoyance with someone.

Discussion

Explain what's going on in these photos.

Fig. 8.8a

Fig. 8.8b

Fig. 8.8c

Fig. 8.8d

Activity

Divide the class into pairs of A and B.

A and B sit opposite each other and spend a minute or two on each of the following tasks:

1. A tells B what he/she did at the weekend. A makes eye contact and B doesn't.
2. A tells B what he/she did at the weekend. B makes eye contact and A doesn't.
3. B tells A what he/she did at the weekend, and both make constant eye contact.
4. B tells A what he/she did at the weekend, and each behaves as normal.

Who normally makes more eye contact, the speaker or the listener?

Discuss how you felt as speaker/listener when the other avoided eye contact.

Gesture

Gestures are actions we make with different parts of our body that can replace or support spoken communication. We each have hundreds of gestures that we use to communicate a vast array of messages.

Discussion

1. What messages can we send with each of the following parts of the body?
   - Head
   - Hands
   - Arms
   - Shoulders
   - Legs
   - Feet

2. How do we communicate the following using gestures?
   - Hello
   - Come here
   - Go away!
   - Stop
   - Money
   - OK
   - I don't know
   - Stupid!
   - Naughty!
   - Quiet
   - Drink?
   - Well done
   - Pleased to meet you

There are a multitude of gestures and gesture combinations. One gesture can have many different meanings, and there are many gestures that mean the same thing. Very subtle differences between similar gestures can have widely different meanings. Be aware that many gestures are culture-specific and can mean very different things in different situations.

> ## Discussion
>
> What different meanings can the following have?
> - A protruding tongue
> - Hands up in the air
> - The V-sign

By becoming more conscious of our gestures and by being clear in their transmission, we can avoid vagueness and misunderstandings. It is useful to observe public speakers and the movements that they make when speaking. Be careful not to overdo gesturing to support speech as it may distract from what you are saying.

Activity

It is possible to have a 'conversation' using only gestures. Try to act out the following role-play without words:

A: Hello.
B: Hello.
A: Are you all right?
B: I'm all right. And you?
A: So-so.
B: What time is it?
A: I don't know.
B: Can you give me some money?
A: No.
B: Please.
A: No!
B: I'm hungry.
A: I don't have any money!
B: I'm cold.
A: Look over there!
B: What, where? I don't see anything.
A: It doesn't matter.
B: Goodbye.
A: Bye.

Alternatively make up your own 'gesture conversation' scenarios.

Discussion

In terms of gesture, a talk pleading for people to donate money to a cause would differ from a talk intended to incite people to revolt. What sort of gestures would you use in each case?

Two heart gestures that have become popular in recent years are the 'hand heart' and the 'finger heart'.

Fig. 8.9a   Fig. 8.9b

▶ Posture

How we stand, sit, walk, lie and generally hold our body communicates a variety of messages:

1. Mood and physical state, e.g. relaxed posture = confidence.
2. How we feel towards others, e.g. two people squaring up to each other aggressively stand upright, shoulders back and head up straight.
3. Status, e.g. soldiers stand to attention in front of a superior officer; in some cultures they bow before royalty; people kneel to pray.
4. Situation, e.g. at an interview we sit upright showing alertness and interest.

Activity

Match the moods to the postures below:

Moods	Postures
Triumph/victory	Arms and legs crossed
Boredom	Hands held tightly in front, fidgeting
Interest	Hands on hips, head up and back straight
Nervousness/shyness	Leaning forward, head cocked
Confidence	Head in hands, elbows on table, shoulders slumped, body sagging
Defensiveness	Arms held aloft, head held high, fists clenched

Are any of these signals ambiguous?

Discussion

What messages are these people communicating?

Fig. 8.10a

Fig. 8.10b

Fig. 8.10c

A look around a classroom often reveals a wide variety of moods, with postures ranging from interest to boredom to utter disbelief!

Team Ireland were praised for their show of respect to the hosts at the Olympic Opening Ceremony in Tokyo in 2021.

Fig. 8.11

Taking the knee has become a popular gesture against racism. First displayed by American football player Colin Kaepernick in 2016, when during the national anthem, instead of standing, he knelt to protest against racial inequality in the USA, it has gone on to be used by sports players around the world and at Black Lives Matter protests.

Fig. 8.12

Territory

Our territory is something we feel strongly about, and it can make us protective and defensive. It is our space, and we communicate it in a variety of ways. Animals leave their scent on trees and bushes to let other animals know who lives there. Humans mark their territory in visual ways.

There are three types of human territory: tribal, family and personal.

Tribal Territory

Primitive tribes occupied a specific area, consisting of a home base and a hunting ground around it. Intruders would have been driven away and members of the tribe communicated their membership by war chants and war paint. Today, the tribe has become the nation, using nonverbal signals such as flags and national anthems to communicate its identity, and

Fig. 8.13

border checkpoints to show its boundary. Another example is football fans, who communicate to rival fans their territory in the stadium with a display of colours, flags, scarves and chanting.

Family Territory

The family territory is the home, with the bedroom as the core where we feel most secure. People who have been burgled, and whose private possessions in their bedrooms were rummaged through, experience a personal sense of having been invaded. The house has a boundary of a wall, fence or hedge. Within the home are other markers of territory – ornaments, furniture, family photographs, wall art, etc. A family often displays its territory outside the home, e.g. when at the beach, towels, rugs, bags, etc. will mark the space to which the family temporarily belongs.

INTIMATE SPACE
Less than 1.5ft (0.45m)

PERSONAL SPACE
15ft (0.45m) – 4ft (1.2m)

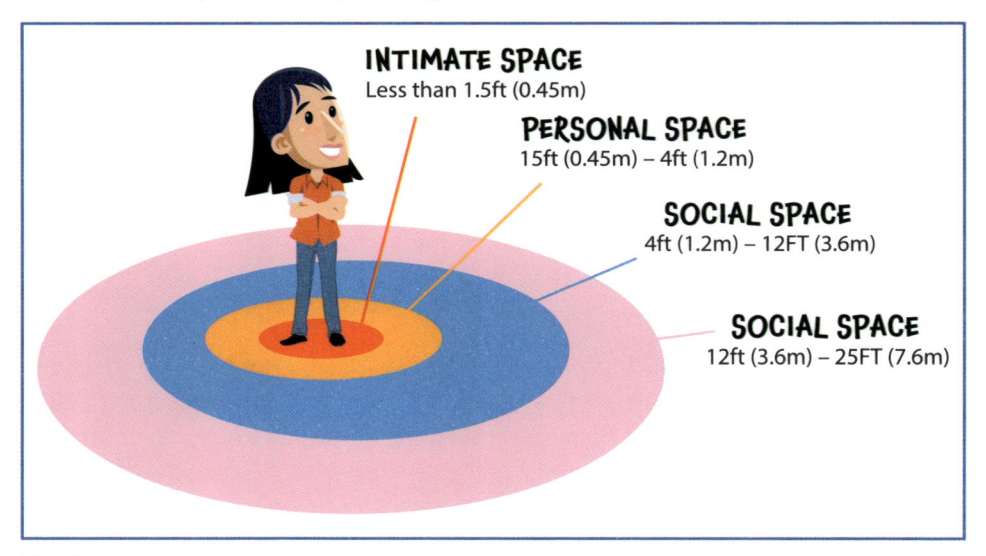

SOCIAL SPACE
4ft (1.2m) – 12FT (3.6m)

SOCIAL SPACE
12ft (3.6m) – 25FT (7.6m)

Fig. 8.14

Personal Territory

Each of us carries an invisible 'space bubble', our own portable piece of territory. We can see this when we get onto a bus or train. If the seats are all empty, except one, the chances are we won't sit next to the only person there. We will always sit where we give ourselves the maximum amount of space.

If someone unknown enters our bubble, we might feel threatened. If someone we know and care for keeps well outside it, we might feel a sense of rejection. Our personal space bubble communicates levels of formality, friendship, intimacy and how comfortable we feel with other people. We have to know and trust someone pretty well before we let them enter our space bubble. Sometimes we have no choice but to let others into our space, for example at a crowded concert or football match. In Mediterranean and North African cultures people usually like to stand closer than Northern Europeans and Americans.

Fig. 8.15

> ## Discussion
> During the COVID-19 pandemic, public health guidelines were to keep 2 metres apart, especially indoors. Many public buildings and public transport reduced the number of seats, so that people had empty seats on either side of them. What effect did this have? How did it feel to be 'socially distancing' from others?

Sitting behind a desk is putting up a barrier and, therefore, distance, between two people. It can give the impression that we are unapproachable. Observe the different interview techniques of television chat show hosts. Some use desks and others don't. Which is more effective?

> ## Activity
> List five people you feel comfortable entering your 'space bubble'. What do they have in common? Discuss your reasons with the class group.

Proximity

Proximity is how close we let someone get to us. It depends on:
1. *Status* – people of high status enter others' space more than vice versa, e.g. teacher and pupil, doctor and patient, Garda and criminal, officer and soldier, employer and employee.
2. *Gender* – women tend to be physically closer to each other than men.
3. *Age* – children enter each other's space more than adults.
4. *Culture* – Middle Eastern and African people get closer to each other than Westerners and some Asians.

Go to YouTube and search 'Seinfeld personal space' to see an amusing video clip from this comedy about the sanctity of personal space.

▶ Orientation

This is how we position ourselves in relation to others, and it communicates how we feel towards them. We sit face to face with someone we like or respect. Giving someone the 'cold shoulder' means we face away from them in a display of dislike or disrespect.

Two people sitting at a table can choose to orient themselves in a number of different ways:
- Side by side
- Face to face across the table
- At right angles to each other at one corner

What are the differences between each of these in terms of formality and intimacy? Consider, for example, which is most appropriate for a job interview. Why did King Arthur have a round table? Consider the typical classroom set-up. Are there alternative ways of arranging the seating for different types of activity?

NVC experts tell us that the direction in which a person's feet are pointing is where they want to go. If they are talking to another person and their feet are pointing towards that person, then they want to be with that person. But if they are talking to and facing someone, but their foot or feet are pointing towards the door, that's where they want to go. If their foot or feet point towards another person, they would rather be talking to them.

Fig. 8.16

Discussion

If a stranger approached you and appeared to be a threat, how would you orient yourself toward him? If he appeared to be no threat, how would your NVC be different?

▶ Physical Contact

Experts say physical contact with others is good for us. It can satisfy emotional needs, increase our sense of self-worth and enhance our relationships as a means of communicating love, affection and closeness. Of course, we all experience different degrees of closeness in our different relationships. For some people it would be perfectly natural to give an affectionate hug to a friend, while to others this would be a source of embarrassment.

Touching defines relationships and communicates social status. But it must be done with tact and respect. Positive touching can be therapeutic and healing whereas negative touching can be dominating and abusive.

Irish philosopher Richard Kearney thinks that the increasing use of digital technologies is causing us to lose our primal need for touch as we become more accustomed to virtual interaction with other people. During the COVID-19 pandemic, social distancing made it very clear how important physical contact is in our lives as we found ourselves even more separated, isolated and 'out of touch' with others since even more of our social interaction moved online.

Fig. 8.17a

Fig. 8.17b

Fig. 8.17c

Fig. 8.17d

There are four types of physical contact, ranging in degree of intimacy:

1. *Functional* – usually done in professional situations, e.g. doctors, physiotherapists, hairdressers.
2. *Ritual* – the most common type of ritual touching is the greeting, e.g. handshake, embrace, nose-rub, kiss on the cheek, 'high five'.
3. *Playful/supportive* – used to indicate encouragement, sympathy and affection, e.g. a pat on the back, touching the hand or arm. This type is open to misinterpretation, especially at work. It may be viewed as patronising, as an invasion of personal space or at worst as sexual harassment.
4. *Intimate* – between parent and child, between lovers.

126 Effective Communication

Handshake Techniques

There are a variety of handshake techniques:
1. The firm handshake
2. The limp handshake
3. The accompanying hand on the other's elbow
4. The accompanying hand on the other's shoulder
5. The accompanying hand on the side of the other's head

Fig. 8.18

Discussion

What does each of these handshake techniques communicate in terms of confidence, warmth and intimacy?

Physical contact varies in the following ways:
1. *Status* – doctors will touch patients and not vice versa (see 'Proximity', p. 123).
2. *Gender* – women in Western societies touch more than men.
3. *Age* – children touch more than older people.
4. *Culture* – Northern Europeans, Americans and most Asians touch less than Southern Europeans and Africans. Most Asian societies are traditionally not touch oriented and public displays of affection are avoided, although in India it is not uncommon to see men holding hands simply as a sign of friendship.

Fig. 8.19

Discussion

You have decided to go on a world trip for one year. At the airport a number or friends and family members have come to bid you farewell. How would you say goodbye to the following nonverbally?
- Your mother
- Your father
- Your boyfriend/girlfriend
- Your sister
- Your brother
- Your closest friend
- A colleague
- Your boss
- A casual acquaintance

This could be done as a role-play if members feel comfortable.

Paralanguage

Sometimes we communicate with the voice but not necessarily with words. There are three types:
1. Vocal qualities
2. Vocalisations
3. Vocal segregates

Vocal Qualities

- Pitch
- Volume
- Stress/emphasis
- Speed
- Rhythm
- Tone
- Accent

All of these can communicate our emotional state, personality, social class, origins and level of education. We can alter the meaning of what we say by infusing it with different tones. We can convey approval or disapproval, warmth, humour, friendliness, dislike, scorn, sarcasm, etc. We can sound serious or playful, firm, seductive, apologetic, angry, etc.

If we are planning on working in a vocation that involves dealing with the public, it is important to be aware of how we speak. A warm welcoming tone in our voice is preferable to sounding bored or impatient.

Activity

1. How would you say, 'We have a half day tomorrow' as a question?
2. Try to say, 'That's absolutely brilliant', first using an enthusiastic and then a sarcastic tone.
3. Try to say, 'Shush, be quiet', first in an angry and then a gentle/friendly tone.

Vocalisations

Sometimes we communicate through noises rather than through speaking. We grunt, groan, moan, shriek, weep, gulp, giggle, laugh, snigger, cry, sigh, whisper, whistle, scream, shout, yawn, sneeze, cough, belch. As with other forms of NVC, they can be ambiguous. For example, what different meanings can a sigh communicate?

Activity

1. What does Homer Simpson mean when he says, 'Doh!'?
2. What noises would you use to communicate the following?
   - Delicious
   - Disgusting
   - Disapproval
   - Frustration
   - Boredom
   - Pain
   - Yes
   - No
   - What?
   - Quiet

Vocal Segregates

This is the use of pause, hesitation and fillers such as 'em'. Many of these we use unconsciously but using pause and hesitation effectively can greatly enhance a speech (see also Chapter 7: Presentation Skills).

Activity

If it feels comfortable, pick one of the following attitudes/moods, and without telling the rest of the class group, try to communicate it through a combination of posture, facial expression, eye contact, paralanguage and gesture. Have the rest of the group guess the emotion.

- Disappointment
- Fear
- Confusion
- Love
- Fascination
- Boredom
- Frustration
- Derision
- Victory
- Piety
- Disgust
- Shiftiness
- Disapproval
- Admiration
- Sexiness
- Cockiness
- Astonishment

Come up with others if you wish.

Silence

In couples who are very close, silence communicates contentment as they may know each other so well they don't need to talk. On the other hand, it can mean awkwardness when two people cannot keep a conversation going. Giving someone the silent treatment is way of slighting someone we aren't pleased with. Teachers may use it to show disapproval in a classroom, usually accompanied by a stare. In Asian countries silence indicates politeness and contemplation.

Depending on the situation, silence can mean:

- Affection
- Reverence
- Attention
- Hesitation
- Embarrassment
- Hostility
- Oppression

The Environment

The design, shape, colour, size, temperature, lighting, smells and sounds of a place can affect how we feel and behave in a particular setting. In this way the environment communicates with us. For example, we should be aware of how we arrange the furniture in a room for a meeting. A room lit with daylight rather than artificial lighting can have a better effect on our work. A brightly lit room is easier to work in than a dark one, but dim lighting can create a romantic or relaxing mood, if that is what we want.

Restaurants use environmental factors to create atmospheres that can determine how long people stay. Fast food outlets use bright lights and uncomfortable seating to prompt customers to leave soon after they've finished eating. Soft music, candles and comfortable chairs are used in more expensive restaurants. Supermarkets have spent time and money researching how light and music affect how we shop.

Feng shui is the ancient Chinese practice of arranging furniture, objects and colours, etc. so that we can feel more relaxed by a balanced energy.

> ## Activity
> 1. Look at the furniture arrangements where you are right now. Is it a comfortable, relaxed environment or not? What makes it so?
> 2. Survey the environmental arrangements in your college canteen. Are there any changes you could make to improve the overall atmosphere?

Time

How we use time communicates something about relationships, status and personality. We tend to spend more time with people we like. An employer will spend more time with an employee who is impressive than with one who is less so. People of higher status tend to keep others waiting, e.g. a doctor will keep a patient waiting, which tells us that the doctor's time is more precious. A person who is always late may be seen as being unreliable. In Western society we are more concerned with punctuality than in many other cultures.

Music

It has been said that music can soothe the savage beast. In other words, music has the power to alter our moods. In general it comes from and appeals to the emotions. It can soothe us, uplift us, invite us to dance, cause us to cry, fill us with joy, passion, anger, etc. Listen to some different styles of music and try to identify what they are communicating in terms of mood and emotion. What do the following styles communicate to you:

- Rap
- Traditional Irish jig
- Psalm
- Punk
- Ambient
- Strauss waltz
- Heavy metal
- Hip-hop
- Reggae
- Bach fugue
- Techno
- Folk ballad

Fig. 8.20

Discussion

How does a live concert communicate differently from a record?

▶ Sounds

Bells, car horns, sirens, drum signals, etc. all communicate various messages.

▶ Smell

Whether they come from a person or a place, smells are powerful communicators, usually either attracting or repelling. The aroma of fine food wafting from a restaurant, the sweet perfume of flowers on a May day, the smell of cigarette smoke on our clothes all provoke emotional responses and give out their own messages. Even though we have lost much of the power of our sense of smell, we still tend to cover up our own unpleasant odours with different soaps, perfumes and oils to make ourselves socially accepted, or to try to attract a partner. We might even deodourise our homes to make them more pleasant to inhabit.

▶ Dance

Dance is an artistic expression using many of the nonverbal techniques mentioned above such as posture and gesture, but it is also much more than that. A famous ballet such as *Swan Lake* is a powerful performance full of emotion and drama. *Riverdance* changed traditional Irish dancing into something much more passionate than it used to be and introduced it to a worldwide audience. What does it communicate to you? (To see it, go to YouTube and search 'Riverdance 1994'.)

Fig. 8.21

▶ Art

Painting, drawing and sculpture are all forms of visual art. They can communicate any number of moods, feelings and ideas, or may just be something attractive to hang on the wall.

Other Nonverbal Signs and Codes

Morse code, semaphore, drum signals, smoke signals, traffic lights and some road signs all use nonverbal ways of communicating messages. Computer technology uses languages that are based on numbers as opposed to words and programs are written in a series of zeros and ones. Shorthand is a system of written symbols used to record speech quickly.

Activities

1. Role-play the following simple situations using only NVC:
   - Waiting at the bus stop in freezing weather
   - A tourist asking directions (doesn't speak the language)
   - A mugging
   - Football supporters at a match in the minutes leading up to and including a goal
   - Ordering a meal in a restaurant
2. Try to spend a break session without using words.
3. **Chinese Miming**
   Everyone sits in a circle, and the first person sends a message by mime to the person on her left. That person passes it on to the person on his left and so on around the circle. Compare the final message with the original.

Chapter Review

1. Give a brief explanation of: eye contact; face-to-face communication and facial expression; gestures; territory; paralanguage.
2. Explain the significance of NVC with regard to cultural differences.
3. Describe ways in which NVC can be ambiguous.
4. Make a list of the NVC types you are now more aware of and consider how you might consciously use them in future.

Answers

The two men in the photographs on page 113 are (Fig. 8.4) José Mujica, President of Uruguay, 2010–2015, and (Fig. 8.5) Luis Lacalle Pou, President of Uruguay since 2020.

On page 115 Fig. 8.6b is the fake smile.

Facial expressions activity on page 115:

Fig. 8.7a Sadness Fig. 8.7b Anger Fig. 8.7c Surprise Fig. 8.7d Contempt Fig. 8.7e Happiness Fig. 8.7f Fear Fig. 8.7g Disgust

Chapter 9
Visual Communication

In this chapter, you will learn about:
- Images
- Visual Language
- Visual Interpretation
- Visual Production
- Posters and Flyers
- Infographics

Fig. 9.1: 17,000 year old cave art in Lascaux, France

▶ Images

Verbal communication uses words to send messages; visual communication uses images. While it is not known exactly how the earliest humans communicated, it is certain that they did paint pictures on the walls of caves. We are not sure what kind of language our early ancestors used, but for thousands of years, the spoken word would have been the main means of communication for humans. In the Middle Ages, especially after the invention of the printing press, the written word became more important as a source of information. With the emergence of photography, cinema, television, video and the internet the image has almost overtaken the written word as a means of communication.

Today we are constantly being bombarded by visual messages in advertising, magazines, on television, film, video, the internet, and we are becoming producers and consumers of visual messages more than ever before on social media.

Images can be used in numerous ways to communicate effectively in order to:

- Educate
- Advertise
- Inform
- Aid meaning
- Express ideas
- Persuade
- Entertain

Fig. 9.2

Activity

Write down one or two examples of the numerous ways in which images can be used as listed above and discuss as a group.

We can often read and understand a visual message more quickly than a written one. An image is easier to remember than words and can cross linguistics barriers. It may also have much more immediate and emotional impact. The image is a very powerful means of communication.

Fig. 9.3

This photograph of the Earth rising above the surface of the moon was taken by astronaut William Anders during the 1968 Apollo 8 mission to the moon. It was the first time the Earth had been photographed from space and is said to have inspired the environmental movement. It continues to inspire today.

Discussion

There is an old saying that 'a picture is worth a thousand words'. What does this mean? Could we ever say that a word is worth a thousand pictures?

Images are not necessarily superior to words, but they are equally important. The most successful communication is when there is a combination of words and pictures, verbal and visual. Some images on their own can be ambiguous and even meaningless. This is why captions are used to explain photographs, and why slogans accompany pictures used in advertisements. In this way, words *anchor* the meaning of the image. Words and images complement each other and should be carefully chosen.

Images with inappropriate but often hilarious captions or quotes in photographs of celebrities and politicians are an endless source of humour on social media.

The Camera Lies

The images seen in Fig. 9.4 show how the camera can cover up the truth of the subject in a photograph. The magazine cover shot shows how image-enhancing software has been used to make Keira Knightley appear more 'beautiful'.

Fig. 9.4

Visual communication also has the power to manipulate, especially in the modern media. Photography, film, television and video as media of communication are deliberately manipulated to produce a specific effect on the viewer. It may be to persuade us to buy a product, to make us laugh or cry, to seduce us into wanting to watch another episode or just wonder at the beauty of the image. It used to be said that the camera never lies, but it does, very effectively.

One major disadvantage of visual communication is that images cannot give detailed descriptions, which words can. Nor can they easily express abstract ideas like hope, fate or knowledge, or complex feelings like resentment or rejection. It is easier to visualise words that refer to concrete objects, such as *dog*, *ball* and *hat*.

▶ Visual Language

Verbal language has rules of grammar and punctuation in order to give it meaning. We don't usually consider visual language to have such rules, but we can look at some of the basic elements of visual communication. These are:

- Colour/light
- Size
- Texture
- Depth
- Perspective
- Boundaries
- Position
- Movement/direction

Colour/Light

Colour is essentially a combination of different shades of light and dark and it can communicate a variety of meanings. Light and dark can affect our moods, lightness being linked with daytime, spring and summer, positive feelings of hope, celebration and joy. Darkness we associate with night-time, winter and negative feelings of fear, despair and depression. Of course, some people love dark colours and might choose to only wear dark-coloured clothes, for example. How we view colour is highly subjective.

Discussion

1. In the film *Reservoir Dogs* the chief characters were named after colours, Mr White, Mr Black, etc. The two unpopular colours were Mr Pink and Mr Brown. Why did no one want to be called by these names? Why was there competition for the name Mr Black?
2. What words, feelings and ideas do you associate with these colours?
   - Red
   - Orange
   - Yellow
   - Green
   - Blue
   - White

When using colour in a visual message, we must remember that it can affect the emotions of a viewer more than other attributes. If used well, it can draw attention to certain aspects of an image. If poorly used, it can damage the overall effect.

Size

In image production, size counts. We tend to notice large images more easily than smaller ones. When designing an image, we need to consider its size in relation to the page on which it will appear.

Texture

Texture refers to the feel or appearance of a surface, or of an image. Look at the table or desk nearest to you. Is its surface rough or smooth, its colour plain or dappled?

Depth

We perceive the world as having three dimensions. In other words, we can see the actual volume of objects which show that they have weight and mass. A square, a circle and a triangle each have two dimensions, but a cube, a sphere and a pyramid each have three.

Perspective

Perspective gives the impression of distance in a picture. A picture of a railway track disappearing into the distance shows perspective by the way the lines appear closer together the further away they are (e.g. see Fig. 2.2 on p. 17).

Boundaries

The boundary of an image is the edge or frame that contains it. Borderlines or designs can enhance a poster, but they can also distract from the main image if they are too prominent.

Position

The positioning of an image in relation to the boundary is quite important. The most obvious thing is to place an image in the centre. When taking photographs of people, we often 'cut off' their feet or the tops of their heads by mistake. Filling the frame of a photograph means not having the object too far away or chopped in two. Do we want to feature someone's face or their entire body in the picture?

> ## Discussion
>
> Look at Leonardo da Vinci's *The Last Supper* and comment on the use of depth, perspective, boundaries and position.

Fig. 9.5

Movement/Direction

Getting a viewer to perceive movement in a still image needs 'visual vibration'. The use of wavy lines is applied to cartoons to show a character moving or shaking, and high-contrast straight or wavy lines can create the illusion of something moving in a particular direction.

▶ Visual Interpretation

As with all forms of communication, an image can have more than one specified meaning. The meaning is determined by a combination of the sender, the receiver and the context. A national flag is literally a symbol of the country it represents. It can also fill one person with patriotic pride, but to another it could represent an offence or a threat. A Union Jack on the Falls Road, a predominantly Republican/Catholic street in Belfast, will have a completely different meaning to one hanging on the Shankill Road, a largely Loyalist/Protestant area. As well as the literal meaning, there is an implied meaning or connotation.

Activity

What is the connotation of this art installation by Spanish street artist Isaac Cordal?

Fig. 9.6

Symbols

A symbol is a particular kind of image or sign that represents something. Initially the meaning is not always clear: it often has to be learned. Then it becomes easily recognisable. Logos, flags, religious images and numbers are all examples of symbols.

Activities

1. What do the following symbols represent?

©   ☭   °C   ⚡   %

a   b   c   d   e

☯   ⚧   ⚕   ☪   ☣

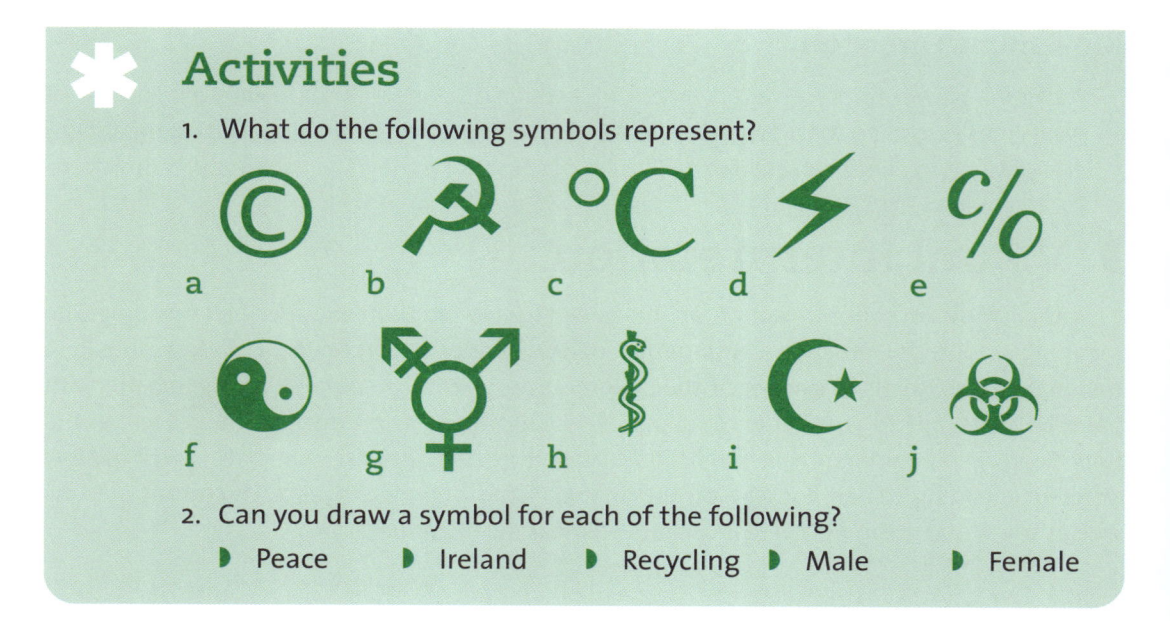

f   g   h   i   j

2. Can you draw a symbol for each of the following?
   - Peace
   - Ireland
   - Recycling
   - Male
   - Female

Logos

Logos are symbols used by companies and organisations to promote easy recognition and are a key part of branding and brand recognition. They may be purely graphic, i.e. use a symbol only, or may combine the organisation's name in a particular style of text such as a trademark.

Discussion

This image went viral a number of years ago. Can you name each brand and plant? What is the implication of the exercise?

Fig. 9.7

Emojis

Emoji comes from the Japanese for 'picture character'. These symbols, first developed in the 1990s, are hugely popular in texts, emails and other forms of online communication. They are predated by emoticons (emotion icons), which used punctuation marks to create facial expressions to express mood and feelings (such as :-) for example).

They have become so widespread that they are considered to be a complete, simple language in their own right. Two of the most popular emojis are the 'face with tears of joy' 😂 and the 'heart eyes' 😍.

As with other forms of communication, and especially with visual communication, emojis can be ambiguous and cause confusion. Additionally, when messages are exchanged between different devices and platforms, they might not appear exactly the same.

> ## Discussion
> Select and view a number of photographs, pictures, advertisements, cartoons and other images from books, magazines and newspapers and discuss how effective they are at communicating a visual message. Discuss their literal meanings as well as their connotations.

▶ Visual Production

In today's highly visualised world, we find that we need to create visual messages or images for college assignments, presentations at work, to promote a business, product or an event, or for social media, where we share our colourful lives with family and friends.

Today's technology means we are now all photographers and filmmakers, using our devices to take shots or shoot videos and edit them to our own taste and standards. Canva is a design tool and app with a whole range of templates to help create flyers, posters, logos, infographics, pdfs and content for social media, all made easy and with a free option for students (www.canva.com).

▶ Posters and Flyers

Posters and flyers can be easily created using readily available software. For example, Microsoft Word has a flyer template. A poster must be large, preferably A2 size, and should have enough impact to compete with other posters in, say, a shop window or community noticeboard. Use appropriate colours, fonts and eye-catching imagery to create the best possible visual message. If you are using text to accompany an image, choose a font that is appropriate for the message.

> ## Activity
> **Font Selection**
>
> Look at the following display of film titles. Is there anything strange about them? The way they are written seems to be at odds with the themes of

the films. For example, *Frankenstein* is a horror film, yet the font used is humorous and playful. Make a similar analysis of the other titles, their connotations and the fonts used and the fonts used to display them.

FRANKENSTEIN

𝕿𝖍𝖊 𝖂𝖎𝖟𝖆𝖗𝖉 𝖔𝖋 𝕺𝖟

Troy

Pulp Fiction

▶ Infographics

Charts, graphs and diagrams are very useful for showing data, statistics and other information in a visually striking way. They can give written assignments, projects and oral presentations a bit of added impact and interest, condensing and clarifying certain types of information. Your computer software makes them fairly easy to create with a range of styles and colours and even three-dimensional effects.

Graphs, Charts and Tables

Line graphs (Fig. 9.8) are useful for showing trends that rise and fall.

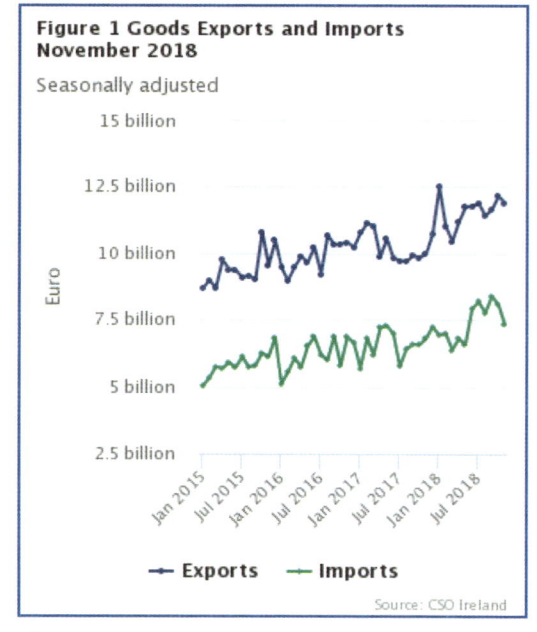

Fig. 9.8

Bar charts (Fig. 9.9) are effective for illustrating differences in quantity. They can be horizontal or vertical.

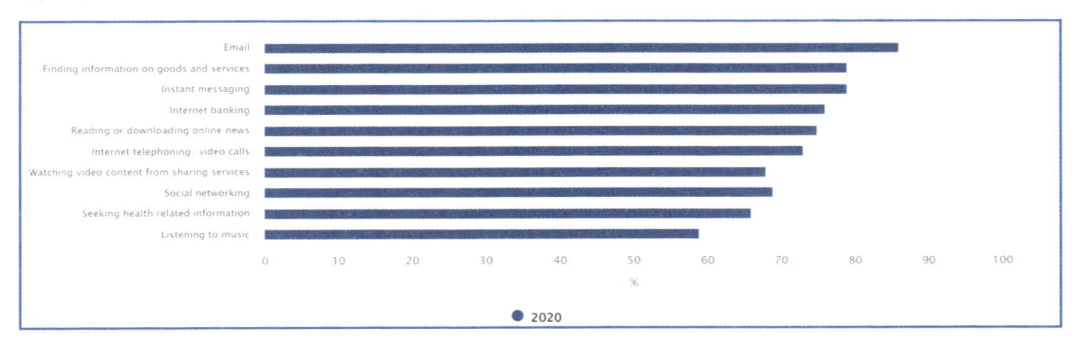

Fig. 9.9

Histograms are similar to bar charts, except the columns represent the frequency of occurrence (how often something occurs) and have no spaces between them.

Pie charts (Fig. 9.10) can be used to display percentages of a whole.

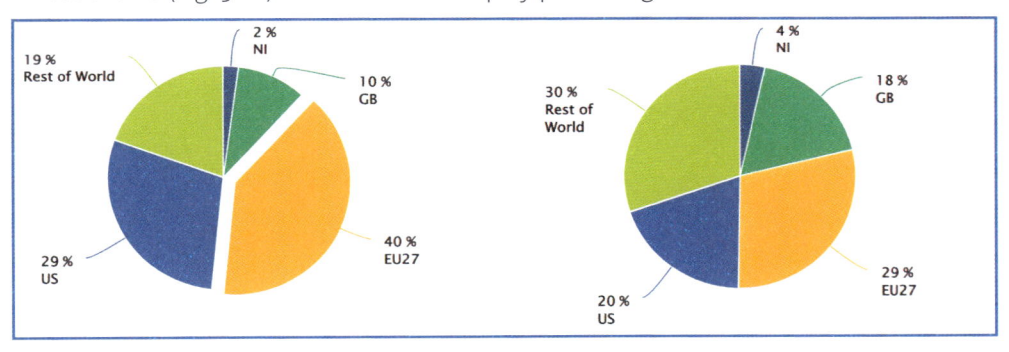

Fig. 9.10

Pictograms (Fig. 9.11), as the name suggests, consists of a picture or series of pictures that can add a touch of humour, although they are not as precise as other kinds of chart.

Colour	Number of Smarties	Frequency
Green		7
Orange		8
Blue		5
Pink		6
Yellow		11
Red		8
Purple		7
Brown		3
	Key ● = 2 smarties	

Fig. 9.11

The following three methods of data representation are not strictly visual, but they do help simplify information.

Organisation charts (Fig. 9.12) are used to show the structure of authority in an organisation.

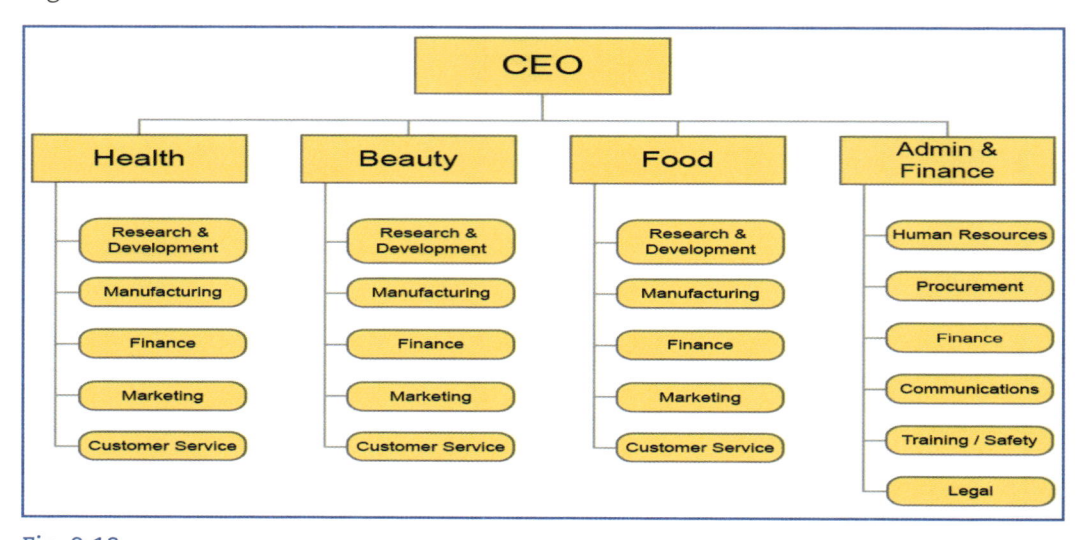

Fig. 9.12

Flow charts (Fig. 9.13) show how an activity is to be carried out in a series of logical stages.

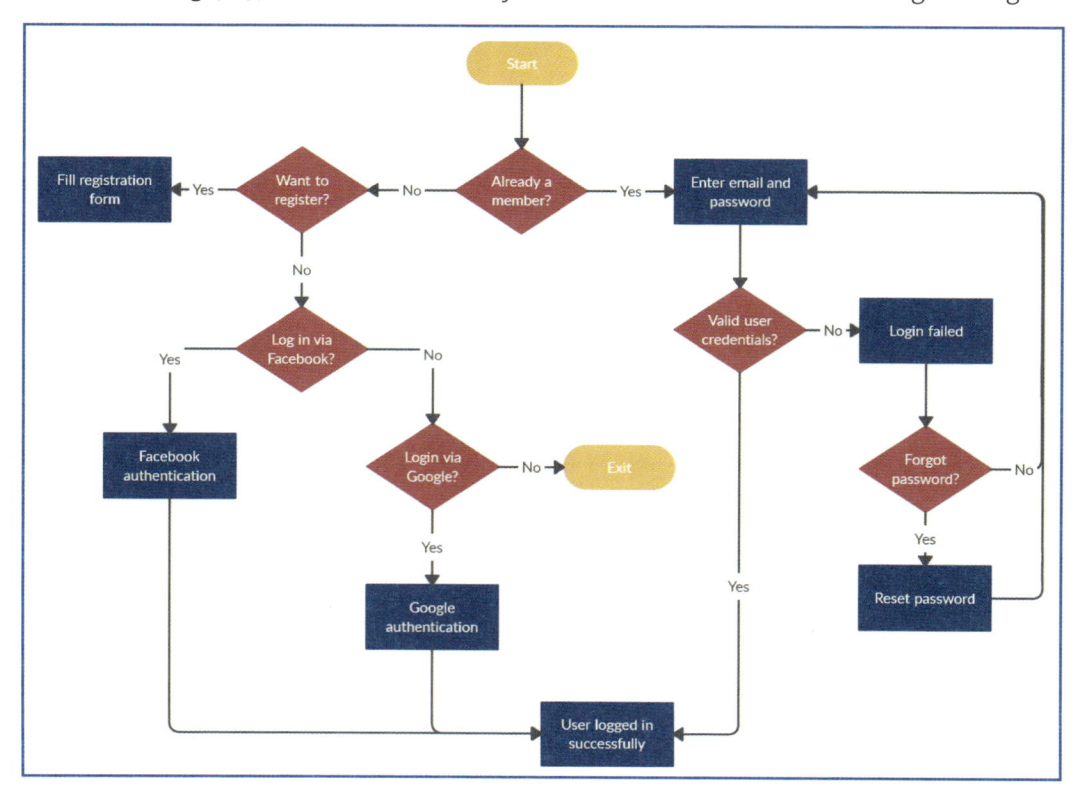

Fig. 9.13

Tables (Fig. 9.14) can be used to compare and contrast data in a clear and simple way.

	Table 1. Compliance with EU ESD Targets 2013-2020 (all numbers in the table are rounded to the nearest kt CO_2eq)	2013	2014	2015	2016	2017	2018	2019	2020
A	Total greenhouse gas emissions without LULUCF	57,903	57,626	59,878	61,546	60,744	60,912	59,897	0.0
B	NF_3 emissions	1	1	1	1	1	1	1	0.0
C	Total greenhouse gas emissions without LULUCF and without NF_3 emissions	57,903	57,625	59,877	61,545	60,743	60,911	59,896	0.0
D	Total verified emissions from stationary installations under Directive 2003/87/EC	15,686	15,953	16,830	17,737	16,896	15,515	14,172	0.0
E	CO_2 emissions from 1.A.3.a. domestic aviation	10	9	10	10	17	17	18	0.0
F	**Total ESD emissions (= C-D-E)**	42,207	41,663	43,037	43,798	43,829	45,379	45,707	0.0
G	**EU ESD Targets**	46,892	45,761	44,630	43,499	40,885	39,807	38,729	37,651
	Distance to target (= F-G)	-4,685	-4,098	-1,593	299	2,944	5,571	6,978	

Note: Shaded cells show data that has been reviewed, and compliance agreed, by the European Commission under Article 19 of the MMR No. 525/2013

Fig. 9.14

Points to remember:
- Always title charts.
- Keep them simple and clear.
- Don't clutter them with too much information.
- Colour looks better than black and white.
- Keep text to a minimum and make it legible.
- Fill up as much of the page as possible.

Diagrams

A diagram (Fig. 9.15) is essentially a drawing or sketch of an object showing its various parts. It would obviously be preferable to see a diagram of the inner workings of a camera than have someone try to explain them to us!

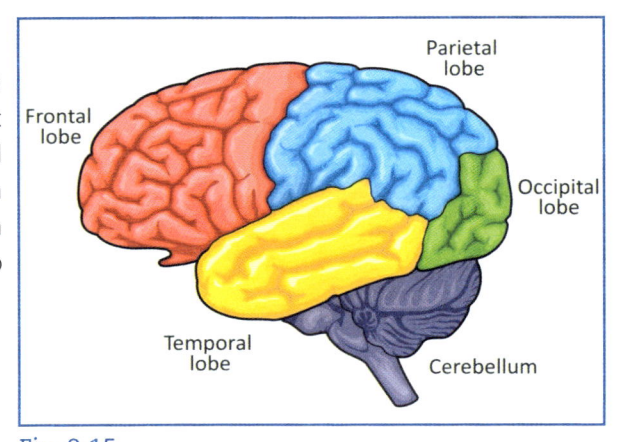

Fig. 9.15

Maps

To show locations, transport networks or any geographical features, maps are ideal (Fig. 9.16).

Fig. 9.16

Activities

1. Produce a poster and/or flyer for one of the following:
   - A concert
   - A newly opened leisure centre/restaurant/shop/business
   - A college social event
   - A sporting event
   - A fashion show
   - A circus
   - A charity/fundraising event
   - Climate change awareness
   - Biodiversity awareness
   - COVID-19 awareness
   - An international day against racism
   - An international day of AIDS awareness

   Think of other causes or occasions, perhaps related to your own vocational studies.

2. Produce a card for one of the following occasions:
   - Birthday
   - Christmas
   - Passing exams
   - Wedding anniversary
   - Condolence
   - St Patrick's Day
   - St Valentine's Day
   - Easter
   - Birth of a baby
   - Mother's Day
   - Father's Day

3. Fig. 9.17 shows the image on a plaque attached to the *Pioneer* spacecraft which is intended as a message from humankind to whoever finds it on its journey through space. What does the image communicate? Do you think it is effective? If you had to convey an image of humankind to extraterrestrials, what would you draw?

Fig. 9.17

4. The US Department of Energy wants to design a sign that will warn people of its nuclear waste dump in Nevada. The waste will remain dangerous for 10,000 years, so the sign must last for that long and keep its meaning for whoever inhabits that part of the world at that time. Consider that about 10,000 years ago humans were evolving from hunter gatherers to farmers. We don't know what language they spoke then, and we don't know what language they will speak 10,000 years from now. Maybe Earth will be populated by extraterrestrials. How would you design a 'Keep Out' sign for the future? What kind of message would you use?

Seven Steps to Create a Visual Message

1. Decide on a communication objective. What do you want to communicate? Do you want to send a message of great meaning and importance, or to entertain, educate, inform, advertise, or would you prefer to express yourself artistically, if so inclined?
2. Decide on an appropriate visual medium/format. What materials will you use and why?

These first two steps may be done in reverse if you already know what medium you want to use but are not yet sure of the message.

3. Decide who is your target audience.
4. Develop your idea. Do a rough sketch/outline. Decide on colours, shapes, size, texture, etc.
5. Refine and polish.
6. Decide if it needs text/verbal support. Keep it short and simple. Choose an appropriate font.
7. Test its impact on your friends/classmates/tutors.

If presenting a visual assignment, you may have to submit support studies to show a record of the process. It should include the following:

1. Written notes recording the process, i.e. the development of your ideas from start to finish – where you got the idea and why you chose it
2. Your communication objective
3. Reasons for choosing your medium/materials
4. Rough sketches/outlines
5. Description of any changes and alterations made during the rough work
6. Reasons you made them
7. What you liked/disliked about your initial ideas/sketches

On submission of the final piece, you should include all rough work and the written record.

Chapter Review

1. What advantages does visual communication have over verbal communication?
2. Why is it important to learn about visual communication?

Answers

Page 140. The answers to the first activity are as follows:
a) Copyright b) Marxism/Communism c) Degrees Celsius d) Electricity (clipart)
e) Care of f) Yin Yang g) Transgender h) Healing and medicine (Rod of Asclepius)
i) Islam j) Biohazard

Part 4
Reading and Writing

Some Examples
- Letters
- Memos
- Reports
- Assignments
- Notices
- Agendas
- Reviews
- Notes
- Postcards
- Poetry
- Stories
- Lyrics

Advantages
- Provides a written record
- Can be used as evidence/contract
- Can be re-read, copied, stored/filed
- Time to conceive and prepare message carefully
- Can relay complex detailed ideas
- Provides analysis, evaluation, summary
- Can confirm, interpret, clarify spoken and visual messages

Disadvantages
- Takes time
- More formal and impersonal than spoken
- Harder to convey tone, emotion
- No instant feedback
- Once sent, difficult to change
- Slow exchange of views/opinions

Chapter 10
Reading Skills

In this chapter, you will learn about:
- The Purpose of Reading
- Types of Reading
- Writing a Summary
- Critical Evaluation

If you don't like to read, you haven't found the right book.

J.K. Rowling

Discussion

1. Make a list of the things you've read in the past 24 hours. Discuss in pairs and then with the class group.
2. What was the last book you read? Discuss with others by giving a short synopsis and a quick review.

The Purpose of Reading

We read primarily for the following reasons:
- Information
- Entertainment/leisure
- Personal contact
- Education

Another very sound reason to read is that it improves our command of the language we speak by increasing our vocabulary and this in turn helps improve our communication skills. Reading helps us to expand our range of words so that we can express ourselves more eloquently.

Our reading will improve by practice and our communication skills will improve by reading. Although it is tempting to take the easy way out and read what is unchallenging, we won't improve unless we read material that introduces us to new words and new ways of expression. Reading regularly and widely is the main thing. Don't always read the same type of material. If you've been used to magazines, try a newspaper. If you read novels, try a work of non-fiction. If non-fiction is your thing, try a comic for a change.

It is also useful to have a good dictionary at hand (in paper, online or as an app) to look up new words.

Fig. 10.1

Reading Self-Check

How well do you read? We all read at varying speeds and levels of concentration and efficiency. Here are some of the most common problems that people have with reading:

1. Reading all kinds of text at the same speed
2. Slow reading
3. Re-reading words or passages
4. Inability to find the main idea in a passage
5. Losing concentration while reading
6. Pronouncing or mouthing words while reading them
7. Study-reading intensely for a long period of time without taking a break

If you do any or all of the above, you have developed some bad habits over the years, but by and large they are problems that can be overcome with a little effort. In the following few pages we will look at some of the ways in which our reading can be improved.

Different Texts, Different Speeds

If you think about what you've read in the past 24 hours you will notice the sheer variety of texts. We don't use the same method of reading for all of them. For example, when looking at a bus timetable we don't read every single word. Rather we scan for the particular piece of information relevant to us. We would use a different method for reading a book. With a novel we would read every word but not as intensely as if we were studying a book for an exam.

Types of Reading

There are four types of reading:

1. Scanning
2. Skimming
3. Normal reading
4. Close reading

Scanning

This is very fast reading to find specific information that is only relevant to our needs. We scan timetables, dictionaries, small ads, noticeboards and telephone directories for specific words or names. We scan newspapers for articles that interest us and web pages on the internet for relevant pieces of information or for links to other pages. Scanning is useful for finding information as part of a research project.

Activity

You've decided you want to learn how to swim so you get a brochure from the local pool. Scan the timetable of the various sessions to find a suitable time for a lesson. Your working hours are 9 am to 5 pm Monday to Saturday with Wednesdays free. You work to 8.30 pm on Tuesdays.

	Monday	Tuesday	Wednesday	Thursday	Friday	Saturday	Sunday
7.30 am	Early Swim	Early Swim	Early Swim	Early Swim	Early Swim	Closed	Closed
9 am	Open Swim	Open Swim	Adults	Open Swim	Adults	Closed	Closed
10 am	Private Booking	Private Booking	Adult Lesson	Child Lesson	Child Lesson	Family	Closed
11 am	Open Swim	Club	Club	Open Swim	Club	Child Lesson	Family
12 pm	Private Booking	Private Booking	Private Booking	Private Booking	Private Booking	Child Lesson	Family
1 pm	Lunch Swim	Lunch Swim	Lunch Swim	Lunch Swim	Lunch Swim	Adults	Family
2 pm	Open Swim	Open Swim	Open Swim	Open Swim	Open Swim	Open Swim	Open Swim
3 pm	Child Lesson	Private Booking	Private Booking	Private Booking	Private Booking	Open Swim	Open Swim
4 pm	Open Swim	Family	Child Lesson	Child Lesson	Private Booking	Open Swim	Open Swim
5 pm	Open Swim	Lane Swim	Open Swim	Lane Swim	Open Swim	Open Swim	Open Swim
6 pm	Family	Open Swim	Family	Open Swim	Family	Closed	Closed
7 pm	Club	Club	Child Lesson	Club	Club	Closed	Closed
8 pm	Adult Lesson	Adult Lesson	Club	Open Swim	Open Swim	Closed	Closed
9 pm	Adults	Adults	Club	Adults	Adults	Closed	Closed

How did you scan the timetable? Did you do it methodically starting from Monday at 7.30 am and carefully work your way down each day? Or did you scan it haphazardly looking all over the place with no apparent system? Having a methodical system can sometimes help us find information more quickly.

Skimming

When we skim-read a passage we swiftly glance across the surface to get an overview of what it is about. Passages may be skipped because they are irrelevant. We skim advertisements, newspaper articles and brochures. For study or research purposes a skim-read lets us know if the material is relevant to our needs, and if it is, we can then go back and read it in detail. Topic sentences are often placed either at the beginning or at the end of paragraphs. When skimming, we can focus on these to get the gist of the text. It is good to skim-read any piece of writing before reading it fully. Then when we go to read it at a normal pace, we will absorb the information more easily.

Signposts

In most textbooks and some news articles, headings, subheadings and headlines indicate what is to follow in the main body of the text, acting as signposts. Words and phrases that are underlined, in **bold**, in *italics*, numbered, lettered or in bullet points are often signposts and are easy to skim-read.

Normal Reading

This is reading at moderate speed, for example novels, letters, newspaper articles and magazines. A lack of speed is considered to be a major reading problem. It is often found that with increased speed comes better understanding. The average person reads at about 240 words per minute with a comprehension rate of about 60 per cent. This means that most of us do not remember 40 per cent of what we read. Most of us could do with improvement in both our speed and comprehension. If you are curious about your reading speed, there is a free test at this website: http://www.readingsoft.com/

Fig. 10.2

When we read, our eyes do not smoothly move across the page from left to right because every now and then they stop very briefly to take in a word or a phrase. These stops are called *fixations* and normally last between one-quarter to one and a half seconds. The number of words we focus on during each fixation is referred to as the *recognition span*. Fast readers can read vertically down a page, fixating on each line just once and taking in its whole meaning. These people have a large recognition span. So obviously the greater the recognition span, the fewer fixations we need and the faster we will read. Slower readers make more fixations because they have a smaller recognition span. Unfortunately, meaning in sentences does not come in single words but in chunks of words, phrases and sentences. When we try to take in meaning, one word at a time, by the time we reach the end of a sentence we have forgotten what was at the beginning. Because the human brain can function much faster than this, we are leaving time for our mind to drift off and think about something else. So we lose concentration and start to daydream.

Activity

Read the following passage slowly, one word at a time, covering up each word in front of the one you are reading:

In…spite…of…what…you…might…think…reading…can…be…improved…by…fixating…on…groups…of…words…rather…than…on…single…words…because…single…words…don't…mean…much…on…their…own.

As you will have noticed, this very slow way of reading makes it more difficult to understand the sentence quickly. We don't find any meaning at all in the first few words and things only start to make sense once we reach the word 'improved'. A more efficient reader will read the sentence in clusters of meaning like this:

In spite of what you might think…reading can be improved…by fixating on groups of words…rather than on single words…because single words don't mean much on their own.

We need to push ourselves to practise reducing our fixation time, and at the same time try to expand our recognition span. This should increase our speed, our comprehension and also help reduce concentration loss.

Re-reading

Re-reading words or phrases in a passage naturally decreases our reading efficiency. To reduce this habit, we can use a pointer when reading. This might seem a little childish, but it helps our eyes move more smoothly across the page. Alternately, we can cover up the lines already read with a sheet of paper, card or another book, and even push it down a little faster than we think we can go. This means we will concentrate better on what we are reading the first time and it helps us break the habit.

These techniques should be practised regularly to improve reading efficiency.

Close Reading

This is reading that is slow and intensive because the text is demanding and needs to be properly understood. We might close-read poetry, class notes, textbooks, instructions for operating equipment or for examinations, leases, contracts and other detailed documents so that we understand them fully.

It is not a good idea to read long difficult passages for more than about 40 minutes at a time. After this, we tend to lose our ability to concentrate, and a short break of five to ten minutes is usually sufficient to refresh ourselves.

Tips for a Close Reading

1. Have a pen, paper and dictionary handy.
2. Start with a skim-read of the entire passage. If it's a book, look at the title, contents, introduction, conclusion, heading and subheadings. Scan the index for specific subjects.
3. Read the passage *actively*. This means asking yourself questions such as:
    (a) Why is it written this way?
    (b) What does the writer mean by this?
    (c) Do I agree with this?
    (d) Do I find this information new, interesting, boring?
    (e) What are the main points?
    (f) Does this make sense
    (g) Is the information correct?
    (h) Is the language formal/informal, subjective/objective, emotive/factual/opinionated?
4. Note information that you already know.
5. Note information that you find particularly interesting, relevant, irrelevant or even ridiculous.
6. Write down, highlight or underline difficult words or passages.
7. Look up any unfamiliar words.
8. When you've read the passage, try to recall it in your mind. What are its main points? Write down what you can remember in your own words.
9. Finally, go over the passage again in case you've missed any important points.

Activity

Read the following article, using all four methods of reading. Scan it first for words you don't understand and underline them. Look them up in a dictionary. Skim the article to get the gist of what it's about. Read it normally to get the details and finally close-read it. What do you think of the ideas in the piece? Is it well written? Can you comment on the writer's style?

> **Social Media and Interpersonal Communication**
>
> Glance around a restaurant and you'll be hard-pressed to find people who don't have their heads down using their cell phones to text, Tweet, or update their Facebook statuses—all while sharing a meal with others at their table.
>
> Social media's effect on our ability to interact and communicate is visible throughout all areas of society, so what does this mean for interpersonal communication? According to Paul Booth, PhD, an assistant professor of media and cinema studies in the College of Communication at DePaul University in Chicago, social media certainly affects how we engage with one another across all venues and ages. "There has been a shift in the way we communicate; rather than face-to-face interaction, we're tending to prefer mediated communication," he says. "We'd rather e-mail than meet; we'd rather text than talk on the phone."
>
> According to Booth, studies have shown that people actually are becoming more social and more interactive with others, but the style of that communication has changed so that we're not meeting face-to-face as often as we used to.
>
> That said, our interactions on social media tend to be weak ties—that is, we don't feel as personally connected to the people at the other end of our communication as we do when we're face-to-face. "So while we're communicating more, we may not necessarily be building relationships as strongly," Booth says.
>
> Three key issues are surfacing regarding the role social media now plays in people's communication styles, Booth notes. First, when we communicate through social media, we tend to trust the people on the other end of the communication, so our messages tend to be more open. Second, our social connections are not strengthened as much through social media as they are face-to-face, so we don't tend to deepen our relationships—they

tend to exist in the status quo. Last, we tend to follow and interact with people who agree with our points of view, so we aren't getting the same diversity of viewpoints as we've gotten in the past.

"Certainly, with every new communication technology comes changes in the style and type of interpersonal communication," Booth says. "Obviously the bigger the influence of the technology, the more changes we see in communication styles."

Far-Reaching Effects

Nicholas David Bowman, PhD, an assistant professor of communication studies in the Eberly College of Arts and Sciences at West Virginia University, says actions that trigger a bad online relationship likely are the same ones that trigger a bad relationship in real life—only the modality has changed. "For example, cyberbullying has largely the same antecedents and behavioral, emotional, and affective consequences as does [noncyber] bullying," Bowman says. "Yet the difference is the 'more'—that is, social media allows for more contact, more communication, and in a more public manner."

In a bullying event, often the person being bullied can remove himself or herself from the environment, at least temporarily. For example, a child being bullied at school can escape the playground when he or she goes home each night. "However, cyberbullying is marked by its persistence," Bowman says. "The bullying messages don't stay in a particular space, such as a playground, but can follow the child home. If we consider that bullying's effects on an individual can build over time, then there is a real concern that increasing contact between bullies and their targets in persistent and digital interactions might exacerbate the problem."

Information Overload

One big concern surrounding social media's impact is communication overload—learning how to handle and make sense of this "more" information we now have.

As Bowman explains, we're getting more information about more people than ever before, and we feel a need to process and perhaps even respond to it all. "In fact, there has been some very early recent data suggesting that teens are perhaps pulling away from Facebook because it's just too much for them to handle," he says.

Another concern lies in technology addiction, when individuals spend more time with their smartphone than interacting with the people around them, to the detriment of those face-to-face relationships. "It may be the parent checking his or her e-mail during a family dinner or the young college student updating Twitter while on a first date," Bowman says. "For these people, they likely feel such a strong sense of identity online that they have some difficulty separating their virtual actions from their actual ones."

With the release of the fifth edition of the DSM [Diagnostic and Statistical Manual of Mental Disorders] Internet addiction now will be listed as a mental illness marked by emotional shutdown, lack of concentration, and withdrawal symptoms, so we may be closer to diagnosing and understanding socially detrimental human-technology relationships.

"However, many of us caution that Internet addiction might be an inaccurate portrayal," Bowman says. "After all, if social media is designed to connect people with people, then is it really a human-technology relationship or is it a human-human relationship mediated by technology?"

Protecting Privacy
One potentially negative consequence of social media is a lack of privacy.
"Because interpersonal communication is changing, we're finding ourselves more apt to share on social media the sort of information we might have previously shared privately face-to-face," Booth says. "We always have to keep in mind that our social networks are searchable—even when privacy settings are set extremely high, it's always possible to find out personal information."

Of course, the negativity surrounding social media is countered by positive influences, including the ability to communicate with more people across greater distances and with increased speed. "Your message can be shared and spread farther and faster than at any other time in human history," Booth says. "We can do a lot of good by spreading positive messages in this way."

Future of Social Media
Experts agree that clinicians must be aware that people are changing the way they communicate. "We may rely on the weak connections we're making on social media more than on the strong connections we might have when we're meeting face-to-face," Booth says.

> What does the future hold for social media and its potential continuous effect on interpersonal communication within society? Bowman believes social media likely will continue to become increasingly integrated into the normal human experience like most of the communication technologies that preceded it. "They will continue to increase the volume of the human communication process, and we will continue to learn how to use them for good and for bad," he says.
>
> "We must remember that social media is really only a decade old. That's very young in the history of communication technology," Booth adds. "It's been influential, but it hasn't really settled into a routine yet. As social media becomes more normalized, we'll stop seeing it as changing things and start seeing it as the way things are. As a society we'll be OK—we've always adjusted to new technology. So whether it's wearable communication media, such as Google glasses, or more cloud computing, we'll change and adapt."

(Maura Keller, *Social Work Today*, May/June 2013 (vol. 13, no 3, p. 10)
https://www.socialworktoday.com/archive/051313p10.shtml)

▶ Writing a Summary

To summarise a message means to condense it down to its main points. Writing a summary shows that you have understood a text and that you can communicate its overall meaning to others. It is a useful skill in that it helps to identify the essential meaning of a piece of writing while leaving out the unnecessary points. It is helpful when doing research for an assignment and you need to rewrite information in your own words.

Here are some guidelines to help you write summaries.

1. Skim-read the text to get the overall gist. Focus on any headings, subheadings, words or phrases in bold and 'topic sentences', which are usually the first or last sentence in a paragraph that encapsulate the subject matter of the paragraph.
2. Do a normal read of the text.
3. Close-read the text, and underline topic sentences.
4. Write one sentence that explains the overall theme.
5. Write down the main idea of each section.
6. Omit specific details such as examples, dates, statistics, etc.
7. Write a draft of your summary, using the key points you identified, keeping to the same order of information as the original and adding words and phrases to link them together, e.g. *then, however, despite this* or *because of this*.
8. Re-read your summary to make sure you've included all the important elements.

9. Rewrite if necessary.
10. Proofread for spelling, grammar and punctuation.

> ## Tips for an Effective Summary
> - Stick to the same tense as the original.
> - Include the author's name and title.
> - If there is no title, create your own from your theme sentence.
> - Be concise: Your summary should be shorter than the original.
> - Don't add your own opinions.
> - Don't try to make it poetic or 'beautiful'. The important thing is to rewrite the main information in your own words.

▶ Critical Evaluation

So much information that we read, especially online, can be untrue, so an ability to analyse and critically evaluate it, be it written, spoken or visual communication, is a useful life skill that can improve our interpreting and problem-solving skills. The analytical process involves a methodical examination of something, looking closely at its different parts to see how each contributes to the whole to evaluate and understand it better. Then we are in a position to make a more informed opinion about its value or worth.

In a piece of writing we need to examine the following:

Structure
- How well is it put together?
- Does it have a good beginning, middle and end?
- Is there a logical sequence of paragraphs and subjects?
- Does it argue a case and, if so, how well is the argument structured?
- Does the author have an agenda, i.e. might he be putting forward one particular point of view or are both sides of an argument presented?
- Do you agree or disagree with the author?

Language
- Is it well written?
- Is the language clear or is it vague or ambiguous?
- Is it subjective (personal) or objective (impartial)?
- Consider the style: is it fluent, easy to read, or does it contain unnecessarily difficult language.
- Consider the tone: is it serious, humorous, factual, creative, formal, informal, etc.?

Information

- Is the information accurate?
- How do you know?
- Identify information that is relevant from that which is not.

Strengths and Weaknesses

- What are the strengths and weaknesses of the piece?

Informed Opinion or Personal Opinion

Informed opinion is always based on facts and when you have done the analysis, you are in a better position to give a more informed opinion rather than just a personal opinion, having read it through without any analysis.

Activities

1. Write a summary of the article 'Social Media and Interpersonal Communication' on pages 156–59 using the process described above.
2. Write a short critique of the same article.
3. Select a variety of pieces of writing such as newspaper/magazine articles, academic articles, blogs, professional documents, essays, etc. and distribute them amongst the class. Singly or in pairs, summarise one article and relay the information to the rest of the class group. Give a critical evaluation of each piece.
4. Read and write a summary of a professional document based on your own vocational area.

Chapter Review

1. Give four good reasons for reading.
2. List five bad reading habits.
3. Explain the four types of reading.
4. What does active reading mean?
5. Why is summary writing useful?
6. List five components of critical evaluation.

Chapter 11
Writing Skills

In this chapter, you will learn about:
- Types of Writing
- Grammar Basics
- Punctuation

Writing is perhaps the greatest of human inventions, binding together people who never knew each other, citizens of distant epochs.
Carl Sagan

Writing as a form of communication probably evolved in ancient cultures as a way of exchanging information, keeping financial accounts and recording historical events.

Activity
Make a list of the things you have written in the past 48 hours.

Types of Writing

Different types of writing require differ approaches and styles. Some are formal and some informal. Some use descriptive language and some use plain language. The following is a list of examples.

Instructive writing, such as a recipe, instruction manual or list of directions, uses clear and simple language, short sentences and avoids any unnecessary words.

> **Activities**
>
> 1. Write out your favourite recipe.
> 2. Write instructions for sending a WhatsApp/SMS message.
> 3. Imagine a friendly English-speaking alien has landed in your classroom. Write precise, detailed and clear directions for how he can get from the classroom to your home.

Descriptive writing uses words that appeal to the senses to create an image in the reader's mind. There is usually a lot of detail. For example, a travel journal might describe the sights, sounds, smells, tastes and other sensations experienced by the traveller to give the reader a vivid impression of the holiday location. The writer's feelings may also be included and figures of speech such as similes and metaphors also add to the description. Precise language, in particular adjectives, should also be included.

> **Activity**
>
> Describe a day or an event during your last holiday. Use as much detail as possible to create a picture in the reader's mind.

Narrative writing tells a story, true or fictional, using a series of connected events. See the Short Story section on page 182 of Chapter 12: Personal Writing.

> **Activity**
>
> Write a short story beginning, 'I woke up this morning…'

Persuasive writing presents a particular viewpoint and tries to convince the reader that the writer's opinion is correct. It may try to convince the reader to do something such as take action, or it might consist of an argument for or against a particular issue. Advertisements persuade people to buy certain products.

Key elements in persuasive writing include:
- Repetition of certain words or phrases
- Facts that support the viewpoint
- An appeal to the reader's emotions
- A clear writing style to eliminate any contradictions in the argument
- Rhetorical questions (questions that make the reader think but don't need an answer), e.g. 'Who would want to live in that place?', 'How can we stand by and let this happen?'

The main goal of persuasive writing is to win over the reader in some way.

Activities

1. Write a short persuasive piece on one of the following statements:
   - 'The use of college computers for social networking should be banned.'
   - 'We must stop using fossil fuels to prevent runaway climate change.'
2. Write some keywords you would use in an advertisement for a new chocolate bar.

Creative writing includes stories, poems and novels as well as non-fiction, and the purpose is for the writer to use their imagination and to express their thoughts, feelings and emotions.

Activities

1. Choose an ordinary household object and pretend it can perceive the world as humans do. Write its thoughts.
2. Think of someone you love and write a poem describing their attributes, good and bad, using similes ('Her eyes shone like stars') and metaphors ('Her eyes were stars').
3. Grab the seventh book from your bookshelf, open it at page seven, choose the seventh sentence, begin a poem/piece of writing with that sentence and write the rest of the piece using only seven lines/sentences.
4. Write about each member of your family but limit the number of words about each to the age of that person, e.g. 17 sentences about your 17-year-old brother.
5. Make two columns on a sheet of paper. In one column make a list of 10 nouns and in the other a list of 10 verbs. Put them into random pairs and write a sentence for each pair. Create a story using all 10 sentences.

Academic writing is usually serious, factually based, objective and aimed at the critical and well-informed reader. Though it is primarily aimed at academics such as professors, teachers and students, it may also be of interest to the general reader. Some academic books that become bestsellers are often called 'popular' or 'pop', such as the genres popular science and popular psychology.

Business writing can vary in style from conversational to very formal, though it is advisable in the first contact to be formal. Information must be presented clearly and concisely to avoid misunderstandings and wasting time and ultimately to make a good impression on a potential client, employer or business partner. Use simple English and see Formal/Business Letters on page 204 and Business/Formal Email on page 263.

Grammar Basics

It would be impractical to cover the grammar of the English language in its entirety in this book, but a few basic points are worth making here.

Sentence

A sentence is often described as a set of words that has a complete meaning. It starts with a capital letter and ends with a full stop, question mark or exclamation mark. For a sentence to have complete meaning, it almost always has to have two things:
1. *Subject* – who or what does the action, or about whom or what something is stated
2. *Predicate* – refers to what the subject is or does

   For example
- The student submitted the assignment.

This is a complete sentence, 'student' being the *subject*, and 'submitted' being the *predicate*; 'assignment' is what is called the *object*. 'Student' is also a *noun* (the name of a person, place or thing)) and 'submitted' is a *verb*, which describes an action or state of the noun. To make this sentence more interesting we can add:
1. An adjective:
   The **brilliant** student submitted the assignment.
2. An adverb:
   The brilliant student **hastily** submitted the assignment.
3. A preposition (and indirect object):
   The brilliant student hastily submitted the assignment **to** the teacher.
4. A pronoun:
   The brilliant student hastily submitted the assignment to **her** teacher.

Capital Letters

The capital letter is used:
- To begin all sentences including direct speech: **H**e said, '**H**ello.'
- For proper nouns, i.e. names of people, countries, organisations, buildings, geographical features, historical events and festivals: **J**im, **E**stonia, **G**reenpeace, the **T**aj **M**ahal, the **A**mazon, the **T**reaty of **V**ersailles, the **E**dinburgh **F**ringe **F**estival
- For proper adjectives, i.e. derived from proper nouns: **F**rench, **T**arantinoesque

- For the personal pronoun '**I**'
- For acronyms: **NAMA**, **UNESCO**
- For well-known geographical regions, e.g. the **N**orth
- For titles of books, newspapers, magazines, television and radio programmes, plays, songs, poems and films (though conjunctions [for example: and, but] and prepositions [for example: of, in] within such titles are not capitalised) e.g. *The **W**izard of **O**z*, ***R**omeo and **J**uliet*.
- For days of the week and for months, but not for seasons of the year: It was a fine Monday morning in March. At last, spring had arrived.

Activity

Rewrite the following putting capital letters in where necessary:

1. paula, robert and i are studying a course at drumlinn college of further education.
2. it's an etb-run college, the course is a qqi course and i'm on vtos.
3. the college isn't far from ballylinane and the m25.
4. next summer we are going on a sponsored hike in the french alps to raise money for concern.
5. i do work experience at setanta designs every tuesday, just behind the customs house.
6. they dyed the liffey green on st patrick's day.
7. the students aren't all irish. one comes from nigeria and another is lithuanian.
8. last wednesday we watched *the power of the dog* starring benedict cumberbatch and kirsten dunst.
9. she said, 'why don't you come in?'
10. last year i went to electric picnic and this year I'm going to the festival of the fires.
11. we had our debs in the royal hotel last june and the dj was rubbish.
12. there's a module in customer service, but we don't have to do german anymore.
13. i want to become a physiotherapist with manchester united when i'm finished.

Answers available on page 283

Latin Terms

Note the frequently used Latin abbreviations:
- i.e. – *id est* (that is)
- e.g. – *exempli gratia* (for example)
- etc. – *et cetera* (and the rest)
- et al. – *et alibi* (and elsewhere) *et alii/alia* (and other people/things)

Phrase

A phrase is a set of words that doesn't always have a complete meaning.

For example, 'to her tutor' is a phrase that doesn't mean anything on its own.

'The brilliant student' is a phrase that could mean something if, for example, it was a response to a question such as 'Who submitted the assignment?'

Confusing Phrases

Beware of using *of* instead of *have*:
- I could of been a contender ✗
- I could have been a contender ✓
- She should of stayed ✗
- She should have stayed ✓
- It would not of been possible ✗
- It would not have been possible ✓

Subject/Verb Agreement

The subject in a sentence must 'agree' with its verb. We cannot say 'The student submit the assignment' because the subject and verb do not agree. So, both subject and verb should be either singular or plural and not a mixture.

These words take the singular: each, every, either, neither, any.

With collective nouns, the singular or plural are both acceptable these days:
- The Government has/have raised taxes again.
- The audience was/were thrilled with the performance.

Activity

Correct the following sentences so that there is agreement between subject(s) and verb:

1. There is 450 students in the college.
2. Hector, together with his sister, Hattie, walk to school everyday.
3. She is one of those designers who likes doing things her own way.
4. The wages they pay is very low.

> 5. The driver and passenger is happy.
> 6. That bunch of flowers have seen better days.
> 7. Which one of you two are the manager?
> 8. All four of them has a PhD.
> 9. Each of them were studying for years.
> 10. *Peaky Blinders* are my favourite TV programme.

Answers available on page 283

Paragraph

A paragraph is a section of writing that usually deals with one specific topic. The writer states the topic in either the first or last sentence. In a handwritten piece the first sentence is indented. When word processing, paragraphs are normally separated from each other by a line space. Paragraphs give a piece of writing a tidy, ordered appearance and make it easier for the reader to read and understand.

Numbers

Newspapers and other publications often pick a style of numbering. For example, when writing numbers from one to nine use words, and from 10 upwards use numbers.

▶ Punctuation

Punctuate the following sentence:
- Woman without her man is nothing

There are two possible solutions:
- Woman: without her, man is nothing.
- Woman, without her man, is nothing.

Two sentences, the same words, yet two different meanings. This is why we punctuate written communication, so that the reader understands clearly and without ambiguity the meaning of the written word. Writing cannot convey meaning like speaking does – with tone of voice, volume, speed, etc. – so punctuation is our best way of doing this. Computer technology can help with automatic checks and predictive writing, but these tools can cause our writing skills to become rusty if we become too dependent upon them. So we still need to know the basics in order to produce clear, meaningful pieces of writing.

Apostrophe (')

The apostrophe is used in the following ways:

Possession

The apostrophe is used to indicate possession in nouns:
- Fred's cat
- The Chief Inspector's slightly shabby raincoat

So we add an apostrophe and an 's'. The same applies for possessors that don't have an 's' in the plural:
- The children's toys
- The women's scarves

However, when the possessor is a plural *with* an 's', the apostrophe goes after the 's':
- The students' assignments
- The ladies' handbags

For possessors that end in an 's' in the singular, we add an apostrophe and an 's':
- The boss's office
- Mr Burns's nose
- *Bridget Jones's Diary*

But if we want to talk about the feet of Moses, we say:
- Moses' feet

The 's' is often omitted when the last syllable of the name is pronounced *-iz*, as in Moses', Bridges'.

Activity

Change the following phrases and add apostrophes where required, e.g. 'the cage of the hamster' becomes 'the hamster's cage'.

1. The goggles of the swimmers
2. The plays of Shakespeare
3. The tomb of Rameses
4. The toys of the children
5. The bones of the dog
6. The Green of St Stephen
7. The wool of the lambs
8. The Square of St Thomas

Answers available on page 283

Note the expressions:
- A fortnight's holiday
- Two weeks' holiday
- One week's time
- One euro's worth
- Five euros' worth
- For God's sake
- For goodness' sake

Also:
- She went to the dentist's.
- We are off to the butcher's.

In each case a word has been left out – surgery and shop.

Contractions/Omission of Letters

The apostrophe is used to indicate that a letter has been left out:
- He doesn't know wha' he's talkin' about. (He does not know what he is talking about.)
- Who'd've thought you'd be head o' the company? (Who would have thought you would be head of the company?)

A word like 'doesn't' is a contraction because it has been contracted, i.e. shortened from 'does not'.

Activity

Rewrite the following, inserting apostrophes and contracting where necessary:

1. I could not eat another thing.
2. They are all we have got.
3. Do you not have your umbrella with you?
4. Who will sit in the back with Sarah?
5. She is the best hope there is to win.
6. It has been raining.
7. Who would have thought you had it in you?

Answers available on page 283

The apostrophe is not used:
- For plurals: 'The band played all their hits' (not hit's); 'Do we have to do Communications?' (not Communication's)
- Verbs: 'She saves her money each week'. (not save's)
- Possessive pronouns: Hers, its, ours, yours, theirs

- Plurals of numbers/years: The 1960s
- Plurals of abbreviations: PCs, B&Bs

'PC's' and '1960's' are frequently used today, but they are incorrect.

Confusables:
- Its = belonging to it:
— The Government did its best to curb inflation.
- It's = it is/it has:
— It's only rock 'n' roll but I like it.
- Whose:
— The man whose wife sang at the opera was wearing green trousers.
- Who's = who is/who has:
— Who's been eating my porridge?

Activity

Insert apostrophes (and an 's' if necessary) in the following sentences:

1. Were tired of reading Shakespeares plays. Cant we read some of Yeats poetry?
2. The buses didnt stop at St Stephens Green because the drivers wage increase wasnt enough.
3. Were goin to Donegal for a fortnights holiday.
4. Ill get an hours work done if Peter doesnt disturb me.
5. Theres nothin but rocks on Mars surface.
6. If Goldilocks hunger hadnt got the better of her, shed have passed by the bears house and none of this wouldve happened.
7. Ive got to go to the doctors cause my tonsils swellings got worse.
8. Heres Dereks jacket. Its covered in dogs hairs.
9. The pubs windows look great but its doors colours dont.
10. For heavens sake if its such a big deal well all go to Helens.
11. The medias got to curtail its habit of prying into peoples lives.

Answers available on page 283

Hyphen (-)

The hyphen is used in many compound words, i.e. words formed by joining two or more other words to make new words, e.g. well-being, merry-go-round.
Compound adjectives are hyphenated when they come before the noun but not after:
- We played a well-known song for the encore.

- The song that we played for the encore was well known.

Phrasal verbs are not hyphenated:
- You need to build up your strength.

But when used as a noun they are hyphenated:
- We enjoyed the build-up to the game.

A hyphen is also used to divide a word that won't fit at the end of a line: dis-connected. Of course, when word processing, this is unnecessary as the words are fitted into the page automatically.

Dash (–)

The dash separates:
1. Words and phrases in the middle of a sentence:
- The band – the best in the country – has just embarked on a world tour.
- Two young men – both beginners – joined the course yesterday.
2. Words or phrases added on to the end of sentences:
- The street has a lively atmosphere – just what we were looking for.
- We drove down the coastline – one of the most beautiful I'd ever seen.

The dash is often regarded as slightly informal. When word processing, use Ctrl and the hyphen key on the numbers keypad on the right for a dash, but put a space either side of the dash.

> ### Activity
> The following passage needs six hyphens and seven dashes:
>
> My sister in law came to stay for the weekend she didn't even ring to warn us! Her husband my brother Harry is a long legged evil looking man he even scares the dog. We watched the semi final on television and then were about to have a big feed of pasta my favourite when we noticed the sell by date on the packet two weeks old!

Answers available on page 283

Colon (:)

The colon:
1. Indicates that something is following on from the previous phrase or sentence:
- You know what will happen if you miss the deadline: you'll fail the assignment.
2. Introduces a series or list:
- Here's what I'm having: soup, lasagne, a side salad, ice cream and coffee.

3. Introduces a quotation:
- As Bob Dylan said: 'Keep a good head and always carry a light bulb.'

Semi-colon (;)

The semi-colon:
1. Is used to separate two parts of a sentence that are too closely connected to be separated by a full stop:
- I love apples; Granny Smiths are my favourite.
- I remember him when he couldn't put two notes together; now he's top of the charts.
- She was delighted; I was delirious.

These could be written as separate sentences.

2. Can sometimes be replaced with a conjunction such as 'but' or 'and'
3. Can also be used for a list in which the items are lengthy:
- John's travels took him far and wide: a week by the sea on a beautiful Greek island; a month exploring the rugged Turkish coastline; three weeks travelling south through the scorched landscape of the Middle East; and finally a month in Egypt exploring the ancient archaeological wonders.

Activity

Put a colon or semi-colon in the following sentences:

1. Out came the sun off came the shirts.
2. We'll need the following a hammer, nails, wood and paint.
3. To err is human to forgive divine.
4. Here's the suspect's description 6'2", brown hair, brown eyes and a moustache.
5. The speaker began 'Good evening, Ladies and Gentlemen.'
6. Luxembourg is a small country France is a large one.

Answers available on page 283

Full Stop, Question Mark, Exclamation Mark

The *full stop* is used:
1. At the end of sentences, normally followed by a capital letter to begin the next sentence
2. After initials: W.B. Yeats
3. After abbreviations: 25 Dec.

There is no full stop in a sequence of capitals – USA, UN, etc.

A sequence of three full stops, called an *ellipsis*, means an omission of a section of text:
- Everyone... seems to have used the internet these days.

A *question mark* is used after questions instead of a full stop and is followed by a capital letter. It is not used after indirect questions.

An *exclamation mark* is used instead of a full stop after exclamations, which usually express some strong feeling, emphasis or humour.

Activity

Put a full stop, question mark or exclamation mark after each of the following sentences:

1. I don't know whether she's in or not
2. Do we know if there is alien life in the Universe
3. Help
4. I wonder if I could borrow your hammer
5. He told me why he was late
6. Don't you dare
7. How far do we have to travel
8. What a great idea

Answers available on page 283

Comma (,)

The following sentences could be very confusing without commas:
1. The discussion over the game continued.
2. The student thought the teacher was going to do very well.
3. The tiger having eaten the children walked on.
4. Granny has eaten Brian.

Where would you put them?

Separating Mark

The comma is a *separating mark*. It separates:

1. Two clauses that could be two complete sentences and are joined by conjunctions such as 'and', 'but', 'or', 'yet' and 'while':
- We wanted to go to the beach, but it had started to rain.
- They booked into a nice hotel, while we had to camp in the field.
2. Descriptive phrases in the middle of a sentence, which are not essential to the meaning of the sentence:

- The novel, a murder mystery, will probably become a bestseller.
- Mrs Malone, who was wearing a bright pink frock, poured the tea.

BUT
- The woman who was wearing a bright pink frock poured the tea.
  (This is essential to the overall meaning.)

3. Items in a list of three or more items, but not before 'and':
- We bought tea, milk, sugar and bread.
- She climbed to the top of the wall, took out her binoculars, scanned the horizon and prepared for the worst.

4. Words that introduce direct speech:
- He said, 'You know, that's the worst sentence I've ever read.'
- 'You know,' he said, 'that's the worst sentence I've ever read.'
- 'You know, that's the worst sentence I've ever read,' he said.

5. Non-essential additions to sentences (including interjections like 'aha', 'oops', 'er', 'um', etc.):
- Aha, there you are!
- Janey Mac, would you look at the state of him?
- It's a really brilliant film, like, you know what I mean?

6. Question tags (also non-essential additions):
- It's cold today, isn't it?
- You saw it, didn't you?

7. Vocatives (addressing a person or thing) and salutations:
- Mr President, I'd like to congratulate you.
- It's nice to see you again, Helen.
- Dear Sandra,

8. Sentence adverbs like 'however', 'nevertheless', 'meanwhile', 'finally', 'at last':
- There is, however, a good reason for studying this.
- Yes, I'd like that.
- No, I disagree.
- Of course, she'll never make the grade.

9. Participial (-ing) phrases:
- Feeling energetic, he went for a run.
- Having completed my QQI Level 5 in Outdoor Adventure Education, I am now ready to work in this sector.

10. Parts of a sentence to avoid confusion:
- The discussion over, the game continued.
- The student, thought the teacher, was going to do very well.
- The tiger having eaten, the children walked on.
- Granny has eaten, Brian.

Incorrect Uses of the Comma

- I walked to the window, it was still open.
- At the end of the game, the players, were exhausted.
- Addresses: 12, Stephen Street.
- People, who live in glass houses, shouldn't throw stones.

Activity

Insert commas in the following sentences:

1. So Joe do you think we have a chance of winning?
2. The doctor a large friendly man prescribed some pills.
3. Singing at the top of his voice Steve prepared a splendid dinner.
4. Josephine meanwhile was reading the paper.
5. 'Don't you think' she enquired 'we should call the vet?'
6. The Delaneys live in number 46 and the Mulligans live in number 45.
7. The train travelling at 120 mph had 14 carriages.
8. Having finished their meal the family took the last bus home.
9. I put on my coat picked up my things bade farewell and left the building.
10. It was like the worst book I've ever read.
11. I told you yesterday we had to submit the assignment.
12. You're finished now aren't you?

Answers available on page 283

Inverted Commas/Quotation Marks (' ') ("")

Use either single '' or double "" marks. If using a quotation within a quotation, use single for the first and double for the second:

- She said, 'In the words of Roosevelt, "The only thing we have to fear is fear itself," and I must say I have to agree.'

Direct Speech

- 'You know,' she said, 'maybe we'll meet up again sometime.'

Punctuation marks, which belong to the quote, remain within the quotation marks.

In a written passage a new speaker is indicated by a new paragraph.

Quotations

Quotations are used for what someone else said or wrote:

- As Descartes said, 'I think, therefore I am.'

Titles

Quotation marks indicate titles of poems, songs, articles in newspapers or magazines and short stories:
- 'The Lake Isle of Innisfree' is a favourite poem of mine.

Irony/Jargon/Slang

Irony, jargon, slang or words that have new or strange meanings can be indicated by the use of quotation mark:
- They consulted a few 'experts' before making a decision.
- Tom said he had to take a 'bio break' during yesterday's meeting.
- The team tried out their 'shock and awe' tactics during the game.
- Many people today are 'woke' to current issues of social injustice.

Activity

Insert quotation marks, if necessary, in the following sentences:

1. It's all right she said everything will be better in the morning.
2. What kind of a word is bodacious anyway he enquired.
3. He used to be a successful film producer, but now he's been cancelled.
4. Give us your rendition of As Time Goes By.
5. Teachers to Strike yelled the headline across the front page.
6. In the words of Samuel Beckett: We are all born mad. Some remain so.

Answers available on page 283

Brackets/Parentheses ()

These are used to enclose explanations, translations, definitions and added information to the text:
- His philosophy was always *carpe deum* (seize the day).

(If an entire sentence in enclosed in brackets, the full stop must come within the final bracket.)

Activities

Bring out the Brackets

Insert brackets as appropriate in the following sentences:

1. The ship if you could call it that will sail at 10.30 p.m.
2. We sat in the shade it was too hot to do anything else drinking ice-cold water.

3. The people who are really stressed these days not counting nurses are senior management.
4. The books both thrillers lay on his desk gathering dust.
5. She shouted after him, '*Ich liebe dich* I love you,' but it was too late. He was gone.
6. This steady increase in temperature known as global warming is set to get worse over the coming century.

Confusing Words

Delete the incorrect words in each of the following sentences:

1. There/their/they're is a group of men outside and there/their/they're carrying umbrellas under there/their/they're arms.
2. I've been/being at this bus stop for 45 minutes and I'm sick of been/being kept waiting.
3. Where/were/we're all going to Donegal, which is where/were/we're we where/were/we're last year for our holidays.
4. There are two/too/to gunslingers coming two/too/to this town. That is two/too/to two/too/to many.
5. It's/its been a long time since the union got it's/its way.

Two Words or One?

Circle the correct word or words in each sentence.

1. Is there a post office near by/nearby?
2. Communications is easy, whereas/where as Maths is hard.
3. She fell in to/into his arms with a heavy sigh.
4. On the count of three, altogether/all together now.
5. When he found it in the river, the briefcase was still intact/in tact.
6. He slammed his fist on the table, there by/thereby breaking his wrist.
7. We have to do a practical as well/aswell as a theoretical exam.
8. Who knows what's instore/in store for us?
9. Don't you get a lot/alot of ice with your drink?
10. In fact/infact Ireland need three points to qualify.
11. Bring an umbrella incase/in case it rains.

12. That holiday has left me deeply in debt/indebt.
13. It will be all right/alright on the night.

More Confusing Words

In each of the following sentences, select the correct word, decide what the other one means and put it in another sentence (it may have more than one meaning):

1. We dropped into the off-licence/license to get some beer for the party.
2. Is this a licensed/licenced premises?
3. She decided to brake/break off/of their relationship.
4. I have an awful pain in my back. I hope I don't have a slipped disc/disk.
5. We saw a fantastic programme/program on television last night.
6. After all the Christmas eating and drinking, he was scared to way/weigh himself.
7. He called to say he'd be late due to a bored/board meeting.
8. Police are investigating an incidence/incident in a city centre shopping mall.

Answers available on page 283

Tip for Effective Writing

Always proofread your writing before sending a message or submitting an assignment. Check for punctuation, spelling and grammar. If in doubt, ask someone else to proofread for you.

Chapter Review

1. What are the main differences between descriptive writing and academic writing?
2. What kind of nouns begin with a capital letter?
3. Explain the difference between a colon and a semi-colon.
4. When should you use apostrophes?
5. When should you use inverted commas?

Chapter 12
Personal Writing

In this chapter, you will learn about:
- Writing as a Response
- Preparation
- Short Story
- Poetry
- Review
- Personal Letters

Writing as a Response

Writing is often done in response to something. Personal writing can be a response to something we've experienced or felt. We might be responding to our own emotions, thoughts or experiences and we express them in poetry, a story, diary, blog, etc. Or we could be responding to events in society that prompt us to write a letter to a newspaper or share our views on social media. A letter of thanks is a response to a favour done or gift received; a review is our response to a film, book, play, etc. Functional writing could be in response to a brief we might have been given by an employer or a college tutor.

Personal Writing

Personal writing is about expressing our own personal experiences, thoughts and feelings. In effect we are communicating our personalities, which should come across in a piece of writing, be it a letter, poem, story, review, etc. It may also stem from simply reflecting on our lives, the lives of others or the world at large and expressing these reflections in writing.

Some people keep journals or diaries in which they regularly express their innermost thoughts and desires. This type of writing can be therapeutic and liberating, helping to unload psychological burdens that we may be carrying. Since we are doing it purely for ourselves, it doesn't matter if its grammar or punctuation is weak.

◗ Preparation

No matter what type of personal writing we are faced with, we all begin with the dreaded blank page and a head seemingly bereft of fresh ideas. How do we start? First of all we need to be clear what we are writing:

1. *Purpose/intention* – what do we want to achieve; what effect do we want to have on the reader?
2. *Topic* – what is it going to be about?
3. *Form* – what way is it going to be written: a poem, prose, story or dialogue? This will be strongly influenced by our purpose.
4. *Language* – the kinds of words we use will create the style, e.g. language using imagery and metaphor suits poetry but not a letter of application.
5. *Personal style* – certain words or expressions that we commonly use, and even the kind of sentence structure we usually employ (long/short, etc.) when we write denote our own particular style.
6. *Punctuation and grammar* – obviously these need to be correct. (See Chapter 11: Writing Skills.)

There are several stages we need to go through to put together a piece of writing.

Plan/Rough Notes

We cannot hope to write a piece from scratch and submit it as it is. There will always be mistakes and room for improvement. A brainstorming session to get all our ideas on the topic down onto a page is useful. We can then link them together by subtopic.

Draft

We then try to organise these notes to give them some kind of shape. We work out how to order each idea, how to begin and end the written piece and how we structure the main points in between.

Redraft/Edit

We might find some words we don't like. We might change them, make additions/cuts, polish, refine, etc.

Fig. 12.1

Proofread

It is wise to get someone else to proofread our work, as they will see the mistakes that we don't notice.

Where Do We Get Our Ideas?

Fig. 12.2

Memory – this is one source of ideas. Experts often say, 'Write what you know.' If we can tap into our memory for experiences, events, etc. we will be truly communicating our own personality.
Imagination – we can imagine scenarios, characters, situations and build a story around them.
Observation – look around you and write about what you see: people, nature, objects, events, etc.

Activities

To get over 'writer's block', try the following:

1. Handwrite three pages about whatever comes into your head without stopping or worrying about spelling, grammar or punctuation. This can free up your inner creative juices and liberate you from your inner censor ('I'm no good at writing'). It can also provide you with some good ideas for a story or a poem.

2. Sit somewhere quietly and simply record in writing everything you see, hear, smell, touch and taste. These ideas can then be developed into a poem or part of a story.

3. Create two characters by giving them names, physical descriptions, jobs, hobbies, habits, likes, dislikes, activities and ways of talking and walking. Put them in a setting. What happens next? Now you have the start of a story.

Short Story

A good story needs to hold the reader's attention and make them want to read on to find out what happens at the end. The beginning and the end should be strong, the former to hook the reader and the latter to leave them feeling satisfied. Sometimes the best stories are the ones we have experienced ourselves. We can always adapt them to make them more exciting and dramatic.

Fig. 12.3

A short story usually has five key elements:

1. Characters

Create a few characters or just one. Make them come alive by describing them and making them say and do things.

2. Setting

Give the story a time and a place. This can help create a mood, e.g. 'A dark stormy night in the woods' evokes a very different mood from 'A sunny afternoon by the sea'. You can also give it a social setting, i.e. what kind of life do the characters lead? Are they wealthy, poor, dull, adventurous, young, old, etc.?

3. Theme

This is the main idea of the story or an underlying message.

4. Conflict

All great stories from Shakespeare's plays to modern soap operas would be very dull without people arguing or involved in some kind of struggle. Introduce conflict early on.

5. Plot

This is what happens to the character(s). It should contain these key elements:
- *Introduction* – setting the scene and introducing the character(s).

- *Problem or conflict* – the character(s) has to deal with this by taking some action. This is sometimes called the rising action.
- *Climax* – the high point of the action, involving some element of danger or the main challenge the character(s) must face. It is a turning point in the story or a change to the main character(s). This should occur near the end.
- *Resolution* – the conclusion to the story with an outcome to see what has happened to the character(s) as a result of the climax. Here the conflict is resolved.

A short story should focus on one event in a person's life. Every sentence should either develop the character(s) or move the plot forward. Use a variety of writing forms to make it interesting: dialogue, description and action. Decide on the type of narration you will use. First-person narration, in which the narrator is part of the story, can make it sound more personal and believable. Third-person narration gives it a more objective, detached feel. Write about what you already know and keep it simple.

Here is a short story written for Twitter in under 140 characters:

> Nothing happened. Then it did. Adventures ensued. Helpers, adversaries came. He lost everything. Then, redemption. He was changed – forever.
> (Tim Lott, Short Story Tweet, *The Guardian* Saturday, 26 January 2013)

Activities

1. Write a short story in under 140 characters.
2. Read this short story and discuss the setting, characters, structure, plot, narration, language, etc. It illustrates how short and simple an effective story can be. What is your opinion of it?

> **Angel**
>
> Sitting on the drippy, cold steps of Penn Station, sharing a smoke with a boyfriend. This Saturday night is scattered with drunks, and for once, we are not the drunkest; we do not smell the worst. Late-night, paranoid tourists don't even stare – a few ask for directions. We are spreading our wet, waiting bodies all over that stone, watching stumbling silhouettes wrestle with the escalator.
>
> She shuffles up the steps with the last of her strength. Her pink sweatpants are tinged with brown, and her feet are buried in city-stained bunny slippers. Her eyes look like they've seen so much sadness they're forever doomed to apathy. They are eyes dazed with the work it takes to stay warm, and weary of the excess of privileged people. I'm looking

> at those glass eyes and thinking that she reeks of survival; that I'm too cold to move, and all I'm doing is waiting for the first train home.
>
> Out comes her wrinkled, begging hand. We turn out our pockets and find nothing. The mouth of the station swallows her descending, dejected frame.
>
> Light another smoke. We are pushing reluctant time forward as it digs its heels in at the dusty smells and sounds of old stories, at the sucking of smoke, at our involuntary shivers.
>
> She's back again. The wrinkled hand, heavy with pleading, is now answering.
>
> She drops four warm quarters into my palm and says, 'Get yourselves a cup of coffee. Merry Christmas.'
>
> The station gulps her up again before we can say thank you.

(Maria Raha, from www.storybytes.com, 1999)

Poetry

Some people think poetry is about the dreary, miserable lives led by the poets who write the stuff, but in fact poetry can be about anything and can be written in a variety of styles including dialogue and free verse (no formal structure).

If you haven't written poetry before, it's probably not a good idea to submit your first piece for a communications assignment. A poem should have something special that will inspire the reader. This could include any or all of the following:

1. Language that is clever, beautiful, rhythmic, humorous or that uses sounds to good effect. Some techniques used for creating effective sounds:

    - *Assonance* – words sharing similar vowel sounds, e.g. 'The fire smouldered in the cold, but the old man couldn't scold her.'

Fig. 12.4

"Oh. Wow. Another sonnet."

- *Alliteration* – words that share the same initial letter or sound, e.g. 'The rich may rule the world but the rebels rightly riot.'
- *Onomatopoeia* – words that sound like what they mean, e.g. 'splash'
- *Rhyme*
2. Imagery that the reader can 'see'. Imagery can be created by:
   - *Metaphor* – an imaginative description comparing something with an object or action that is not literally applicable, e.g. 'the whispering breeze'
   - *Simile* – a comparison using the words 'like', 'as' or 'than', e.g. 'she sang like an angel'
3. Emotions that will inspire, move or entertain the reader
4. Ideas that will provoke thought

As with all personal writing, you should tap into your own memories and experiences for subject matter.

> ## Discussion
>
> Read this poem by Seamus Heaney and consider the use of memory, observation and the senses as writing aids. Look also at his use of imagery, sounds and language. What does the poet say about poetry?
>
> **Digging**
> Between my finger and my thumb
> The squat pen rests; snug as a gun.
>
> Under my window, a clean rasping sound
> When the spade sinks into gravelly ground:
> My father, digging. I look down
>
> Till his straining rump among the flowerbeds
> Bends low, comes up twenty years away
> Stooping in rhythm through potato drills
> Where he was digging.
>
> The coarse boot nestled on the lug, the shaft
> Against the inside knee was levered firmly.
> He rooted out tall tops, buried the bright edge deep
> To scatter new potatoes that we picked,
> Loving their cool hardness in our hands.
>
> By God, the old man could handle a spade.
> Just like his old man.

> My grandfather cut more turf in a day
> Than any other man on Toner's bog.
> Once I carried him milk in a bottle
> Corked sloppily with paper. He straightened up
> To drink it, then fell to right away
> Nicking and slicing neatly, heaving sods
> Over his shoulder, going down and down
> For the good turf. Digging.
>
> The cold smell of potato mould, the squelch and slap
> Of soggy peat, the curt cuts of an edge
> Through living roots awaken in my head.
> But I've no spade to follow men like them.
>
> Between my finger and my thumb
> The squat pen rests.
> I'll dig with it.

(Seamus Heaney, from *Death of a Naturalist*, 1966)

Poetry Online (Video)

Hearing poetry read aloud can be far more satisfying than reading it. Go to YouTube and search these poems to hear their poets recite them:
- Seamus Heaney, 'Digging'
- Allen Ginsberg, 'Howl'
- Benjamin Zephaniah, 'Faceless'
- Dylan Thomas, 'Do Not Go Gentle into that Good Night'
- Kae Tempest, 'Brand New Ancients'

▶ Review

The purpose of a review is to give an *informed* opinion and criticism of a book, play, film, album or concert. There should be sufficient detail to let the reader decide whether or not they want to go and see/buy it. A film review, for example, should contain information about the following:
- *Director* – have they created a good film? How? Compare it with other films by them.
- *Actors* – have they played their parts well?

Fig. 12.5

- *Characters* – are they believable and well developed? What kind of characters are they? Heroic, funny, sad, evil, etc.?
- *Plot* – is it exciting, suspenseful, realistic, full of holes, complicated? The ending should not be revealed.
- *Setting* – where and when does it take place?
- *Genre* – what type of film is it (comedy, drama, science fiction, thriller, etc.)? Is it a successful example of its genre?
- *Script* – is it well written? Perhaps you could give a good quote or two from the film.

Sometimes a film review might have further information about the budget, soundtrack, lighting, cinematography, special effects, awards, etc.

A book review should contain information about:
- *Author* – compare the book with other works by the same author
- *Language* – is it simple/complicated, easy/hard to read, well written/poorly written/beautifully written?
- *Style* – is it snappy, slow, fast-paced, a page-turner, gripping, 'unputdownable', dull, exciting, etc.?
- *Characters* – see film review (above)
- *Plot* – see film review (above)
- *Setting* – see film review (above)
- *Genre* – see film review (above)

An album review should contain information about:
- *Recording artist/band/singer*
- *Genre* – folk, rap, rock, pop, hip-hop, classical, etc. Is it a successful example of its genre?
- *Different songs/pieces of music* – are they moving, exciting, sad, etc.?
- *Lyrical content* – are the words any good?
- *Sound quality/production* – is it raw/polished, clean/distorted, etc.?
- How it *compares* with other albums by the same artist or of the same genre

A concert/gig review should contain information about:
- *Artist/band/singer/musicians* – did they play, sing, dance well?
- *The performance* – was it entertaining, funny, moving, beautiful, etc.?
- Whether the performer(s) *related* to the audience
- *Special effects* – lighting/explosions, etc.
- *Sound quality* – e.g. could you hear the lyrics/various instruments?
- *Audience reaction* – were they happy, pleased, ecstatic, underwhelmed, etc.?

Activity

Read the following review of *Donnie Darko* and discuss the reviewer's references to the director, actors, characters, plot, genre, etc.

Donnie Darko

It is early October 1988, and the US presidential election is on. Donnie Darko (Jake Gyllenhaal) is a likeable, sleepwalking, troubled teenager who might be schizophrenic. He lives with his family in leafy suburban Middlesex, Virginia and goes to the local high school. One night a six-foot evil-looking rabbit called Frank leads him out of the house on a sleepwalk and tells him the world will end in 28 days, 6 hours and 42 minutes. He arrives home the next morning to find a jet engine has crashed into his bedroom. Miraculously, none of his family is hurt, and had he been in bed he surely would have been killed. But strangely no airplane with a missing engine is found. As he tries to work out what all this means, Frank continues to haunt him and instructs him to commit various acts of destruction. At the same time he has to deal with the assorted characters in his life. His parents (Mary McDonnell and Holmes Osborne) are naïve, but compassionate and tolerate his insulting behaviour because they know he is ill. His sister, played by real-life sister, Maggie Gyllenhaal, is as sweet and sarcastic as you'd expect. His science teacher has to stop a conversation he has with Donnie about time travel because it is veering into religious territory. Donnie soon starts going out with Gretchen, the new girl in class played by Jena Malone, and an awkward romance starts.

Gretchen: 'You're weird.'

Donnie: 'Sorry.'

Gretchen: 'No, that was a compliment.'

Directed by first timer Richard Kelly, this has become something of a cult favourite since its release in 2001. Its success partially lies in the fact that it doesn't fit neatly into any one specific genre but manages to dip into high school drama, black comedy, supernatural sci-fi, romance, psychological thriller and because of this it remains free from clichés and utterly unique.

> Jake Gyllenhaal is superb as the central character, giving a subtle yet emotionally powerful performance as a highly intelligent but disaffected teenager searching for answers and questioning authority. The film is also peppered with some wonderful minor characters and subplots to keep the interest up. Drew Barrymore plays the liberal English teacher who gets fired for teaching literature that is considered to be offensive; Patrick Swayze is a smug motivational guru who has a nasty skeleton in the closet; Katherine Ross is Donnie's psychiatrist, who prescribes him drugs and, in one of the film's funniest scenes, hypnotises him and foolishly asks him what he thinks about at school. One character, the isolated Grandma Death, might just have the answers to Donnie's probing questions. The performances are all impeccable, played with conviction and doing justice to the fabulously witty script.
>
> As the film counts down the 28 days, after which we expect some kind of apocalypse (coinciding with Halloween), the tension builds and Donnie's questions about fate, chaos and time travel force us to ask, is he really living in some parallel time sequence or is he delusional and hallucinating? At one point he asks Frank, 'Why are you wearing that stupid bunny suit?' to which Frank replies, 'Why are you wearing that stupid man suit?'
>
> The film's ending, with Tears for Fears' 'Mad World' playing over various characters chewing over their actions or overcome with emotion, is incredibly moving, leaving the viewer with many questions on many levels yet strangely satisfied. Hilarious, heart-breaking, surreal, profound and thought-provoking, this is as much a treat for those with enquiring minds as it is for the hopelessly romantic. Some people will find it a little too strange and puzzling, but for those who want something beyond the ordinary, this is just the ticket.

(Martin Scott, 2005)

▶ Personal Letters

With the communications revolution in full swing and new technologies appearing all the time, letter writing would appear to be a dying art. Today it seems much more efficient to send an email, text message or to telephone. Yet there is something special about receiving a personal letter from someone. Somebody has taken the time and effort to put pen to paper, to compose words with more thought than goes into a text message or email, to buy a stamp and to post it in a postbox. An email can be deleted at the touch of a button, whereas a letter can be read and re-read and may be stored away to be discovered years later. How many text messages or emails will be found and savoured in years to come?

A personal letter, be it a letter of thanks, condolence or congratulations, should be handwritten. Its purpose is to express personal thoughts, and if it is typed then it becomes less personal, and the less personal, the less its effect. The receiver of a handwritten letter will note and appreciate personal touches.

The informal nature of personal letters means that the rules are not as strict as for formal letters. Nevertheless, a basic layout is required.

Sample Personal Letter

> 49 Bridge Street
> Bray
> Co. Wicklow
> Ireland
>
> 23.9.21
>
> Dear Philip,
>
> It was great to see you and Erica in Boston over the summer holidays. Thanks for putting us up in your house for the week. We really had a brilliant time. Next year you can come and stay with us, and I'll show you some Irish hospitality.
>
> I've just started a course at a college of further education so I'm really busy studying hard and making lots of new friends. I'm working part-time in a local café at the weekends, but I make sure I have time for socialising too! I bought myself a new bike last week with some of the money I saved from working in the States. It's great for getting to college every day and for keeping fit, though the traffic can be pretty dangerous at times.
>
> Give my love to Erica, Ted and Sue.
>
> All the best,
>
> Martin

Layout

The sender's address goes at the top right-hand side of the page. The date goes below this. The salutation goes below the date but on the left-hand side. Indent the first and all subsequent paragraphs. There are a variety of ways you can close a personal letter depending on how well you know the recipient. 'Yours sincerely' may be too formal for some people. 'Yours affectionately' can be used for close relations or friends, or simply 'Yours' for a close friend. For people we know well, familiar endings such as 'Love', 'All the best' or 'Best wishes' are also typical.

Thanks

A letter of thanks not only shows appreciation for a favour or a gift, but it also acts as an acknowledgement of receipt. It does not have to be very long, but it should be sincere and contain a personal touch. It may be used as a reply to invitations, on receipt of gifts/presents, after weddings, parties and visits or in response to help given or acknowledgement of an expression of condolences. Two short paragraphs are sufficient.

Paragraph 1

Suggestions:
- 'Many thanks for the book you sent me. It was very kind of you. I haven't been able to put it down since...'
- 'Thank you very much for the wedding present you gave us. It is proving to be so useful.'

Paragraph 2

This could contain some simple news about yourself or about the receiver:
- 'It was so good to see you...'
- 'I have been really busy lately studying hard at college...'

Condolences

A letter of condolence can be a difficult and sensitive piece of writing. It is important to find the right amount of sincerity, without going over the top and sounding false. It should contain words of sympathy:
- 'I was so sorry to hear about the death of...'
- 'We were shocked to hear the sad news about...'

Words of comfort:
- 'She was a wonderful person, kind and generous...'
- 'We are thinking of you at this sad and difficult time...'
- 'He was a good friend and will be greatly missed.'

If appropriate, some offer of assistance:
- 'If there is anything I can do...'

To personalise a letter of condolence, we can include a personal memory we ourselves had of the deceased or an anecdote about a time spent in their company: 'I remember the time when...'

Congratulations

Offering congratulations is a simple matter and may be used for the following occasions: passing exams, an engagement, a wedding, a promotion, the birth of a child, a new home.

Some useful phrases:
- 'We wish you every success in your new position'
- 'I am delighted to hear the good news'
- 'We were overjoyed to hear the news about the birth of your son'
- 'I'm sending you my hearty congratulations'
- 'You should be proud of such a fine achievement'
- 'Well done!'
- 'Congratulations!'

Tip for Choosing What to Write

Some people are naturally more imaginative than others and have no problem finding inspiration to write a story or a poem. If you feel you aren't that creative, writing a book or a film review might be easier – or maybe a personal letter. Remember that a teacher will have to read any number of pieces of personal writing so you should try to make it as original as possible.

Activities

Confusing Words

In each of the following sentences, select the correct word, decide what the other word means and put it into another sentence (it may have more than one meaning):

1. There is ample/amble opportunity to get to know each other.
2. Tourists can wonder/wander through the beautiful gardens at leisure.
3. She didn't except/accept my apology.
4. The film had a powerful effect/affect on me.
5. There was a full compliment/complement of members at the meeting.

6. He was completely disinterested/uninterested in the game.

7. There was a continuous/continual flow of water from the tap.

8. Don't loose/lose your keys.

Lost in Translation

The following are signs poorly translated into English. Work out what is wrong with them, what each is trying to communicate, then rewrite them to make their meaning clear.

Swiss restaurant menu:
Our wines leave you with nothing to hope for.

Rhodes tailor:
Order your summers suit. Because is big rush, we will execute customers in strict rotation.

Bucharest hotel lobby:
The lift is being fixed for the next day. During that time we regret that you will be unbearable.

Athens hotel:
Visitors are expected to complain at the office between the hours of 9 and 11 am daily.

Chapter 13
Workplace Documents

In this chapter, you will learn about:
- Application Form
- Curriculum Vitae
- Letter of Application
- Formal/Business Letters
- Other Formal Letters
- Memorandum
- Invoice
- Press Release
- Leaflet/Brochure

At some time in your career you are bound to come across various types of documents that relate to the workplace, such as letters, memos and invoices. You may be required to produce such documents. Therefore, it is important to know how to prepare and write them. Most workplace documents follow certain formats and use language that is clear and concise. This chapter will look at how to create these.

Application Form

Filling in a job application form sounds simple enough, but many opportunities are lost due to carelessness.

Tips for Filling in Application Forms

1. Make a photocopy of the original and fill it in first. If you make mistakes, you have a chance to correct them.
2. Skim-read the whole form before completing it.
3. Keep handwriting as neat and clear as possible.
4. Word process it, if possible, to make it look more professional.
5. Check all instructions, e.g. using block capitals, ink colour, etc.
6. Don't rush it.
7. Double-check all your information for accuracy.
8. Include information that is accurate – you might have to explain it in an interview.
9. Get someone to proofread it when finished.
10. Make a photocopy of the completed form for your own use, e.g. to prepare for the interview.
11. Take the same care in addressing the envelope.

Sample Job Application Form

Job Title: _____

Surname: _____

First Name(s): _____

Title (Mr, Ms, etc.) _____

Address: _____

Telephone Number: _____

Mobile Number: _____

Email: _____

EDUCATION

List in reverse chronological order.

Schools/College	Dates	Subjects/Courses	Results/Grades

EMPLOYMENT
Current/most recent position
Dates
From: _____ To: _____
Name and address of employer:
_____
_____
_____
_____

Job Title: _____
Main duties and responsibilities: _____
_____
_____
_____
_____

Previous employment
List in reverse chronological order.

Name and address of previous employer(s):	Dates	Position held
_____	_____	_____
_____	_____	_____
_____	_____	_____
_____	_____	_____
_____	_____	_____
_____	_____	_____

Have you ever suffered from any serious illnesses? _____
If so, give details: _____
_____

Do you have a full current driving licence? _____
Have you ever been charged for a driving offence or been involved in a serious accident?
If so, give details: _____
_____

Have you ever been convicted of a criminal offence?_____
If so, give details: _____
_____
_____

Language proficiency:_____
Computer proficiency:_____
How did you learn about this vacancy?_____
Have you worked for this company before?_____
If so, when?_____

INTERESTS

Give details of any interests, pastimes and achievements:
_____
_____
_____
_____

Outline your reasons for wanting this position:
_____
_____
_____
_____

Additional information that you think might be relevant:
_____
_____
_____
_____

Signature: _____ Date: _____

▶ Curriculum Vitae

Latin for 'course of life', a curriculum vitae, or CV, is a document giving a brief account of your life to date relevant to a work situation. It should be word-processed, neatly presented, well laid out, putting the important information first and all of it relevant. There are various ways of presenting a CV, but it should be no longer than two or three A4 pages.

Layout

A CV should contain the following information:

Personal Details

Name, address, phone number, email

Personal Profile
This is a brief summary (50 words maximum) of your unique selling points (USPs), skills and qualities that should encourage the reader to read further. Try to tailor it to the job for which you are applying. It could include an overview of your:
- Education
- Experience
- Skillset

Education
List in reverse chronological order, in other words the most recent first. Include names and addresses of schools and colleges, dates, course/award titles, subjects/modules and final third-level dissertation/thesis if relevant. Do not include primary school.

Employment History
List in reverse chronological order with dates, names and addresses of employers, job titles or descriptions/responsibilities. Keep job descriptions brief.

Further Training
Add any other courses you have done outside of mainstream education such as first aid, ECDL, manual handling. Include dates, name and address of the place you completed the training.

Hobbies and Interests
Include pastimes, memberships of clubs, societies, organisations, positions of responsibility, community groups and voluntary work.

Achievements/Awards
This section could include any medals, awards or prizes won, for example sport, debating or other competitions.

Additional Information
Here you could include other skills and abilities that might be useful such as computer or language proficiency or full clean driver's licence.

References
Here the following line can be used: 'References available on request.' Be prepared to give details for references when asked.

General Points for CVs
1. Be truthful.
2. Apart from the personal profile, avoid long paragraphs and sentences.
3. When listing skills and job details, avoid using 'I' sentences. Instead use:
   - 'Excellent communication skills'
   - 'Worked as...'
   - 'Dealing with customers...'
   - 'Responsible for...'

Sample CV

STEPHEN LOUGHRAN

Riverside House, Bridge Street, Bandon, Co. Cork.

086 1234567   sloughran@fastmail.com

PERSONAL PROFILE

Highly skilled horticulturalist with excellent attention to detail, motivated and flexible with a desire to experiment with new crop varieties. A good team player, able to work on own initiative, striving for high standards and efficiency.

EDUCATION

2020–2021	Drumlinn College of Further Education, Drumlinn, Co. Monaghan QQI Level 6 in Organic Horticulture Grade: Distinction
2019–2020	Drumlinn College of Further Education, Drumlinn, Co. Monaghan QQI Level 5 in Organic Horticulture Grade: Distinction
2019	Leaving Certificate
2013–2019	Kinsale Community School, Kinsale, Co. Cork

FURTHER TRAINING

2021	First Aid Response course, Irish Red Cross, Cork

EMPLOYMENT HISTORY

2018–2019	Ballywhelan Organic Farm, Dunderrow, Kinsale, Co. Cork	
	Responsibilities	Sowing seeds
		Crop maintenance
		Harvesting crops for market
		Selling produce at weekly market
2017–2018	Coughlan's Bar, Bridge Street, Bandon, Co. Cork	
	Position	Barman
	Responsibilities	Serving customers
		Cash and card handling
		Ordering stock
		Opening and closing premises
		Cleaning premises

2016–2017	Supervalu, Riverview Shopping Centre, Bandon, Co. Cork	
	Position	Storehouse assistant
	Responsibilities	Stacking shelves
		Stock-taking
		Ordering stock
		Taking deliveries

HOBBIES AND INTERESTS
- Swimming, music, reading
- Member of Sandycove Swimming Club, Kinsale
- Volunteered for Kinsale Arts Festival 2018

ACHIEVEMENTS/AWARDS
- Took part in 1 mile swim to raise money for Cork Simon Community
- Photography – winner West Cork People under 18 Photo of the Year Award 2017
- Chess – School Chess Champion 2018

ADDITIONAL INFORMATION
- Excellent command of French
- Full clean driver's licence

REFERENCES
- References available on request

LinkedIn

LinkedIn (www.linkedin.com) is a professional networking site where jobseekers can post CVs, employers can post job advertisements and also find suitable applicants. Members can create profiles for themselves, like digital CVs, and there are opportunities to connect with others who share the same professional interests.

Useful Websites

The following websites are useful for information on jobs and career advice:
- www.monster.ie
- www.jobs.ie
- www.irishjobs.ie
- www.recruitireland.com
- www.indeed.com
- www.employee.ie

▶ Letter of Application

Many applications are now made directly online or by email but often employers still require a letter, sometimes called a cover letter, to accompany your CV. It will be the first impression you make on an employer so it should be well written and presented. Its purpose it to encourage the employer to read your CV and to be impressed enough to invite you for an interview. Here are a few guidelines:

1. Find out the name of the person to whom you should apply and address the letter to that person.
2. Find out the details of the job, e.g. title and specifications.
3. Use language that is formal, positive, enthusiastic and confident.
4. Use short and simple sentences.
5. Send copies of any references or certificates and keep the originals.
6. Keep copies of all letters you send.

Layout

The layout of a letter of application is as follows:

Paragraph 1

- Say that you would like to apply for the job.
- Say where you found out about it.

Paragraphs 2 and 3

- Say why you would like the job.
- Say why you are qualified for the job and refer to any specific details on your CV.
- Say what skills and qualities you can bring to the job.

Paragraph 4

- Say you can supply more information if required.
- Say when you are available for an interview.
- Say you look forward to their reply.

Sample Letter of Application

The Bungalow
Dock Road
Dunmore East
Co. Waterford
Tel: 086 7724391

20 May 2021

Shane Cochrane
Manager
Tramore Outdoor Education Centre
Tramore
Co. Waterford

Re: Assistant Instructor Position

Dear Mr Cochrane,

I would like to apply for the job advertised in the *Examiner* on Friday, 14 May.

As you can see from my CV, I have just completed a QQI Level 5 Outdoor Instructor Award, during which I greatly improved my skills in kayaking and rock-climbing as well as developing group facilitation and instruction abilities.

I am highly motivated and outgoing and have always been interested in the outdoors. I believe this job would give me the opportunity to further develop my skills and to share my enthusiasm with your clients.

If you require any further information, please do not hesitate to contact me. I am available for an interview at any time and look forward to your reply.

Yours sincerely,

_____
Sandra Twomey

Formal/Business Letters

All formal and business letters should be typed/word processed. When typing a letter, it is useful to use the fully blocked style. This means everything – address, date, salutation, etc. – starts from the left-hand margin and is frequently used with open punctuation. In other words, only the body of the letter contains commas, full stops, etc. The style of business letters today is short and to the point. Software that provides templates for formal letters is available on most computers.

Sample Business Letter

E-Zee
Internet Services and Web Design
31 Main Street
Co. Kilkenny
Email: ezee@ireland.com
Tel: 056 2144781   **1**

Ref BO/RD   **2**

13 March 2022   **3**

Ms Tanya Fitzpatrick
Principal
Drumlinn College of Further Education
Drumlinn
Co. Monaghan   **4**

Re: Quotation for design of website   **5**

Dear Ms Fitzpatrick,   **6**

Thank you for your enquiry of 4 March concerning our web design services which were recently advertised in the *Irish Times*.

Although we are a relatively new company, we already have a reputation for a fast, efficient service, state-of-the-art technology and a design team that has many years' experience.

I have consulted with my chief designer and am pleased to submit a quotation for the requirements you outlined in your letter. I hope this meets with your approval. Please do not hesitate to contact me if you require any further information.   **7**

Yours sincerely   **8**

Brian O'Neill   **9**

Brian O'Neill
Manager   **10**

Enc   **11**

Layout

The layout of a business letter is as follows:
1. The sender's address, unless the paper has a company letterhead, which will include the address, phone number and email address
2. A reference, which is used for filing purposes and is usually the sender's initials (optional)
3. The date displayed as follows: 9 March 2022. The 'th' after numbers is usually omitted these days and avoid abbreviations such as: 9/3/22
4. The recipient's name, title and address
5. The heading if required: 'Re: Quotation for design of website'
6. The salutation:

- 'Dear Sir/Madam' (if the recipient is not known)
- 'Dear Sir' (if the recipient is known to be male)
- 'Dear Madam' (if the recipient is known to be female)
- 'Dear Mr Fitzpatrick or Ms Fitzpatrick' (if the recipient's name is known)
- 'A Chara' (if the recipient is not known)

7. The body of the letter. A simple rule is to keep it clear, concise and courteous. If it can be written in three paragraphs, that is enough, with one main idea per paragraph. The breakdown of the body of the letter should be as follows:

- Paragraph 1: State the background or context of the letter:
  — 'Thank you for your letter of 13 July last in which you stated...'
  — 'I would like an estimate for...'
- Paragraph 2: The reason for writing, the main thrust of the message.
- Paragraph 3: Round off with an indication of an expected outcome, or further communication:
  — 'I look forward to hearing from you at your earliest convenience'
  — 'Please do not hesitate to contact me, should you require any additional information'

8. Complimentary closure:
   — 'Yours faithfully' if begun 'Dear Sir/Madam'
   — 'Yours sincerely' (sometimes shortened to 'Sincerely') if started with 'Dear Mr/Ms', etc.
9. Signature (handwritten)
10. Name and title of signatory (typed/word processed)
11. Enc for an enclosed document or Encs for more than one

General Guidelines

1. Always make notes or do at least one rough draft before you start to write your letter.
2. Use an appropriate tone.
3. Proofread.
4. Spelling, grammar and punctuation must be correct.
5. Use good quality paper and a matching envelope, if possible.
6. Keep copies of all letters you send.

Other Formal Letters

Letter of Enquiry

1. Make sure you give complete and precise details about the information you require.
2. Ask someone to proofread your letter as if they were the recipient.

Reply to an Enquiry

1. Begin with a reference to the enquiry.
2. Information can be presented clearly by using numbered or bulleted headings.
3. As above, ask someone else to proofread.

Letter of Complaint

1. Reasons for sending:
- On receipt of shoddy goods
- On receipt of poor service
- Environmental nuisance/disturbance
- To record your annoyance
- To seek an end to a situation
- To seek redress for damage/inconvenience caused
2. Always write a complaint as soon as possible after the situation or event.
3. Begin with a statement of regret.
4. When you are complaining, use a tone that is polite but firm.
5. Explain the inconvenience caused to you and the dissatisfaction you felt using I-statements, not you-statements, e.g. 'I was very distressed when...', not 'You caused me great distress...'
6. Avoid being offensive, rude or overly dramatic.
7. Supply details to support your complaint – dates, times, numbers, documents, etc.
8. Offer a suggestion of how the matter might be rectified, e.g. by compensation, refund, replacement, repair, etc.

Letter of Adjustment (Reply to a Complaint)

1. Whether a complaint is justified or not, always be tactful.
2. If it is justified, accept responsibility, offer an expression of regret, an explanation, an apology and an intention to rectify the matter by compensation.
3. If it is not justified (and be absolutely certain that it isn't), politely make this clear.
4. If a complaint is mishandled, it could result in loss of business, loss of goodwill or adverse publicity.

Memorandum

A memorandum (memo for short) is a brief message used internally in organisations to convey or request information, to confirm spoken communication or to give instructions. The word comes from the Latin for 'something to be remembered'. It can often be quite informal in style, depending on the organisation. Today memos are mostly sent by email, but for a hard copy, A5 paper is normally used, since a memo is such a short document, although A4 is also acceptable. As in business letters, a reference number/initial can be used, 'Cc' indicates copies sent to other parties and 'Enc' means there is an accompanying note or document. A memo may be typed or handwritten and deals with just one item of business.

Many companies have their own standardised memo forms. There are a variety of items that may be included on a memo but generally the following are the most important: the sender, the recipient, the date and the subject matter. Open punctuation and fully blocked style is usual today.

Sample Memo

MEMORANDUM

TO	All Staff
FROM	P. Jacob
DATE	10 August 2022
SUBJECT	New Computer Software

The new computer software has just been installed. As most staff members will be unfamiliar with its operation, I would suggest a demonstration for an hour on Thursday, 15th at 10.30 am in the main office. Des Griffin has kindly volunteered to show us how to use it.

Invoice

An invoice is a document given to a customer or client, which serves as a record of goods or services provided to them. The vendor needs to keep a copy as a sales record and the customer should retain a copy as a purchase record.

Layout

An invoice should include the following:
- The word 'invoice', often in capitals or bold
- Company name, letterhead/logo, address, phone number, email and website
- Company number
- VAT registration number if VAT registered
- Invoice number – each invoice should have a unique number
- Date

- Date payment is due, usually 30 days after the invoice date
- Customer/client name
- Description of goods/services including quantities, units of measure, etc. with cost per item
- Subtotal
- VAT, if required
- Total amount due
- Bank details

Sample Invoice

INVOICE

Cloughjordan Community Farm
Cloughjordan
Co. Tipperary

Tel: 023-450710
Email: info@cloughjordanfarm.ie
www.cloughjordanfarm.ie

Number 539702   Tax Reg No: 1234950T

23 October 2022

To:
Treacy's Garden Centre
High Street
Roscrea
Co. Tipperary
Tel: 021 4779686

Invoice # TG002

Payment due: 23 April 2022

Quantity	Description	Unit Price	Total
5	Set Radar over-wintering onions	8.00	40.00
7	Bag Record seed potatoes	12.45	87.15
2	Empire apple trees	14.80	29.60
		Subtotal	€156.75
		Total	€156.75

Bank Details:
Allied Irish Bank
Main Street
Cloughjordan
Co. Tipperary

Account No: 1234567 • Sort Code: 95-42-16 • IBAN: IE33AIBK93123487654321 • BIC: AIBKIE2D

Press Release

A press release is a written message for the media to announce a news item, an event such as a concert or festival, awards, new products or services or the opening of a new business. It is a useful promotional document and, if done well, increases the likelihood of your news story being published in a media outlet such as a newspaper.

Sample Press Release

PRESS RELEASE
EMBARGO: FOR IMMEDIATE RELEASE

Transition Town Kinsale Invites You to Put the Spring in Your Step

Put the spring in your step at the annual festival fair organised by Transition Town Kinsale this St Patrick's weekend.

Local music, foods and a series of free-to-attend workshops will take place at Transition Town's 5th annual Spring Fair, which will take place at Temperance Hall, Kinsale, on Saturday, 19th March next from 10 am to 5 pm.

You can sample some delicious local food at the 5-K Café or participate in workshops on composting and seed sowing. Come and learn how to make useful items from recycled materials. Measure your own carbon footprint and watch a locally made film on the issue. Later on, be entertained by local performers such as Snatch Comedy and local band The Good Rain at the Springamagig, Kinsale College Amphitheatre, 8 pm-10.30 pm. Raffle and spot prizes galore.

'Transition Town Kinsale has been at the forefront of creating a thriving, resilient and sustainable community since it started in 2006. Sign me up!' (Jeff Boyden, Mayor)

ENDS

For further information contact Donal Creed on 086 1234567, donalcreed@fastmail.com
http://www.transitiontownkinsale.org

Transition Town Kinsale (TTK) is a voluntary community initiative, established in 2006, working to help make the transition from a dependency on fossil fuels to a low-carbon future. Our vision is a resilient, self-reliant and sustainable town.

TTK has achieved a reputation abroad as being the birthplace of the global Transition movement with hundreds of villages, towns and cities around the world preparing to follow the same path towards local sustainability.

Layout

A press release should contain:
- Headline
- Main body

Headline

Create an eye-catching headline that will make the reader interested and want to read further. It should be clear and to the point. Use a bold or upper-case font to highlight it. A subhead can go underneath in italics giving a little more information.

Main Body

Write the press release as you would like it to appear in the publication. Save the newspaper editors and reporters time by giving them all the important details in the first paragraph using around 25 words and answering the questions: who, what, why, when, where and how. Any additional content should elaborate on it. Start with the date, venue and town. Use as much factual information as possible and write in clear, short sentences and simple language. Include a quote from a reliable source and add a single line about the organisation and contact information at the end. A link to a website is useful.

▶ Leaflet/Brochure

A promotional leaflet/brochure is a good way to promote a business or an event with eye-catching images and some simple basic information. It is usually on a trifolded A4 page, which can be created using Canva (www.canva.com) or in a Word document either by selecting 'Landscape' orientation in Layout and choosing three columns or simply going to Word templates and searching for 'Brochure'.

Layout

A leaflet/brochure should contain the following:
- Key information about the service/product
- Unique selling points (USPs) of the service/product provided
- A catchy headline
- An eye-catching appealing image(s) – consider appropriate colours, shapes, font styles, etc.
- Contact details, e.g. address, phone, email, website
- Simple, easy-to-read text

Tips for Effective Documents

Check you have the correct document layout.

- Keep information clear and concise.
- Always proofread for punctuation, spelling and grammar.

Sample Leaflet

Who We Are

About Us
Locally grown, chemical free, fresh fruit and vegetables grown and delivered to your door and at local farmers' markets.

Contact Us
Phone: 087 1234567
Email: greenthumbs@fastmail.com
Web: www.greenthumbs.com

Juicy cherry tomatoes

Biodiversity
At Green Thumbs we work with nature, using locally sourced soil nutrients such as seaweed, manure and homemade compost and we encourage pollinators such as bees and butterflies, ensuring a bountiful harvest every season.

Green Thumbs
Gort na Broc
Borris
Co. Carlow

Green Thumbs

Local, seasonal, fresh fruit and vegetables.

Activities

Writing Practice

1. Fill in the application form on pages 196–8 as if you were applying for a job in your own vocational area.

2. Create/update your own CV using the guidelines and sample in this chapter.

3. You are working in a department store. Write a memo to your colleagues informing them about your Christmas party including dates, times, venue and cost.

4. Write a memo to your classmates informing them that there is a student council meeting next week. Include the date, time and room.

5. You are the manager of a company/organisation (select appropriate vocational area). Write a memo to your staff informing them:
   - Of some new equipment that has been installed with instructions for use/suggestions for a demonstration at a specific time and place

   OR

   - About the importance of punctuality in the workplace, as some staff have been arriving late and leaving early

6. Find an advertisement for a job related to your area of study and write a letter of application for it.

7. Write a letter applying for work experience.

8. Write a letter of complaint to a travel company about a disastrous holiday they sold you.

9. Write a letter of complaint to a company/organisation about poor service/shoddy goods you received from them.

10. Create an invoice for a service or goods supplied by you/your company (select appropriate vocational area).

11. Write a press release for the launch of a new service/product by you/your company (select appropriate vocational area).

12. Create a leaflet/brochure promoting an activity/business (select appropriate vocational area).

Confusing Words

In each of the following sentences, select the correct word, decide what the other word means and put it into another sentence (it may have more than one meaning):

1. Write to the personal/personnel manager.
2. Who is the principle/principal of this college?
3. The forest was very quiet/quite at night-time.
4. No dogs are aloud/allowed.
5. The award ceremony will precede/proceed the speeches.
6. You can hire/higher a car at the airport.

7. It looked like a scene/seen out of a disaster movie.

8. The couple decided to steel/steal away in the dead of night.

Lost in Translation

The following are signs poorly translated into English. Work out what is wrong with them, what each is trying to communicate, then rewrite them to make their meaning clear.

Leipzig elevator:
Do not enter the lift backwards, and only when lit up.

Yugoslavian hotel:
The flattening of underwear with pleasure is the job of the chambermaid.

Moscow hotel, next to cemetery:
You are welcome to visit the cemetery where famous Russian and Soviet composers, artists, and writers are buried daily except Thursday.

Austrian skiing hotel:
Not to perambulate the corridors in the hours of repose in the boots of ascension.

Hong Kong dress shop:
Ladies have fits upstairs.

Chapter 14
The Report

In this chapter, you will learn about:
- Types of Report
- The Short Report
- References
- Language and Format
- Choosing a Topic
- Research

Like other forms of written communication, reports vary in length, content, format and style depending on the purpose for which they are intended. Essentially a report is a presentation of facts following an investigation or examination. For example, the manager of a company may ask for a report on the company's sales figures for the past year. A fire officer might be asked to carry out a report into the adequacy of the fire safety procedures in an organisation. Large corporations and state bodies often commission lengthy reports that take many months to prepare and are the size of a book.

Types of Report

Routine Reports

These are submitted routinely, are brief and often written on specially provided forms, for example a doctor's reports on a patient or a teacher's report on a student.

Special Reports

Special reports are normally carried out and written for a specific purpose. For example, a fire officer may be called into a firm to investigate the necessary improvements needed so that a building meets the requirements of the fire department. These reports are usually short and may be approximately 500–1,000 words in length. Some reports may be so brief that they take the form of a memo.

Long Reports

As the name suggests, these are lengthy documents often taking the form of a book. Large corporations and state bodies will commission long reports and they may take many months to prepare, for example the 'Report of the Commission of Investigation into Mother and Baby Homes' in Ireland was published in 2021.

Reports may also be categorised as *formal* or *informal*.

▶ The Short Report

The short structured report consists of the following components:
1. Title
2. Terms of reference
3. Methodology
4. Findings
5. Conclusions
6. Recommendations
7. Appendix/Appendices
8. Bibliography

Items 6–8 are not always included.

Title

Use a separate cover page and a short title stating precisely what the report is about, e.g. 'Report on Fire Safety at Dun Laoghaire Music Centre'.

Terms of Reference

This states the purpose of the report or why it was carried out. If the report is simply to provide information, the wording would be as follows: 'As requested by the management, to investigate the adequacy of the fire safety procedures and facilities at the centre.'

If the report is required to make recommendations, then the wording would be as follows: 'As requested by the management, to investigate the adequacy of the fire safety procedures and facilities at the centre and to make any necessary recommendations.'

Methodology

This is how the report was carried out and should state what kind of research was done (see page 219 for research methods). The methodology section can range in length from one sentence to a few short paragraphs.

Findings

This is the main body of the report and shows the results of the research or investigation. The information here must be factual and presented in a clear, objective and impersonal style. Avoid using the first or second person pronouns 'I', 'me', 'my', 'you' and 'your'. This keeps the language impersonal and helps avoid biased statements.

For example, write 'This report' instead of 'My report', 'In conclusion' instead of 'I can conclude that'.

Factual statements must be supported by evidence of research. (See References on page 218.)

Divide the findings into logically sequenced sections, using subheadings for subsections and bullets and/or numbers for lists.

Use visual supports such as charts, diagrams, photographs or drawings to help present the findings and enhance the overall presentation of the report, but only use them if they are relevant.

Conclusions

These must be based on the findings and summarised into three or more main points. They should be unbiased, supported by the facts presented in the findings and should answer the questions in the terms of reference. They should be written in descending order of importance.

Never introduce new information in the conclusion.

Recommendations

Not all reports need to make recommendations, so include them only if they are relevant or part of the terms of reference. They should be positive suggestions for future implementation that could improve a situation or an organisation. List them in descending order of importance. See page 230 for an example of how a finding must progress logically to a conclusion and from there to a recommendation.

Appendix/Appendices

This contains any additional information such as results of a survey or questionnaire, questions asked in an interview or notes taken during an observation.

Bibliography

A bibliography is a list of all the secondary research sources you have used for your report and should go at the end of the report. Its purpose is twofold:
1. To show that you have done some research
2. To acknowledge the creators of the work you have used

Different source types require different entries. Here is the layout using the Harvard Style of bibliography.

Books

Author surname, initials. (Year of publication) *Title of book*. Edition (if applicable). City (or area/country): Publisher.

Example: Harvey, N. (2022) *Effective Communication*. 5th edn. Co. Tipperary, Ireland: Boru Press.

Newspaper Articles Online

Author surname, initials. Year of publication, 'Title of article', *Newspaper name*, Date, Available at: URL (Downloaded Day Month Year)

Example: O'Brian, C. 2022, 'Instagram plans new tools to boost teen safety', *The Irish Times*, 7 December 2021. Available at: https://www.irishtimes.com/business/technology/instagram-plans-new-tools-to-boost-teen-safety-1.4748871 (Downloaded 25 February 2022).

Websites

Author/editor surname, initials. (Year of publication) *Page Title*. Available at: URL (Accessed Day Month Year).

Example: Crumbie, A. (2021) *What is fast fashion and why is it a problem?* Available at: https://www.ethicalconsumer.org/fashion-clothing/what-fast-fashion-why-it-problem (Downloaded 19 December 2021).

Pamphlets, Brochures, Leaflets

Title (Year of publication) Place of Publication: Publisher.

Example: *Ireland's Environment, Take Action Now*! (2000) Wexford: Environmental Protection Agency.

Edited works

These are books with a selection of essays by different authors.

Author(s) surname, initials, Year of publication, 'Title of essay/chapter', in [name of editor(s)], (ed(s).) *Title*. Place of publication: Publisher.

Example: Fiske, J., 1991, 'Postmodernism and Television', in Curran, J. and Gurevitch, M. (eds.) *Mass Media and Society*. London: Edward Arnold.

DVDs

Title [DVD] (Year of publication) Place of publication: Publisher.

Example: *Body Language* [DVD] (2001) Galway: Simply Communication.

Emails

Sender's surname, initials, (Year of publication) Email to name of recipient, Day month of communication.

Example: Brophy, J., (2021) Email to Nicholas Harvey, 14 April.

For a more extensive list of bibliography entry types, see UCD Library Harvard Referencing Style: https://www.nmhs.ucd.ie/sites/default/files/harvard_guide_november_2018.pdf

To save time, the website www.citethisforme.com will create bibliography entries for you.

▶ References

A report should be written in your own words. Under no circumstances should passages of text be copied, word for word, from other sources, and passed off as your own work. This is plagiarism and is a serious breach of academic honesty, which could result in your work being cancelled. You need to show evidence of the research carried out and this is done by including references to other works and written material. Here are the main types of referencing.

Quotations

Quotations must be taken from the original text word for word. Short quotations should be placed within quotation marks and be followed by the author's surname, year of publication and page number.
Example:

> 'A report should be written in your own words.' (Harvey, 2022, p. 218)

This means the quotation is taken from a book by someone by the name of Harvey, published in the year 2022, and is taken from page 218. The reader can then refer to the bibliography and check the details of the book.

Long quotations (three lines or more) are separated from the rest of the text and indented.
Example:

> A report should be written in your own words. Under no circumstances should passages of text be copied, word for word, from other sources, and passed off as your own work... You need to show evidence of the research carried out and this is done by including references to other works and written material. (Harvey, 2022, p. 218)

Words omitted from a quoted piece are indicated by an *ellipsis* (...). This is useful if a passage contains words in the middle that are irrelevant, and you want to leave them out.

Quotations from an interview should be presented the same way, but followed in brackets by the name of the interviewee and the word 'interview' and if possible, the date the interview took place.

A *citation* is a reference to another author's work, which must include the year of publication.
Example:

> Harvey (2022) states that a report should be written in your own words.

Again, the reader can then check in the bibliography for books by Harvey.

▶ Language and Format

The language of a report should be formal, objective (unbiased) and impersonal. To avoid personal language you can use the passive voice, e.g. 'A survey was conducted' instead of 'I conducted a survey'.

Consider the reader and use language and terminology that they will understand. If you use any technical terms, add a glossary at the back to explain them.

Use a standard formal font to make your report easy to read, size 10 point to 12 point for main text, 14 point or 16 point for main headings. Be consistent throughout the report – don't use a variety of fonts.

▶ Choosing a Topic

If you have the option of choosing a topic, then choose something that interests you and that is easy to research. Begin by brainstorming the topic and writing down everything you already know about it. Follow this by working out what information is missing. This will be the start of your research.

Fig. 14.1

▶ Research

You cannot write an assignment based purely on what you already know, or from class notes and handouts. You have to go and do some thorough research yourself. The strength or weakness of an assignment often rests upon how much research has been done, how it has been carried out and how it is presented. Extensive and relevant research will yield a good result.

There are two types of research:
1. *Primary research* – information that is gathered first-hand by means of surveys, interviews, questionnaires, observation, experiments and testing

2. *Secondary research* – Information that is gathered from material that has already been produced by someone else, e.g. books, brochures, leaflets, magazines, newspapers, websites, reports and other research papers

Fig. 14.2

Primary Research

There are two types of primary research:
1. *Qualitative research* refers to quantities, for example, data that can be measured and turned into statistics. Surveys and questionnaires are typical forms of quantitative research and often require a large number of participants. This type of research answers the questions who, what and where. The results can be displayed in charts or graphs.
2. *Qualitative research* is about how good or useful something is and is often based upon people's opinions and behaviour. For example, you might conduct an interview or set up a focus group to find out people's attitude to something. Fewer numbers of participants are needed and as the results are not measurable, they are presented in written form. It answers the questions why and how. Observation is another example of qualitative research.

A combination of both can be very useful to get a complete picture. For example, market research might be done on how many people bought a certain product (quantitative) and then some of these might be interviewed to find out why they bought it (qualitative).

Types of Quantitative Research

Survey

A survey is a way of collecting information, usually by means of a questionnaire, from a sample of the population. A sample here means a selection, such as a group of people being asked how they might vote prior to an election. Surveys can be carried out by post, by telephone, email or online using free online software such as SurveyMonkey (www.surveymonkey.com) or using Microsoft Forms. Before carrying out a survey, consider the pros and cons of each method, e.g. telephone surveys might prompt interviewees to hang up; email surveys can be efficient but sometimes respondents can be slow to reply.

Questionnaire

A questionnaire is a method of collecting data using a series of questions and should be designed so as to be as concise and user-friendly as possible. If possible, do a test run on classmates or friends and make any necessary adjustments before undertaking the real survey. You should aim for 20–30 respondents for a short, structured report.

When designing the questionnaire, consider the following:
1. Exactly what information is required?
2. Who will supply the information?
3. Will the respondents understand the questions and be able to answer them?
4. Are the questions clear and unambiguous?
5. In what sequence should the questions be arranged?
6. Is the layout clear?
7. How will the results be formulated, i.e. in tables, charts, graphs, etc.?

If distributing questionnaires, try to get them filled out and returned by respondents immediately rather than leaving them in locations where they may go missing or simply be ignored.

Layout
The layout of the questionnaire is as follows:
1. Title of survey
2. Some factual questions
3. More complicated, multiple-choice questions
4. Open-ended questions
5. Identification questions (age, gender, nationality, etc.)

Types of question:
Closed-ended questions require an answer of either yes or no. Boxes may be used for the respondent to tick. Tick boxes like these are very user-friendly, as respondents don't have to spend too much time thinking or writing.
Example:
Do you drive a car?   Yes ☐   No ☐

Multiple-choice questions supply a number of possible answers from which the respondent can choose. Leave a space for 'other' in case there is an option you haven't considered.

Example:
How do you travel to work:
By bus ☐
By car ☐
By train ☐
By bike ☐
On foot ☐
Other (please specify) _____

Open-ended questions give the respondent the option of giving a more lengthy and detailed reply, so remember to leave a few lines before the next question. Use a limited number of these questions as they can be time-consuming for the respondent and are also difficult to quantify unless some answers are the same, in which case they can be converted into statistics.

Example:
What improvements would you like to see? _____

_____

Scaling questions ask the respondent to rate something. There are three types of scale:

1. The *Likert Scale* asks the respondent to agree or disagree with something.
   Example:
   The Internet is a useful means of research.

Strongly agree	Agree	Neither agree nor disagree	Disagree	Strongly disagree

2. The *Semantic differential Scale* presents the respondent with a scale of two opposing adjectives, and they indicate with a mark on that scale their attitude toward a specific issue or product.
   Example:
   Kinsale Leisure Centre is:
   Well maintained _____ **Poorly maintained**
   A mark on the very left means the respondent thinks it is very well maintained and on the very right, poorly maintained. A mark in the middle indicates average.

3. The *Staple Scale* consists of one adjective in the middle of a numbered scale.
   Example:
   Do you think the staff in the centre are:

-5	-4	-3	-2	-1	friendly	+1	+2	+3	+4	+5
-5	-4	-3	-2	-1	helpful	+1	+2	+3	+4	+5
-5	-4	-3	-2	-1	efficient	+1	+2	+3	+4	+5

Sample Questionnaire

Questionnaire on Social Media Use

1. Which of the following social media do you use?
   - Facebook ☐
   - YouTube ☐
   - WhatsApp ☐
   - Instagram ☐
   - TikTok ☐
   - Snapchat ☐
   - Twitter ☐
   - Pinterest ☐
   - Other (please specify) _____

2. How often do you check your social media feed?
   - Several times a day ☐
   - Once a day ☐
   - Several times a week ☐
   - Once a week ☐
   - Once a month ☐

3. How much time do you spend on social media during each visit?
   - Less than 30 minutes ☐
   - 30 minutes to one hour ☐
   - One to two hours ☐
   - More than two hours ☐

4. How many 'friends' do you currently have? _____

5. How many of your friends have you met in person? _____

6. What do you mainly use social media for?
   - Keeping in touch with friends ☐
   - Keeping in touch with family ☐
   - Meeting new friends ☐
   - Sharing photos/videos ☐
   - Sharing information ☐
   - Entertainment ☐
   - Networking ☐
   - Staying up to date with news and current events ☐
   - Other (please specify) _____

7. Are you concerned with privacy issues around social media?
   - Yes ☐   No ☐

8. Are you concerned with security issues around social media?
   - Yes ☐   No ☐

9. Have you ever experienced bullying while on social media?
   - Yes ☐   No ☐

10. Have you modified your settings to make them as safe as possible?
    - Yes ☐   No ☐

11. What improvements would you like to see in your social media experience?
_____
_____

12. Social media is a fun way of keeping in touch with people but it is also a huge time-waster.
    Strongly agree ☐
    Agree ☐
    Neither agree nor disagree ☐
    Disagree ☐
    Strongly disagree ☐

13. To which age group do you belong?
    Under 18 ☐
    18–24 ☐
    25–34 ☐
    35–50 ☐
    Over 50 ☐

Analysis of the Results

When the surveys and questionnaires have been completed and collected, they need to be analysed and the results presented. Some results, for example responses to closed-ended questions, can be simply converted into charts.

Suppose there were 20 respondents to the questionnaire and the results for question 2 were as follows:

How often do you check your social media?
- Several times a day   5
- Once a day   10
- Several times a week   3
- Once a week   2
- Once a month   0

Now you have a frequency table showing how respondents replied to question 2 and the results can be converted into percentages as follows:
- Several times a day   25 per cent
- Once a day   50 per cent
- Several times a week   15 per cent
- Once a week   10 per cent
- Once a month   0

Charts

The results of this can be presented using either of the two types of charts below.

Bar Chart

A bar chart works well for this type of question as the data is displayed quite clearly.

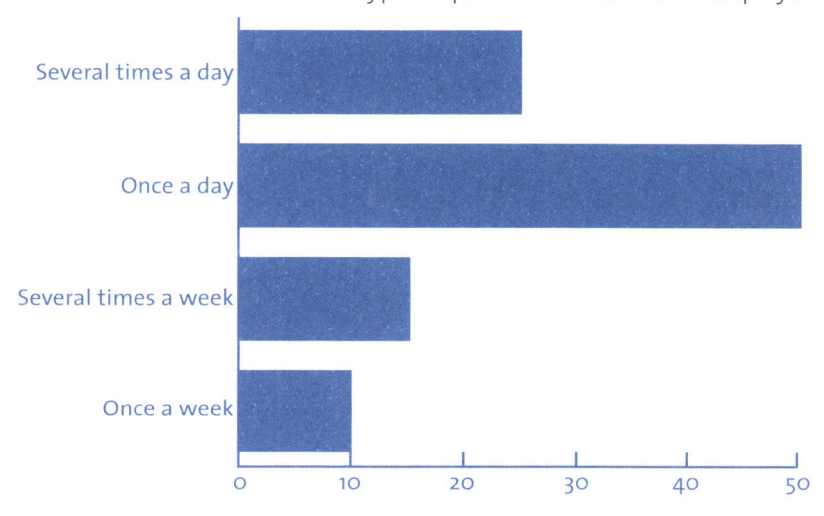

Fig. 14.3 How often do you check your social media?

Pie Chart

A pie chart is also effective for this question, again because the information is clear and can be read and understood quite quickly.

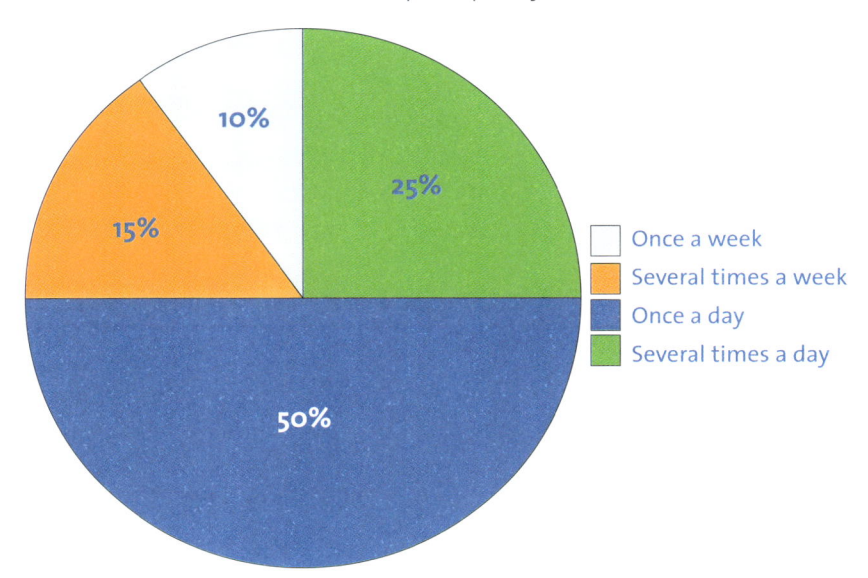

Fig. 14.4 How often do you check your social media?

For more on charts and graphs, see Chapter 9: Visual Communication.

Types of Qualitative Research

Focus Group

A focus group is where you bring a group of people together to discuss and determine their attitudes, opinions and beliefs on a certain topic. It is often used for market research to determine how popular or effective a new product or service will be.

Interview

If you decide to interview someone, consider how you will conduct the interview. If you are going to meet the person face to face, you should contact them by email or phone, to request and set up a meeting. It is useful to follow up an email with a phone call. It is also possible to conduct an interview over the phone. Whichever way you decide to proceed, you need to be prepared. The seven questions in the Questionnaire section on page 221 will apply here also. It is important to know exactly what information you are looking for.

Always prepare a list of questions before the interview. If you arrive ill-prepared, you will appear unprofessional and the interview will take longer. Some people might get annoyed if you are unprepared, as they will feel their time is being wasted. If well prepared, you can tell an interviewee how long the interview might take. It is worth considering that they may find the work you are doing useful and therefore a professional approach on your part will increase their co-operation.

Decide how you will include the information from your interview in the main body of your assignment. You might quote the interviewee in relevant sections (see 'Quotations' page 218), or refer to points made by them (see 'References' page 218). Avoid simply reproducing the interview at the end.

Observation

This means observing people, activities, organisations, events, patterns of behaviour, objects, etc. and making careful notes of your observations.

For example, in a childcare observation, a detailed factual account is written about what the child says, does, how it behaves, plays and interacts with other children, describing the tones of voice, facial expressions and body language used; an observation could be made of a particular bus route, such as what times and how many people get on and off at a particular bus stop during the day.

Experiment

An experiment is a test carried out in a controlled procedure to determine the truth or otherwise of a hypothesis. It can vary from an informal test to see what is the most regularly visited social media sites by students in a particular college to a rigorous scientific test using measuring equipment in a laboratory.

Fig. 14.5

Secondary Research

Secondary research involves finding information that someone else has already written or produced that is relevant to the topic of your report.

Sources

If you are researching an organisation, your first source of secondary research will be from within the organisation itself in the form of company reports, policies, statements, the website, press releases, databases, etc. Of course, not all of these may be made public but there is no harm in asking.

IPA Yearbook

The *Institute of Public Administration Yearbook* contains an extensive database of Irish companies, state bodies, public and private organisations, both national and international, as well as a detailed calendar of events and a wealth of useful statistical information (www.ipa.ie).

Central Statistics Office

The Central Statistics Office (CSO) is a government agency that provides statistics on all social and economic trends in Ireland (www.cso.ie).

Other Sources

- The internet
- Newspapers and journals
- Books
- Government departments
- State agencies

- Reports
- Brochures and leaflets
- Audiovisual media

When starting your secondary research, all four types of reading will come into play (see Chapter 10: Reading Skills). To recap, skim to get an overview, scan to locate specific facts and details, read at a normal pace for general understanding and close-read for more difficult material.

When you find material that you think is useful, skim-read the following in particular:

- Title
- Table of contents
- Introduction
- Conclusion

These will give you a broad overview of what the material is about. Scan the table of contents, index or the bibliography for more details.

As soon as you start to use published material for research, it is crucial to record the following:

- Title
- Author(s)/producer(s)
- Date of publication/broadcast
- Publisher
- Place of publication

For information retrieved online, record the title of the page or article, the author if there is one, the URL or address and the date you accessed the website. This information will be included in your bibliography.

Sample Short Structured Report

REPORT ON FIRE SAFETY AT DUN LAOGHAIRE MUSIC CENTRE

Terms of Reference
As requested by the management, to investigate the adequacy of the fire safety procedures and facilities at the centre and to make any necessary recommendations.

Methodology
The local fire officer was contacted and requested to make a visit to the centre for a consultation with the centre's Health and Safety Officer.

He made a thorough inspection of the building to check fire-fighting equipment, alarm system, fire exits, notices and procedures for fire drills and emergency evacuation, and reported to the Health and Safety Officer.

Members of staff were asked if they recognised the different types of fire extinguisher, if they knew how to operate them and if they were well acquainted with the evacuation procedures already in place.

Findings

Present position
- There are five fire exits in the centre. Each room in the centre is within walking distance of a fire exit.
- The alarm system is functioning properly.
- Fire notices in rooms are old and worn, and difficult to read clearly.
- No fire drill has taken place in the past two years.
- There are three fire hoses, and seven fire extinguishers in the building, three water, two dry chemical and two carbon dioxide (CO_2) extinguishers. None had been tested in the past four years. One of the water and one of the dry chemical extinguishers were faulty and one of the CO_2 extinguishers was almost empty. The rest of the extinguishers were in order.
- Staff members do not know the difference in appearance between the three types of fire extinguisher in the centre, nor their uses for different classes of fire.

Conclusions
- No one is up to date with the emergency evacuation procedures. Staff are not sure which exits correspond to the different rooms.
- It is not known if all the fire-fighting equipment is in full working order.
- Members of staff do not know how to use the various types of fire-fighting equipment.

Recommendations
- Devise new procedures for fire prevention and emergency evacuation.
- Design new fire notices for each room indicating which exit is to be used from each room.
- Invite the local fire officer to the centre to:
  — Talk to all staff about the various uses of each type of fire extinguisher, and to give a demonstration of each
  — Advise on the upgrading and purchasing of new fire-fighting equipment.
- Purchase new fire-fighting equipment.
- Appoint a member of staff to be Fire Officer, in charge of fire prevention and safety and to maintain equipment and notices.

Thomas O'Sullivan
Date: 20 February 2022

Note how there is a logical progression from Findings to Conclusion to Recommendation:
- *Findings* — Staff members do not know the difference in appearance between the three types of fire extinguisher in the centre, nor their uses for different classes of fire.
- *Conclusion* — Members of staff do not know how to use the various types of fire-fighting equipment.
- *Recommendation* — Invite the local fire officer to the centre to talk to all staff about the various uses of each type of fire extinguisher, and to give a demonstration of each.

This sample shows a very short structured report giving a simple layout. The report required for the QQI Level 5 Communications module needs to be a good deal longer and more detailed with evidence of research.

Activity

Write a report on your place of work experience. Here are some suggested guidelines for topics:

1. The history and background of the organisation/company/business
2. The ownership and management
3. Identification of the key personnel, their duties and responsibilities
4. A full description of the organisation/company/business, its buildings, facilities, resources, access, security, maintenance, daily routine, e.g. opening and closing times
5. The impact of the organisation/company/business on the local community, economy, culture, environment, etc.
6. A survey of the clients and customers, their use of the facilities and how they rate them, etc.
7. A SWOT analysis, i.e. a list of strengths, weaknesses, opportunities and threats
8. Conclusions and recommendations on any improvements that would enhance the organisation/company/business

Tips for Effective Reports

- Start your report good and early. It's better to spend a little time on it each week than a lot of time on it during the final week.
- Give yourself plenty of time at the end to put together the table of contents and bibliography, and for proofreading, etc.
- Keep a record of your secondary research as you do it, i.e. websites, authors, titles, etc.
- Keep the language clear and concise.
- Always draft, redraft, edit and proofread.
- Keep it accurate and factual.

Activities

1. **Confusing Words**

   In each of the following sentences, select the correct word, decide what the other word means and put it into another sentence (it may have more than one meaning):

   1. I'm going to give him a peace/piece of my mind.
   2. The king's rain/rein/reign lasted for only two years.
   3. The speeding juggernaut collided with a stationary/stationery car at the side of the road.
   4. I wonder weather/whether the weather/whether will get any better.
   5. We did an in-debt/in-depth study of the situation and then wrote a report.
   6. I think I've past/passed all my exams.
   7. I'm off to the club to practise/practice my moves.
   8. My car is bigger then/than your car.
   9. She thought/taught English as a foreign language in Spain for a year.

2. **Lost in Translation**

   The following are signs poorly translated into English. Work out what is wrong with them, what each is trying to communicate, then rewrite them to make their meaning clear.

   Swedish furrier shop:
   Fur coats made for ladies from their own skin.

Tokyo car rental brochure:
When passenger of foot heave in sight, tootle the horn. Trumpet him melodiously at first, but if he still obstacles your passage tootle him with vigour.

Acapulco hotel:
The manager has personally passed all the water served here.

Sign in Germany's Black Forest:
It is strictly forbidden on our black forest camping site that people of different sex, for instance, men and women, live together unless they are married with each other for this purpose.

Norwegian cocktail bar:
Ladies are requested not to have children in the bar.

Chapter Review

1. What is the purpose of a report?
2. Briefly explain the meaning of:
    (a) Terms of reference
    (b) Methodology
    (c) Findings
    (d) Conclusion
    (e) Recommendations
3. Give a brief explanation of primary and secondary research.
4. What is the purpose of a bibliography?
5. List the ways in which the findings of a survey can be presented.

Part 5

Communication Technology

Some Examples
- Computers
- Internet
- Social Media
- Email
- Smartphones

Advantages
- Speed over distance
- Cheap to use
- Convenient (once set up)
- Good sources of information
- Can store information easily
- Global access
- Mobility

Disadvantages
- Expensive to buy/set up
- Open to abuse
- Impersonal
- Open to misunderstanding and misinformation
- Loss of real face-to-face communication and social skills
- Dependent on power/technology/coverage
- Privacy and security issues

Chapter 15
Communication Technology

In this chapter, you will learn about:
- Communication Technology Timeline
- Convergence
- Ownership and Control
- Impact on Society
- Fake News
- Privacy and Security
- Regulation
- Children
- Environment

> *It has become appallingly obvious that our technology has exceeded our humanity.*
>
> Albert Einstein

> *New technology is not good or evil in and of itself. It's all about how people choose to use it.*
>
> David Wong, author

Fig. 15.1 "So when do we go online?"

▶ Communication Technology Timeline

1831   Louis Daguerre developed first form of photography
1844   Telegraph invented by Samuel Morse
1876   Telephone invented by Alexander Graham Bell – first message: 'Watson, come here I want you.'
1879   Light bulb invented by Thomas Edison
1883   George Eastman produced the first camera film roll, paving the way for amateur photographers
1894   First radio message sent by Guglielmo Marconi
1901   First transatlantic radio transmission
1926   Television invented by John Logie Baird
1943   First working computers built
1946   ENIAC (Electronic Numerical Integrator and Computer), the first general purpose computer, invented
1957   ARPA (Advanced Research Projects Agency) set up by US State Department in response to Soviet launch of Sputnik satellite
1959   Silicon chip developed
1962   First Telstar satellite broadcast
1971   15 computers connected by ARPANET
1972   First email sent
1973   First handheld mobile phone produced by Motorola

1978	First successful personal computers sold
1982	Birth of the internet
1989	World Wide Web developed by Tim Berners-Lee
1993	Internet accessible from private homes
1995	Telecommunications digitalised – sound, images and data travel the world at high speed
1996	Dramatic increase in mobile phone use
2002	New Year's Eve – 8 million text messages sent in Ireland
2004	Almost half of all Irish adults use the internet and 96 per cent of children aged between 10 and 14 own a mobile phone; Facebook founded by Mark Zuckerberg
2005	YouTube created
2006	Twitter created
2009	One billion internet users worldwide; social media overtakes email as the most popular means of communication; WhatsApp founded
2011	Zoom founded
2012	One billion Facebook users worldwide
2020	Two billion WhatsApp users globally; 300 million daily Zoom meetings
2021	500 hours of video per minute uploaded onto YouTube

▶ Convergence

There are so many communication tools available these days that it is impossible to include them all in one section of a communications book, and the rate at which new devices and applications are being created means that some of this information will be out of date after a couple of years.

The communications revolution has been about communications technologies (CT) coming together to form new, faster, cheaper and more powerful means of exchanging information. The technologies associated with the telephone, television and computer have converged to bring us the internet. Mobile phones and television both use computer technology to speed up their basic functions. The borders between telecommunications, the internet and mass media are disappearing. Unified messaging is a means of accessing all of our messages and information using one device such as a mobile phone, computer or TV set.

All these technologies have transformed and continue to transform our lives. Education, business, work, health, travel, shopping, entertainment, culture and socialising are all utterly different from what they were 30 years ago.

The history and development of CT is one of ever-increasing speed and efficiency of communications over ever-greater distances at ever-decreasing costs, and in 2021 around 63 per cent of the global population were using the internet and 84 per cent had a mobile phone.

Communication Technology 237

Fig. 15.2

Activity

Technology Appropriateness

With so many technologies available today, it is important to choose the right tool for the right job. Do you phone, text, video call, email, use social media or instant messaging? Some technologies are more appropriate for formal and work situations and others are better for personal and leisure. Which technology (if any) would you choose for the following situations and why?

Fig. 15.3

1. Your employer needs three quotations for a new printer.
2. You want to let your colleagues know about the annual Christmas party. *Text message*
3. You are booking a holiday. *Social Media. (Booking.com)*
4. You need to call an urgent meeting at work tomorrow morning. *email / Phone call*

5. You want to ask someone out on a date. Social media / Text.
6. You need to check your bank account details. online
7. You are running 30 minutes late for dinner with your friends and need to let them know. Text / call
8. You are giving a talk at your old school about the course you are now studying and what to provide details about the course. email
9. You need to let your employer know that you are sick and cannot come to work. email
10. You want to find out what your partner is wearing to the Halloween party. text
11. You need to inform class representatives of the next student council meeting.
12. Your employer wants suggestions from staff for improved staff facilities at work.
13. You are due to meet a client for a business lunch, but she doesn't know where the restaurant is so you need to give her directions.
14. You want to invite your friends to your birthday party.
15. You have written up the new staff rota but need to run it by your colleagues to make sure it's OK. Many of them are away on holiday.
16. You want to publicise your new business venture.
17. You are planning a conference in Berlin with a group of volunteers from five different EU countries.
18. You want to share news of your engagement with your friends.
19. You are discussing plans with family members, who live in different parts of the country, to go to your cousin's wedding in Edinburgh.
20. Your sister, who lives in Australia, has just had a baby. You and your parents want to see her and the new baby.
21. You want to get your CV checked before sending it for a job application. There is no one nearby who can do it for you, but friends living a few miles away might be able to help.

Ownership and Control

Some of the world's biggest and wealthiest companies are at the forefront of today's communications technologies such as Amazon, Apple, Facebook, Google and Microsoft. When such a huge amount of the information that we share is being channelled through a small number of corporations, it's good to know who owns what.

The following tech giants replaced the big oil companies at the start of the century to become the wealthiest corporations in the world. According to Harvard professor and author Shoshana Zuboff, they are the richest companies in the history of humanity.

Fig. 15.4

Alphabet (Google)

Google was set up by Larry Page and Sergey Brin in 1998 as a search engine, now the most widely used in the world, so much so that 'to google' has become a verb. It is also the most visited website in the world. The company has expanded over the years to include the following services:
- Gmail
- YouTube
- Google Maps
- Google Earth
- Google Docs
- Google Chrome – web browser
- Android operating system for mobile phones

Amazon

Founded by Jeff Bezos in 1994, Amazon's interests are in e-commerce, cloud computing, artificial intelligence and live streaming. It owns:
- Alexa – a virtual assistant for playing music, answering questions and providing news and other information
- Audible – an audiobook and podcast service
- IMDb – Internet Movie Database
- Amazon Web Services – cloud computing

Apple

Founded in 1976 by Steve Jobs, Steven Wozniak and Ronald Wayne, Apple focuses on electronics, computer software and online services. The following are some of its products and services:
- Mac computers
- iPhone
- iPad
- iPod
- iCloud
- Apple Watch
- Apple TV

Meta (Facebook)

Set up by Mark Zuckerberg in 2004, Facebook has become the most popular social media service in the world with over 2 billion users. Its app was the most downloaded in the 2010s. It has come under criticism for not dealing adequately with false information, not curbing hate speech and for invasion of privacy. During Donald Trump's 2016 US Presidential election campaign, the data of 87 million Facebook users was used for psychological profiling and they were subsequently targeted with tailored advertisements. It has been accused of influencing elections and undermining democracy.

In 2021, a former Facebook employee turned whistleblower, Frances Haugen, claimed that Facebook got rid of its programme to deal with misinformation and that Instagram is particularly dangerous to teenagers because it allows social comparison of their physical looks and body shapes. In 2022, Haugen appeared before an Oireachtas Committee and stated that dangerous social media content leads to eating disorders and self-harm, that Facebook is not updating its algorithms to reduce hate speech and that Ireland's Data Protection Commissioner wasn't enforcing GDPR strongly enough to protect people's privacy. (See also Chapter 18: Legislation.)

In 2021 Facebook's parent company changed its name to Meta, but in early 2022 it lost users for the first time. Amongst its products and services are:
- Facebook social media service
- Instagram
- WhatsApp
- Oculus – virtual reality products

Microsoft

Bill Gates and Paul Allen founded Microsoft in 1975 to produce personal computers and it now offers numerous products and services such as:
- Windows
- Office – a suite of apps that includes Word, Excel, PowerPoint, OneDrive and Teams
- Xbox – home video game consoles

- Outlook Express – email service
- LinkedIn – professional networking service
- Skype – Voice over Internet Protocol (VoIP) service for free computer to computer calls
- Internet Explorer – browser
- MSN (Microsoft Network) – web portal and online news and information service
- Bing – search engine

As we can see from the above, the 'Big Five' tech giants own and control a vast number of services and products that millions of people use every day to communicate and exchange information. In many ways they make our lives highly entertaining, informed (and sometimes misinformed) and convenient but together they control up to 90 per cent of social media, book sales, online entertainment, computer and mobile phone operating systems and advertising from online searches. During the COVID-19 pandemic, their profits soared as our working and social lives and our consumption patterns moved online because of lockdowns.

Each one has come under a lot of scrutiny and criticism in recent years. Facebook and Google have been accused of privacy violations, Amazon of mistreatment of employees, Apple of not paying taxes and Microsoft of being a monopoly.

Impact on Society

The internet has changed and continues to change the way we live and work. This section looks at some of the key areas undergoing a transformation.

Business

E-commerce is the buying and selling of goods on the internet. In 2012 over half of Irish businesses were using the internet for making purchases and 30 per cent of their purchases were being made online. Businesses use the internet in other ways such as for advertising, banking and communicating with customers. Social networking has become an important means of reaching new customers and word of mouth recommendations on social media sites are regarded as a key method of expanding and maintaining a customer base.

Fig. 15.5

During the COVID-19 lockdown online business activity soared, and e-commerce for Irish retailers grew by 159 per cent, compared with 32 per cent between 2017 and 2019. One key component of this was the increase in online shopping by the wealthy over-65s who up until then hadn't been enthusiastic online shoppers.

Entertainment

Remote working became essential for many employees during the pandemic as people had to self-isolate at home. Since then it has developed into a common practice for employees to spend some days working from home. Cloud computing enables access to documents and other files online without having to commute to and physically be in the office or other place of work. (See also 'Videoconferencing', page 246.)

Remote working became essential for many employees during the pandemic as people had to self-isolate at home. Since then it has developed into a common practice for employees to spend some days working from home. Cloud computing enables access to documents and other files online without having to commute to and physically be in the office or other place of work. (See also 'Videoconferencing', page 246.)

Fig. 15.6

Remote working became essential for many employees during the pandemic as people had to self-isolate at home. Since then it has developed into a common practice for employees to spend some days working from home. Cloud computing enables access to documents and other files online without having to commute to and physically be in the office or other place of work. (See also 'Videoconferencing', page 246.) The internet is continuously changing the way we access music, films and television programmes. The sale of CDs and DVDs has declined dramatically in the last decades, and this is being replaced by cheaper and more convenient digital downloads and online streaming. We watch and listen to these forms of entertainment on a variety of devices and platforms. The big TV streaming services are Amazon Prime, Disney Plus, Apple TV and Netflix, which is now the largest and also the world's biggest internet media and entertainment company with over 200 million subscribers globally. The top music streaming services are Apple Music and Spotify. Spotify has come in for criticism from musicians for not paying adequate royalties for their songs, highlighting one of the more negative aspects of online entertainment.

Bands, singers and other recording artists used to get income from recordings of their music sold in the form of vinyl records or CDs, but with so much music available for free online, musicians have to rely on concerts and touring to earn most of their income and not from actual music sales.

Gaming is now the most popular form of entertainment, having overtaken the film industry in 2018 in terms of earnings. Highly realistic and sophisticated three-dimensional multiplayer games involve players taking on roles, participating with other members of 'guilds' and forming social connections across the globe. The benefits include developing creativity and strategic thinking, increasing brain speed and multitasking skills as well as social benefits such as building relationships. The downsides include addiction, loss of real face-to-face interaction and contact with strangers.

News and Information

From online newspapers and journals, to blogs, wikis, citizen journalism and social media, the internet is awash with huge amounts of news and information available from across the world at our fingertips. We are the most informed and educated humans in the history of humanity. We are also potentially the most misinformed unless we use our critical thinking skills to determine what information is true and what is false.

An advantage of online news compared with 'old media' such as newspapers and television is that due to its speed its news tends to be more up to date. A newspaper article can be old news one hour after it has been published, but online versions are often being updated by the minute. News can come directly from the source either from a professional reporter at the scene of an event or from a 'citizen journalist', e.g. someone recording a video on their smartphone and sharing it on a social media page.

A *blog* (short for weblog) is a diary-like information website either created by an individual sharing their opinion on some topic or an organisation such as a media company, university, think tank or special interest group with a number of authors creating 'multi-author blogs' (MABS).

A *wiki* (from the Hawaiian for quick) is a community-created online publication, which any member of a group or team can write, upload and edit. Wikipedia, the online encyclopaedia, is the seventh most visited website on the internet and the only one in the top 10 that is non-commercial, being funded mainly through donations.

Podcasts are audio programmes that can be downloaded and listened to at the time of the user's choosing. They usually feature discussions or interviews on a particular topic or theme, are easy to access, are mostly free and there are so many now available to choose from there is a subject to suit every taste.

Social Media

Social media has become the most popular form of online communication, allowing people to connect with family, friends and strangers, and exchange text, photos, videos and other information across a wide spectrum of platforms. In 2022 the following were the main reasons for using social media in order of popularity:

1. Keeping in touch with friends and family
2. Filling spare time
3. Reading news stories
4. Finding content
5. Seeing what's being talked about

Fig. 15.7

6. Finding inspiration for things to do and buy
7. Finding products to purchase
8. Sharing and discussing opinions with others
9. Making new contacts
10. Watching live streams

Social media use is changing the way in which we communicate, socialise, do business and interact with our communities and the world around us, and it has become a key topic of conversation in the early 2020s. Social media as a technology is still in its infancy, and we are still trying to find our way around it as it continues to throw up issues and problems for society, individuals and governments.

Social Media Use in Ireland

According to DataReportal, the number of social media users in Ireland in 2021 was 76 per cent of the total population. WhatsApp and YouTube are the most popular, followed Instagram and Facebook. Statistics for January 2021 show the following social media use in Ireland:
- YouTube – 89 per cent
- WhatsApp – 79 per cent
- Facebook – 78 per cent
- Facebook Messenger – 67 per cent
- Instagram – 62 per cent
- Twitter – 44 per cent
- LinkedIn – 39 per cent
- Snapchat – 34 per cent
- Pinterest – 31 per cent
- TikTok – 30 per cent

There has been a significant amount of research on the negative impact of social media on our lives. It has been shown to be addictive as there is a chemical reaction, a dopamine hit, in the brain similar to the effect of cocaine when users scroll and see 'likes', shares and posts. This has consequences for the person's real life, and

Fig. 15.8

their work, relationships, health and moods can all suffer as a result. One study found that 5–10 per cent of social media users in the US are addicted. Another negative impact is the reduction in attention span, affecting users' ability to concentrate for long periods of time.

Social Media Disorder is a term used to describe negative psychological outcomes as a result of use or overuse of social media. It is especially prevalent amongst teenagers, and symptoms include depression, anxiety and low self-esteem. Due to the way social media works, people can openly share their thoughts, opinions, feelings and values, as well as photos of themselves, things that previously would not have been so public. As a result, there is the possibility for judgement, discrimination and cyberbullying, which can cause any or all the above-mentioned symptoms.

Social media uses algorithms (a set of steps used to solve a mathematical problem or complete a computer process) to sort posts in our news feed based on their relevance to us and determined by the content of our former posts, shares and 'likes'. In other words, they feed back to us what we send out, and we are fed posts that the algorithms think we will like. This keeps our attention, keeps us scrolling and can be used to post advertisements that are relevant to us. This is how social media make money. They harvest huge amounts of users' information and then sell it to advertisers who pay the social media company to advertise on their platforms. The user becomes the product.

Social media is the perfect vehicle for the operation of surveillance capitalism, a term coined by Shoshana Zuboff. It is when our online behaviour and activities, be they Google searches, social media posts or raw personal data, are monitored, collected and stored to determine our values and tastes and predict future behaviour. This data is sold to advertisers, who then target us with advertisements that match our lifestyle. According to Zuboff, it involves not just predicting our future behaviour but ultimately intervening 'in order to nudge, coax, tune and herd behaviour toward profitable outcomes' (Zuboff, 2019, p. 8).

Another aspect of social media algorithms is that we begin to inhabit a 'filter bubble', a cultural or ideological space online that isolates us from content that we might disagree with due to the algorithm feeding us content based on our previous usage. This creates a narrow range of topics that we are exposed to and results in a lack of diversity of information. The danger is that we are no longer confronted by information that could broaden our interests or challenge our opinions and we develop a one-sided point of view. Similarly, we can become part of online communities that only share our viewpoints and we don't mix with those who disagree with us. These communities are sometimes referred to as 'echo chambers', where our comments are confirmed and 'echoed' back to us by other members of our community. Some researchers believe that filter bubbles and echo chambers are responsible for the increased polarisation and division in society, especially between liberals and conservatives in the USA.

Discussion

Which social media platforms are most popular in your class group? What are the pros and cons of each one? In the opinion of the class, does social media increase social connections or does it increase loneliness?

Fig. 15.9

Videoconferencing

Videoconferencing, videotelephony or, informally, video chat allows people to communicate remotely via the internet using a computer or smartphone with a video camera, microphone and speakers. It can save time, travel and carbon emissions, as people can meet without having to be in the same place. Despite its occasional flaws, such as 'frozen screens', poor audio quality and delays often due to limited Wi-Fi connection, it has become a very popular means of communication.

During the COVID-19 lockdowns there was a major increase in usage, as it enabled people to continue to work from home and avail of distance education as well as socially connect. As the pandemic wore on, some people began to suffer from 'Zoom fatigue' and studies have shown that video calls require us to use more energy than face-to-face communication. We have to work harder to focus on nonverbal communication, such as tone of voice and facial expression, we can become anxious during long silences, and we often feel pressure to 'perform' as we are aware we are being watched by a group of people. For some, remote working and education was a lifeline during the pandemic. For other, it was a struggle.

Discussion

In pairs, discuss your own experiences with video calls, remote working and online classes. Have they been positive or negative? Share your thoughts afterwards with the class group.

▶ Fake News

Misinformation has always been around, but the dissemination of fake news has become much more prevalent due to the increase in social media use. Studies have shown that online false information spreads faster than the truth. A study by MIT (Massachusetts Institute of Technology) found that false information is likely to be retweeted on Twitter 70 times more than the truth. One aspect of this is the 'novelty hypothesis'. People like to spread and share novelty information rather than old news, and fake news is often more surprising than real news and has the novelty factor. Algorithms can't tell the different between what's true and what's false information, so the more false information that is posted and shared, the faster and wider it spreads.

It is possible to factcheck information that might seem dubious using any number of factchecking websites such as Snopes, FactCheck.org, PolitiFact and Wikipedia.

Deepfake

Technology has reached the stage where it can create convincingly real images of people. With Deepfake technology an image or video of a person can be swapped with another person's face or body. This is often done for entertainment value, but the technology can be used more insidiously to add the face of a celebrity onto the body of a porn star, which could then be used to blackmail the celebrity whose face appears in the video. It could also be used to make videos in which politicians appear to say things they wouldn't normally say, but which could convince voters to vote against them in an election.

Go to YouTube and watch the video of Barack Obama explaining the risks of Deepfake technology. You won't believe what he says in this video!

It is important to question the reliability of websites we visit and not to take online information at face value. Ask yourself the following questions to help determine the validity of the information you find:
- Is the same information on other (reliable) websites?
- If it's an organisation/company, who are they, what do they do and what is their ethos?
- Who is the author? Are they qualified in the area they are writing about? Do they have an agenda?
- Are there contact details?
- Is the information well written and presented?
- Does it use persuasive language?
- Is it biased?
- Is it up to date?
- Does it have references to other sources indicating that proper research has been carried out?

The URL (web address) can also tell us about the author/organisation. For example, if the extension is .com, it is usually a commercial organisation, and a .org is usually a non-profit organisation.

▶ Privacy and Security

From the relatively harmless but irritating spam (email advertising) to serious crimes such as identity theft, the internet comes with a number of privacy and security risks. What was once private information is becoming public, whether it is photos on social media sites or the publicising of confidential documents by whistleblowers.

Online surveillance can come in many forms: cookies passing on data for the purpose of targeted advertising based on searches; the harvesting of personal data by tech companies to sell to advertisers; government agencies and internet service providers monitoring our online activities; cybercriminals or hackers trying to steal personal data.

Even with a firewall protecting your computer from unwanted intrusion, once online, your device is not 100 per cent protected. Anyone with the right kind of software could be looking at the contents of your computer. Details of online searches may be passed on to third parties for the purpose of advertising and huge amounts of data has been accessed by security and intelligence agencies. Hackers can break into computer systems and steal personal data. In 2021 the Health Service Executive (HSE) was the victim of a cyberattack in which their IT systems were infiltrated, sensitive data was encrypted and the hackers demanded a ransom for it to be released.

Malware and viruses are transmitted with email attachments or downloads and can cause damage to computers. Children can inadvertently access pornography or violent images. Information exchanged online can travel far on the internet, so it is important to take precautions to make surfing as safe as possible.

Tips for Safe Surfing

- ▶ Use up-to-date anti-virus software.
- ▶ Don't share personal/sensitive information online.
- ▶ Don't share your birthday on social media sites. It could be used to access bank accounts along with other personal details retrieved from other sources.
- ▶ If possible, avoid using public Wi-Fi, such as in a café or hotel. If you do, always log out of any accounts or sites.
- ▶ When asked for credit card details, make sure the page is secure: an 's' will appear after the 'http' in the URL and a padlock icon should also appear in a corner of the browser.
- ▶ Use strong passwords. A long sentence or phrase of gibberish with upper and lower case letters, numbers and symbols is good.
- ▶ Change passwords regularly.
- ▶ Don't open attachments or links in unknown emails.
- ▶ Do an online search for senders'/callers'/texters' identities.
- ▶ Check to see if your email account has been compromised here: www.haveibeenpwnd.com.

- Use two-step/multifactor authentication on key websites/online accounts.
- Think before you click.

Fig. 15.10

Regulation

The original designers and creators of what evolved into today's internet wanted a system that enabled the free exchange of information without any centralised controlling authority. Today it functions more or less in this way. However, some regulation is necessary to make it safe to use. Internet regulation is clearly difficult for a medium that crosses all national boundaries. In many countries where freedom of expression is highly valued, any attempt at censorship is seen as contrary to the Universal Declaration of Human Rights. Most countries, including Ireland, operate some form of regulation, to keep online activities as safe as possible.

Examples of Irish organisations that help in this regard include:
- Digital Rights Ireland (www.digitalrights.ie), which is 'dedicated to defending Civil, Human and Legal rights in a digital age'
- Webwise (www.webwise.ie), which focusses on keeping the internet safe, especially for children navigate the online world
- CyberSafeKids (www.cybersafekids.ie), an Irish charity helping children, parents and schools
- Hotline.ie (www.hotline.ie), which combats illegal online content

Finding a balance between freedom of expression, one of the key ideals of the internet, and regulation, such as censorship to prevent harmful content such as hate speech and racism, is a challenge.

Illegal internet use that can be reported includes:
- Child pornography
- Child trafficking
- Racism and xenophobia

- Incitement to hatred
- Financial scams

For more on legislation dealing with communication technology, see Chapter 18: Legislation.

▶ Children

A report in 2021 by Irish charity CyberSafeKids found that up to 81 per cent of children aged 8 to 12 have social media accounts, 92 per cent have a smartphone and 15 per cent say their parents have no parental rules. It also found that 28 per cent of children have friends or followers who are strangers. YouTube and TikTok are the most popular sites amongst young children and posting videos is one of the most common activities.

Fig. 15.11

Most children felt positive about their online lives and generally felt safe, but some children have had negative experiences online. The following are some of the negative experiences and the percentage of children who had them:
- Contact from strangers whilst gaming – 61 per cent
- Cyberbullying – 29 per cent
- Seeing something online that bothered them, that they wouldn't want their parents to know about (e.g. violence/sexual content) – 22 per cent

Children can be protected from harmful web content by:
- Parents understanding how their children use the internet
- Supervision of internet activities
- Communication with them about their activities
- Placing the computer in a 'busy' area of the home
- Filtering/blocking/parental control systems

During the COVID lockdown, when children were restricted from normal social activities, the internet provided a lifeline for keeping in contact with friends and for attending online classes.

▶ Environment

Electronic waste, or e-waste, refers to discarded devices, from computers and laptops to smartphones and hard drives. Global e-waste is growing by 3–4 per cent annually and is caused by tech companies encouraging upgrades, shorter product lifecycles and falling prices, and the disposal of our old devices. Irish households produce an average of 52 kg of e-waste every year, the third highest rate in Europe. If not disposed of properly, e-waste can release toxic chemicals into the environment as well as contributing to landfill overload. Solutions include keeping a device for a long as possible until it becomes unusable; recycling with a certified e-waste recycling facility; buying a second-hand device; and reusing or reselling the item if it is still in good working order.

Fig. 15.12

Coltan is a mineral that is used in mobile phones, personal computers and game consoles. The Democratic Republic of Congo possesses 64 per cent of the global supply. The mining of coltan in Congo has led to it being labelled a 'conflict mineral' because it has been mined and smuggled illegally by militia groups who have used child labour to extract it by hand from underground. Unregulated mining in Congo causes pollution of lakes and rivers, soil erosion and a diminishing number of mountain gorillas in the region, as miners hunt them for food. Solutions include recycling old devices and removing the coltan for reuse and making sure tech companies use coltan that is ethically sourced.

The CT industry produces up to 3.5 per cent of global CO_2 emissions, about the same as the aviation industry. The energy use of the internet is caused by the manufacture and shipping of devices and the cooling systems of data storage centres. The average website produces 1.76 g of CO_2 per view and a one-hour Zoom call produces the same emissions as a petrol-driven car travelling 2 km. Increasing use of the cloud for storing data means that more data centres are needed. In 2022, Ireland had 55 data centres with another 44 under construction. By 2028 data centres will consume 29 per cent of Ireland's electricity and by 2030 CT will account for 51 per cent of global electricity and 23 per cent of emissions.

Every email we send, every photo and video we upload, every song we listen to contributes to this energy consumption, and video and audio streaming in particular make up to 63 per cent of internet traffic and is the fastest growing driver of data consumption.

Already the big tech companies are making efforts to reduce their carbon footprints, with Apple and Facebook claiming to use 100 per cent renewable energy.

Tips for Reducing Your Online Carbon Footprint

- Delete old and unwanted emails as you go.
- Unsubscribe from unwanted newsletters.
- Turn off YouTube auto-play.
- Avoid using video when you only need audio.
- Power down devices when not in use.
- The smaller the device, the less power usage – use a smartphone or tablet for quick tasks and searches instead of a laptop or desktop.

Discussion

Go to YouTube and enter the following search terms to see these videos on social media and its pitfalls:

- 'Social Media Addiction Steve Cutts'
- 'Look Up Gary Turk'

What do you think of these videos? How do they make you feel? Are they accurate portrayals of life in the technology age?

Chapter Review

1. How can you check the reliability of online information?
2. What are filter bubbles?
3. What are the downsides of social media?
4. How can users maintain their privacy and security online?
5. In what ways are social and working lives being changed by the internet? I don't think this has really been explored, as working from home has increased dramatically during the pandemic. I think this is partly due to cloud computing so people don't have to be physically in an office to access files, and file-sharing websites, but the only working element discussed is videoconferencing. (Cloud computing is mentioned only as a service Amazon provides). I suggest including something on remote work or else changing the question or dropping the `working' bit.
6. Explain how algorithms work on social media.

Chapter 16
The Telephone

In this chapter, you will learn about:
- Telephone Technique
- Voicemail
- Smartphones
- Mobile Etiquette
- Text Messaging
- Health Risks
- Fax

Discussion
What are the key differences between talking to someone on the telephone and talking to them face to face? Brainstorm as a class.

The telephone was primarily created to enable people to talk to each other over distances which were too great to be heard directly. It has evolved from the old landline device with wires and dials to the push button mobile to the smartphone, a miniature computer with touch screen interface, virtual keyboard and a huge range of uses. The telephone is the most widely used communications device in the world and it is estimated that in 2021 there were over 6 billion smartphone users globally.

Fig. 16.1

Since the 1950s there have been several failed attempts to introduce the videophone into the mainstream market, with the belief that everyone would want one. Now we can use smartphones to make video calls for free. What are the advantages and disadvantages of being able to see (or be seen by) the person at the other end of the line?

▶ Telephone Technique

While today's smartphones have multiple uses, it is still important to be able to talk to someone on a phone effectively, especially in the workplace. A lot of time and money can be wasted when a telephone call is badly made, and often business can be lost due to poor telephone technique. Customers must be impressed, and a telephone call may be their first impression of an organisation/company. Improving our telephone skills and telephone manner is simple and can help us avoid being misunderstood or losing business.

A number of simple rules apply:

1. Speak clearly – phone line quality can vary greatly due to the different types of phones in use today. Many people, unconsciously or not, adopt a 'telephone voice', speaking more slowly, politely and neutralising their accent in order to be clear.
2. When making a call, be clear about what you want to say and how you want to say it.
3. Have a pen and paper handy.
4. Make notes of the information you need to give and receive.
5. Keep records of calls – in case you make two calls to the same person by mistake.
6. Pave the way for further contact – there may be new and unexpected developments, or simply more business to be done.
7. Be patient.
8. Use good manners at all times.
9. Use an appropriate tone of voice.
10. Try to be as efficient as possible, avoiding delays.
11. Apologise for any delays.
12. Empathise with the caller.

Discussion

Answering Calls

1. In some countries, people answer the phone by just stating their name. Is this a good idea?
2. What are the pros and cons of each of the following ways of answering the phone? Discuss the suitability of each one in social and vocational contexts.
    - 'Hello.' (This can range in tone from friendly to abrupt.)
    - 'Hello, Drumlinn College of Further Education, Orla speaking.'
    - 'Drumlinn College of Further Education, Orla speaking, how can I help you?'

- 'Drumlinn College of Further Education, good morning.'
- '6319075.'

Placing Calls

What are the pros and cons of each of the following statements in placing calls? Discuss their suitability in social and vocational contexts.

- 'Hello, may I speak to Mr O'Reilly, please?'
- 'Is Sharon there?'
- 'Hi. My name is Joe Dunne. Is Alan there, please?'
- 'I was wondering could I speak to Simon?'
- 'Hi, I was looking for Tanya Wallace.'

Remember that when using the telephone, the person at the other end cannot see our non-verbal signals, so we should remember to be aware of the tone and pitch of our voice. Try to sound friendly and interested.

Activity

If the facilities are available, make some real phone calls. If not, do some role-plays. Here are some suggestions:

- Make an enquiry (e.g. travel times and costs)
- Make an appointment (e.g. dentist, doctor)
- Make a reservation or cancellation
- Make a complaint or apology
- Make a date
- Offer congratulations or sympathy
- Enquire about a service (e.g. plumbing, window-cleaning)

Leaving/Taking Messages

If the person we want to speak with is unavailable, it is appropriate to ask to speak to someone else who may be able to help, or we may be asked to leave a message. Usually we will be asked for our name and number, and we will be contacted later on. However, messages can go astray or be taken down incorrectly. It is advisable to find out who is taking the message. Exchanging names establishes rapport between two people and also acts as a kind of guarantee that it will be passed on. Depending on the type of call, it may be more courteous to call again, especially if we require information or are selling something. In these cases, we can find out when the person will be available for us to call again.

When taking a call, if the person asked for is unavailable, we should find out if anyone else can help. If not, we should take down the following information:

1. Who the message is for
2. Caller's name and company/organisation
3. Caller's number
4. Date and time of the call
5. Reason for the call, i.e. the message

It is important to *repeat this information* back to the caller. It only takes a minute and is worth it to prevent mistakes. If you have one, fill out a phone message slip. A caller should never be left on hold for too long without frequent voice contact, or she may wonder if she has been cut off or forgotten about. If she has been waiting for a few minutes, we can give her the option to continue to hold or leave a message.

Sample Phone Message Slip

Message for _____
Telephone Message _____
_____
_____
Caller _____
Of _____
Number _____
Time received _____
Date _____
Message taken by _____

▶ Voicemail

Some people are still terrified of leaving voice messages and yet they are a regular part of daily communication. One reason we find them so disconcerting is that there is no feedback, and it feels as if we are speaking into a void. The best thing to do is leave a simple message with our name, number and just a few details.

When creating your own voicemail greeting, make sure your message is clear. A voicemail greeting can be formal such as might be used for a business:

▶ 'You have reached [name and/or company name]. Thank you for calling. Please leave your name and number and I will return your call as soon as possible.'

It can also be informal:
- 'Hi, [name] here. Sorry I can't take your call. Please leave your name and a brief message and I'll get back to you as soon as I can.'

Smartphones

With a huge range of apps, internet access and multimedia functionalities such as music player and camera, smartphones allow computing and connecting far above and beyond the normal calling and texting of the original mobile devices.

This raises many questions and concerns about the impact of smartphones on our lives. Are we spending too much time on our devices and not enough time actually connecting with others face to face?

The most popular English-language messenger apps in 2022 were WhatsApp and Facebook Messenger, with 1 billion users accessing WhatsApp every day. The image-sharing apps Instagram and Snapchat are also hugely popular, with over 210 million Snapchat snaps and 95 million Instagram posts every day. This illustrates the growing popularity of image-sharing software.

Fig. 16.2

Discussion

Is the growing popularity of photo-sharing an indication of the human need for face-to-face communication? Or is it because the image can communicate more, and more easily, than words?

Mobile Etiquette

Knowing how to use our devices effectively and with respect for other people is as important as knowing how to get the most from the technology. For example, should we interrupt a face-to-face conversation to take a call? It has been said that by doing so, we are telling the person we are with that we have more important things to do. Frequent interruptions caused by mobile phone use may also damage our ability to focus for any length of time.

Tips for Considerate Mobile Phone Use

- Avoid loud private conversations in public places.
- Obey 'No Mobiles' signs.
- Loud notifications and some ring tones may be distracting or irritating to others – use respectfully.
- Switch to the vibrate setting when in public places.
- Switch off or to airplane mode when in quiet spaces.
- Try to avoid accidental dialling, aka pocket dialling.
- Keep texts concise.
- Proofread texts.
- Respect others by not answering the phone when in an important conversation or a meeting.
- When driving, pull over when you need to text or use your device.

Text Messaging

Text messaging was the unexpected success story of mobile telephony when it first arrived in the 1990s. By the 2000s it was the most widely used form of mobile communication. It is an interesting combination of the chattiness of the spoken word and the physical display of writing. Its immediacy is one of its greatest appeals and yet this speed is what sometimes causes messages to be poorly conceived by the sender and misunderstood by the receiver. Emojis sometimes help, but they cannot replace the support of tone of voice or facial expression. With this in mind, it is good advice never to text when under the influence of alcohol or when angry.

What do the following emojis mean:

With texting, the normal rules of spelling and punctuation tend to be dropped and a whole new form of writing has developed.

Activity

What do the following abbreviations mean:

- NE1
- LOL
- LMK
- IMHO
- FOMO
- ROFL
- AFAIK

Such linguistic creativity can be fun and useful for quick informal exchanges but may occasionally be slipped by mistake into more formal contexts such as letters, reports and college assignments.

Another concern is that predictive texting might be eroding literacy skills as users become more dependent on this facility than thinking for themselves about grammar, spelling and punctuation.

Text messaging apps such as WhatsApp and Facebook Messenger are more popular than SMS (Short Message Service) because they are cheaper, since they use the internet as opposed to a phone network.

Fig. 16.3

Health Risks

There has been much debate regarding the potential health threat, due to radiation, from mobile phones. The manufacturers usually say that their research shows no correlation between mobile phone use and damage to human health. However, hundreds of independent studies show a possible link between mobile use and cancer, anxiety, increased blood pressure, sleep loss and heating of the brain. With the arrival of 5G networks, concerns about their impact on health have caused much debate, with some jurisdictions delaying the rollout until more evidence is collected.

The debate about mobile phones' impact on health is still ongoing, but expert advice is to err on the side of caution.

Tips for the Safe Use of Mobiles

- Keep calls short – no longer than 15 to 20 minutes at a time.
- Young people should use them only for essential purposes.
- Employers who require employees to use mobiles should make them aware of the risks.
- Consider the SAR (Specific Absorption Rate – amount of radiation the body is exposed to during mobile use) when buying a new mobile.
- Avoid texting while driving or crossing the street.

Fig. 16.4

> ## Activity
> Make a list of the advantages and disadvantages of mobiles and smartphones under the following headings:
> - Work
> - Leisure
> - Family/home life
> - Health
> - Security
> - Socialising
> - Relationships
> - Language/communication
> - Education

Fax

A fax machine is really a long-distance photocopier that can send copies of documents electronically via the telephone line to another machine anywhere in the world. It has all but been replaced by scanning and attaching documents to email (see Chapter 17: Email) but for the moment it is still in use. Dial the receiver's fax number, insert the document, whereupon it feeds through, sending a copy to the receiver for the price of a phone call. Sometimes a cover sheet is sent with the message. It usually includes details such as the sender's name, receiver's name, date, subject heading and whether it is a routine or an urgent message.

Chapter Review

1. List five rules for an effective telephone technique.
2. What is a suitable way of answering the phone in a vocational/formal situation?
3. What information needs to be recorded when taking a phone message?
4. What are the advantages and disadvantages of texting?
5. What precautions should we take to avoid health risks associated with mobile/smartphone use?

Chapter 17
Email

In this chapter, you will learn about:
- Using Email
- Business/Formal Email
- Email Etiquette
- Spam
- Phishing

Fig. 17.1

Email, short for electronic mail, is a fast and reliable way of sending written messages over the internet. In fact it predates the internet and was an important tool in its development. The first emails were sent in 1965 as part of experiments with the first inter-computer communications in the USA. With the growth of the internet, email has become one of the most popular forms of communication and is hugely important in the world of work.

Like any online communication platform, email is not a secure way of communicating and should be treated accordingly.

▶ Using Email

Checking for New Mail

Log on to your email account and check the *Inbox, Mail* or *Check Mail* (depending on the email program you use) to read any new emails received.

Sending

To write an email to someone, click on *Compose, Create Mail, New Message* or *New Mail* and a mail window will appear.

There are two main sections to an email: header and body. The header consists of the following:

To/Recipients: Write the recipient's email address in here, making sure it is spelled correctly.

Cc: This stands for 'carbon copy' and relates to sending the message to more than one person. Separate each recipient's email address with a comma or semi-colon.

Bcc: This stands for 'blind carbon copy' and relates to sending the message to more than one person but with their email addresses remaining invisible to all recipients.

Subject: Type in a subject keyword or phrase here to let the recipients know what the message is about.

The body of the email is where you type your message. When you've finished, click *Send*.

Replying

It is good to reply to emails as promptly as possible. Since it is such a fast method of communicating, there should be no excuse for not replying quickly. Even one line acknowledging receipt of a mail is enough. When replying, just click on *Reply* whereupon a box with the original message opens, into which you can type your new message. After composing the new message, click *Send*. The *Reply to All* option will send the message to everyone who received the original message, if there was more than one recipient.

Forwarding

To forward a message, click on *Forward*, whereupon the message is copied into a new mail, and you just fill in the name of the new recipient. One problem with forwards is that you might be exposing someone's private email addresses to others without their consent. To avoid this, delete the original sender's email address.

Attachments

The attachment facility enables us to send pictures, word-processed documents, spreadsheets, scanned images and even programs by attaching any of these to a mail we are sending. Large files can take a long time to send. Many computer viruses can be transmitted via attachments, so *never open an attachment from someone you do not trust or know*. If it is infected, it could cause serious damage to your computer. We know we have received an attachment when a paper clip appears beside the message in the *Inbox*. Ensure you have anti-virus software on your device so it can block any viruses you could potentially download or import through a document you are sent.

To send an attachment, open a new email message and click on the paper clip icon or on Attachment or Attach or something similar. A new window will open from which you can find and select a folder or file from your computer that you want to send. Either double click on the file, or click Attach, Open or Choose File and it will return you to your email with the file attached. You might have to click OK to return to your email. Write your email message and send it as normal.

Address Book/Contacts

As you collect email addresses you can store them in your address book/contacts folder to save you having to remember them.

▶ Business/Formal Email

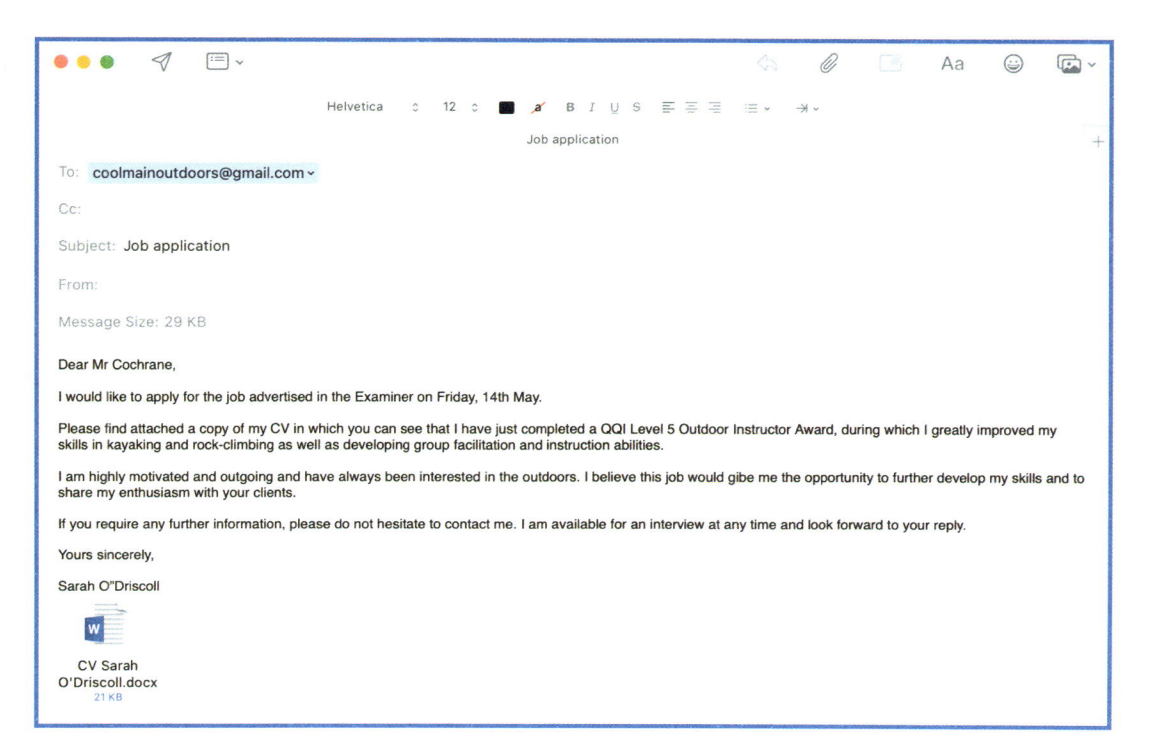

```
Helvetica    12    B  I  U  S
                  Job application

To:     coolmainoutdoors@gmail.com

Cc:

Subject:  Job application

From:

Message Size: 29 KB

Dear Mr Cochrane,

I would like to apply for the job advertised in the Examiner on Friday, 14th May.

Please find attached a copy of my CV in which you can see that I have just completed a QQI Level 5 Outdoor Instructor Award, during which I greatly improved my
skills in kayaking and rock-climbing as well as developing group facilitation and instruction abilities.

I am highly motivated and outgoing and have always been interested in the outdoors. I believe this job would gibe me the opportunity to further develop my skills and to
share my enthusiasm with your clients.

If you require any further information, please do not hesitate to contact me. I am available for an interview at any time and look forward to your reply.

Yours sincerely,

Sarah O"Driscoll

       [W]
    CV Sarah
  O'Driscoll.docx
       21 KB
```

The normal rules of letter writing usually do not apply to email. So how do we write a formal email, say as a business communication or a job application? There are no fixed rules here, and very often the style is still informal and chatty. The sender's address and the date will automatically be sent with the email and the sender writes the subject in the subject box. However, whereas people seldom start an email with the traditional 'Dear Sir' or finish with 'Yours faithfully', we cannot begin a job application with 'Hi John'. The current standards are 'Dear' or 'Hello' followed by a name (Mr/Ms, etc.), and the close is 'Best regards' or 'Kind regards' followed by the sender's full name. You might receive a reply in a far more informal tone than in the mail you sent, but it is better to err on the side of formality at the outset. Let the prospective employer or client set the tone from then on.

Email Etiquette

Due to its speed, email is slightly less formal than normal mail, and messages are written, like texts, in a mixture of spoken and written communication styles. Here are a few golden rules for good email behaviour:
- Use an appropriate email address.
- Use an accurate and concise subject.
- Keep messages concise.
- Respect your recipients.
- Proofread your messages.
- Avoid using capital letters (aka flaming).
- Use paragraphs and bullet points to make it easier for your recipients to read.
- Be aware of your tone and especially avoid irony and sarcasm.
- Avoid negativity and offensiveness.
- Never send an email when angry or under the influence.
- Reply as soon as possible and within one day if possible.
- Use greetings and closures appropriate to your recipient.
- Keep to one email thread per subject, i.e. don't change the subject in a thread.

Spam

Spam is junk email. Because email is inexpensive, spammers send out millions of such emails a day. Some email providers use anti-spam techniques, but they are not 100 per cent effective. If you receive emails from people who have included a large recipient list, request that senders use Bcc instead of To or Cc to keep your address private.

▶ Phishing

Emails pretending to be from your bank, email provider or other organisation asking for your personal details is called phishing. Such emails often ask you to click on a link. If you receive a suspicious email from an unknown source, double-check the email address and/or the website where it originated.

Discussion

In groups of four or five, discuss the following questions.
1. What advantages and disadvantages have you experienced with email?
2. What suggestions and recommendations would you give to others using email?

Activity

1. Go online and find three jobs related to your vocational area.
2. Copy and paste the details of the jobs with contact details and the URLs into a Word document.
   Or
   Take screenshots of the pages and insert the images into a Word document.
3. Type '(Your vocational area/course title) Jobs', e.g. 'Childcare Jobs' at the top of the document and your name in full at the bottom.
4. Edit the document to make it as neat and legible as possible.
5. Save the document as '(Your vocational area/course title) Jobs'.
6. Log in to your email account.
7. Write an email to a friend saying that you have found three possible jobs and asking them what they think.
8. Sign your full name at the end of the message.
9. Attach the '(Your vocational area/course title) Jobs' document to your email.
10. Type '(Your vocational area/course title) Jobs' in the subject box.
11. Send the email.
12. Either print out the document and the email or take a screenshot of the email and upload all the documents to your learning platform, e.g. Moodle.

Chapter Review

1. What is phishing?
2. How would you start and close an email applying for a job?
3. Name five components of email etiquette.

Chapter 18
Legislation

In this chapter, you will learn about:
- Data Protection
- Electronic Communications Regulations
- Freedom of Information (FOI)
- Defamation
- Copyright
- Health and Safety
- Road Traffic Act 2006
- Prohibition of Incitement to Hatred

With the increased use of communications technologies, new legislation has been put in place and old laws updated to regulate how they are used. This chapter looks at the key legislation in Ireland that relates to communications and communication technology.

Data Protection

Everyone has a right to privacy and the protection of their personal information. Many organisations hold information about us such as banks, health authorities, Social Welfare, Revenue, insurance companies and employers. Data protection law helps keep this information safe. The General Data Protection Regulation (GDPR) came into force in the European Union in 2018 and as an EU Regulation has a direct effect in Ireland.

Together with previous data protection legislation, it is known as The Data Protection Acts 1988–2018. These provide citizens (data subjects) with rights regarding their personal data and give responsibilities to those organisations (data controllers) who keep the data. Sometimes data controllers employ other organisations (data processors) to process the data on its behalf.

Personal data is information relating to a person or information that can identify a person. Examples include name, contact details, date of birth, IP address, PPS number, audiovisual recordings, access cards and location data.

As data subjects, we have the following rights:

- The right to be informed if, how and why our data is being processed
- The right to access, i.e. to get a copy of the data
- The right to rectification, i.e. to correct inaccurate data
- The right to erasure/right 'to be forgotten', i.e. to have the data deleted
- The right to restrict processing, e.g. to limit how our data is being used

Fig. 18.1

- The right to data portability, i.e. to copy, move or transfer our data safely
- The right to object, i.e. to prevent our data being processed in certain circumstances and an absolute right to stop it being used for marketing
- Rights in relation to automated decision-making and profiling, i.e. without human intervention where it might significantly affect us

Data controllers have the following obligations:

- To process data lawfully, fairly and transparently
- To process it for one or more specific and lawful purposes
- To limit the data to what is necessary
- To keep it accurate and up to date
- To store it for no longer than necessary
- To protect against unauthorised or unlawful processing, accidental loss, destruction or damage
- To supply a copy of the data to an individual on his/her request

The Data Protection Commission is the national independent authority responsible for upholding the rights of individuals to have their data protected and to ensure that data controllers comply with data protection legislation.

In order to comply with GDPR, websites must:

- Seek users' consent before using cookies
- Provide information about the data tracked by the cookies
- Store consent provided by users

- Allow users to continue to use the website even if they refuse to allow cookies
- Make it easy for users to withhold consent

For more information, visit http://www.dataprotection.ie

Electronic Communications Regulations

The Harassment, Harmful Communications and Related Offences Act 2020, sometimes referred to as 'Coco's Law' (after Nicole 'Coco' Fox Fenlon who took her own life after a period of sustained cyberbullying), makes it an offence to:

- Distribute or publish any threatening or grossly offensive communication about another person or send any threatening or grossly offensive communication to another person with intent to cause harm and intentionally or recklessly seriously interferes with the other person's peace and privacy or causes alarm or distress to the other person
- Take, distribute, publish or threaten to distribute intimate images without consent, with intent to cause harm
- Record, distribute, publish or threaten to distribute intimate images without consent and which interferes with the peace or privacy or causes alarm, distress or harm

Fig. 18.2

Penalties for such offences include fines and/or imprisonment.

Related to this, under the Child Trafficking and Pornography Act 1998, sexting, the sharing of sexually explicit images, is illegal for anyone under the age of 18.

The following are due to be enacted as of 2022:

1. The Online Safety and Media Regulation Bill will deal with harmful online content

    https://www.gov.ie/en/publication/d8e4c-online-safety-and-media-regulation-bill/#online-safety

It seeks to establish the office of a Digital Safety Commissioner to oversee and regulate procedures for removing harmful digital communications, to provide codes of practice and set up an advisory committee.
2. EU Digital Services Act

In 2022 the European Parliament voted in favour of the Digital Services Act which will:
- Deal with illegal online content
- Tackle the spread of false information
- Make social media platforms responsible for their algorithms
- Make it easy for users to refuse targeted advertising

Freedom of Information (FOI)

Under the Freedom of Information Act 2014 (which repealed the former 1998 and 2003 Acts), members of the public have a legal right to official information held by all public bodies unless they are specifically exempt. Exemptions include certain records held by the courts, the Criminal Assets Bureau, the Defence Forces and some records held by An Garda Síochána.

Citizens have the following rights:
- To access information held by government departments and other bodies where the FOI applies
- To have personal information relating to them changed if it is incorrect, incomplete or misleading
- To obtain reasons for any decisions that affect them

Public bodies are entitled to charge a fee for the search and retrieval of the information with the exception of a request for one's own personal information.

For more information, visit http://foi.gov.ie

Defamation

The Defamation Act 2009 protects individuals from having their reputation damaged by the publication of false statements. A defamatory statement is defined as a 'statement that tends to injure a person's reputation in the eyes of reasonable members of society'. The law generally affects publication by the media such as newspapers, magazines, TV, radio and electronic media such as blogs, internet articles and social media. Such defamation can be in the form of text, images, sound recordings or video.

Article 40.6.1.i of the Irish Constitution guarantees freedom of expression, but defamation is one limitation on freedom of expression.

The right to one's good name or reputation is also protected by the Irish Constitution, and a damaged reputation can lead to difficulties that could negatively affect an individual's family and working life.

For a statement to be defamatory:
- It must be published
- It must be false
- It must refer to the complainant

Claims for defamation can be made to clear one's good name or to seek damages as compensation. They can be expensive, requiring a solicitor, evidence and proof that damage has actually been caused.

With the growth of social media use, the number of defamation cases has increased in recent years. Social media users do not always check the information they share online because it is so easy to do so without due consideration, and awards of up to €75,000 in damages have been made in some cases.

The Government has committed to review and reform Irish defamation laws to ensure a balance between freedom of expression and the protection of reputation. The media argue that the current law inhibits freedom of the press to investigate high-profile figures and corporations due to the threat of costly legal proceedings and is often used to censor the media. They believe that it restricts worthwhile investigative journalism. A government report is due for approval at the time of publication.

For more information, visit http://www.defamationireland.com

▶ Copyright

The Copyright and Related Rights Act 2000 protects certain works from being exploited without the permission of the creator of the work. Exploitation refers to copying, distribution, making available to the public, lending, renting, translating, arranging or adapting the work. These restrictions enable the creator to charge a fee to reproduce the work. Works include:
- Literature, music, art and drama
- Film, sound recordings and broadcasts
- Computer software
- Performances

"MY DOCTORAL THESIS LOOKS LIKE A FAKE? SCANDALOUS! I'LL HAVE A WORD WITH THE BLOKE I BOUGHT IT FROM!"

Fig. 18.3

Exceptions to copyright include:
- Fair dealing, such as when the work is used for purposes of research or review
- Education, such as a passage of text used in an exam or a schools anthology
- Libraries, which have limited rights to copy under certain conditions

Copyright is automatic and occurs as soon as a work has been created. Proof of creation, which might be needed in an action for infringement, can be achieved by the creator posting the work to him/herself by registered post and keeping the envelope sealed. This shows that the work was created before the stamp date.

In 2019, the European Union issued a directive to standardise copyright law across the EU and modernise it for the digital age. The proposed changes include:
- Improved access to online content across borders
- More opportunities for use of copyright material in education, research and cultural heritage
- Better protection for content creators, such as musicians, writers and the press

They will also give more responsibility to content providers such as search engines and social media to prevent misuse of copyright material.

There has been opposition to the new proposals, especially by big tech companies such as Google who believe that material uploaded to the internet will need to be checked by lawyers, meaning a much slower internet experience.

The directive has yet to be transposed into law by EU member states.

For more information, visit the Copyright Association of Ireland at https://www.icla.ie/

Health and Safety

Under the Safety, Health and Welfare at Work Act 2005, both employers and employees have a responsibility to ensure that the workplace is kept free from hazards and dangers.

Employer's Duties
- Manage and conduct all work activities so as to ensure as reasonably as practicable the safety, health and welfare of people at work
- Design, provide and maintain a safe place of work with safe access and exit and which uses safe plant and equipment
- Provide information, instruction, training and supervision regarding safety and health to employees
- Provide and maintain welfare facilities for employees at workplace
- Prevent risks to others at the workplace such as visitors, customers, suppliers and sales representatives
- Have plans in place for emergencies

Employee's Duties

- Comply with relevant laws and protect their own safety and health as well the safety and health of anyone who may be affected by their work
- Ensure that they are not under any intoxicant that might endanger themselves or others while at work
- Cooperate with their employer regarding safety, health and welfare at work
- Use correctly any item provided for protection
- Participate in safety and health training offered by their employer
- Report any dangerous situations, practices or defects that might endanger a person's safety, health or welfare
- Refrain from any improper conduct that could endanger their safety or health or that of anyone else
- Employers are also required to produce:
    1. **A Risk Assessment which:**
        - Identifies any hazards in the workplace
        - Assesses the risks arising from such hazards
        - Identifies the steps to be taken to deal with any risks at the workplace
    2. **A Safety Statement which:**
        - Is based on the risk assessment
        - Contains details of people in the workforce who are responsible for safety issues
        - Is made available to employees
        - Should be reviewed by employers on a regular basis

Visual Display Units

Irish health and safety legislation also makes provisions for the safe use of computers under the regulation 'Display Screen Equipment' or visual display units (VDUs). Under the regulation, employers have a responsibility to:

- Ensure the use of the equipment is not a source of risk for the employee
- Evaluate the safety and health conditions of the workstation in particular with regard to eyesight, physical difficulties and mental stress
- Inform the employee about any risks associated with work at VDUs
- Provide any necessary training to employees who are to work at VDUs
- Carry out further analysis of a workstation if any new equipment or technology is introduced
- Inform employees of their entitlement to an eye test before work at a VDU and at regular intervals thereafter

Breaks

Employers should plan the activities of the employees to ensure work at VDUs is periodically interrupted by breaks or changes of activity that reduce work at display screens.

- Rest breaks should be taken or changes in work patterns initiated before fatigue sets in.
- Employees should not sit in the same position for long periods.
- Short frequent breaks are preferable to longer breaks taken occasionally.
- Breaks should be taken away from the VDU.
- No single continuous period of work at a VDU should, in general, last for more than one hour.

Fig. 18.4

Further information is contained in Schedule 4, Regulation 72, 'Minimum Requirements for all Display Screen Equipment' of the 'Guide to the Safety, Health and Welfare at Work (General Application) Regulations 2007.'

These include regulations concerning:
- Display screen
- Keyboard
- Work desk or work surface
- Work chair
- Space requirements
- Lighting
- Reflections and glare
- Radiation
- Noise
- Heat
- Humidity
- Employee/computer interface

For more information see:
- Health and Safety Authority: www.hsa.ie
- Citizens Information: http://www.citizensinformation.ie/en/employment/employment_rights_and_conditions/health_and_safety/health_safety_work.html

Road Traffic Act 2006

Under this Act, it is an offence to hold a mobile phone, including sending or reading a text message, while driving in a public place. It also includes the use of any in-vehicle communication device, information or entertainment equipment. A mobile phone may be used if phoning 999 or 112, or in an emergency.

Prohibition of Incitement to Hatred

A proposed reform of the Prohibition of Incitement to Hatred Act 1989 will make it an offence to share hate speech online. The law aims to deal with online speech that is racist, anti-LGBTQI+ or offensive to religious groups, members of the Travelling community or disabled people. The new law will provide for the protection of freedom of speech.

Chapter Review

Outline the main features of each of the following:
- Data protection
- Electronic communications regulations
- Freedom of Information
- Defamation
- Copyright
- Health and Safety

Appendices

▸ Appendix 1

Activity: One-way Communication

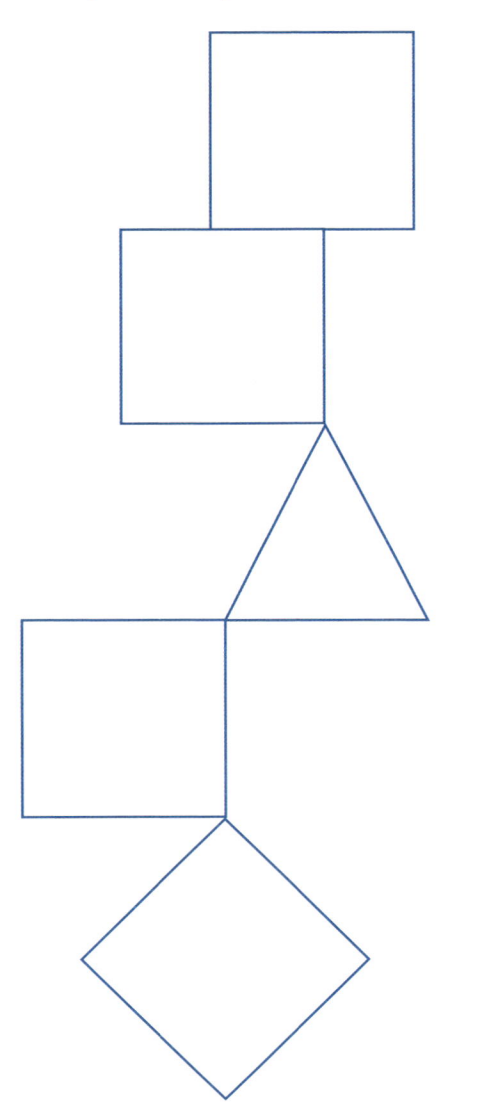

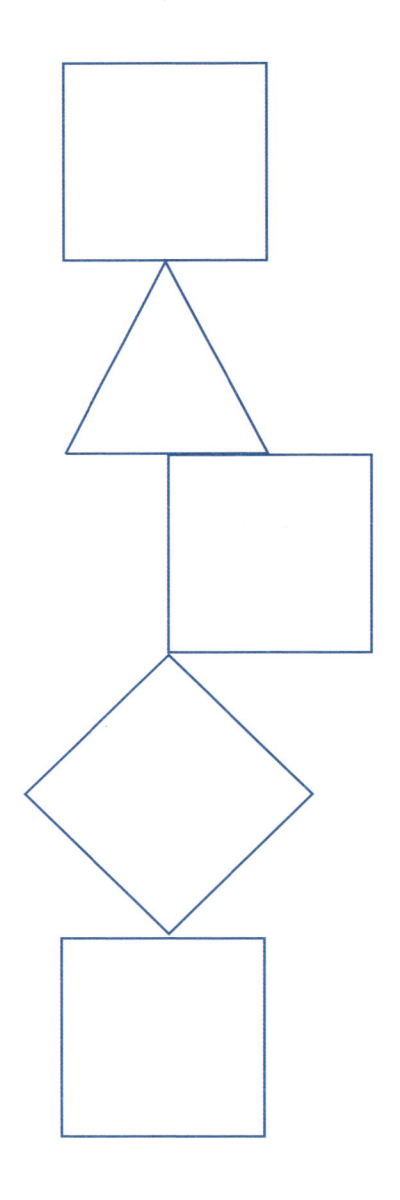

Appendix 2

Gibbs' Reflective Cycle

Gibbs' Reflective Cycle

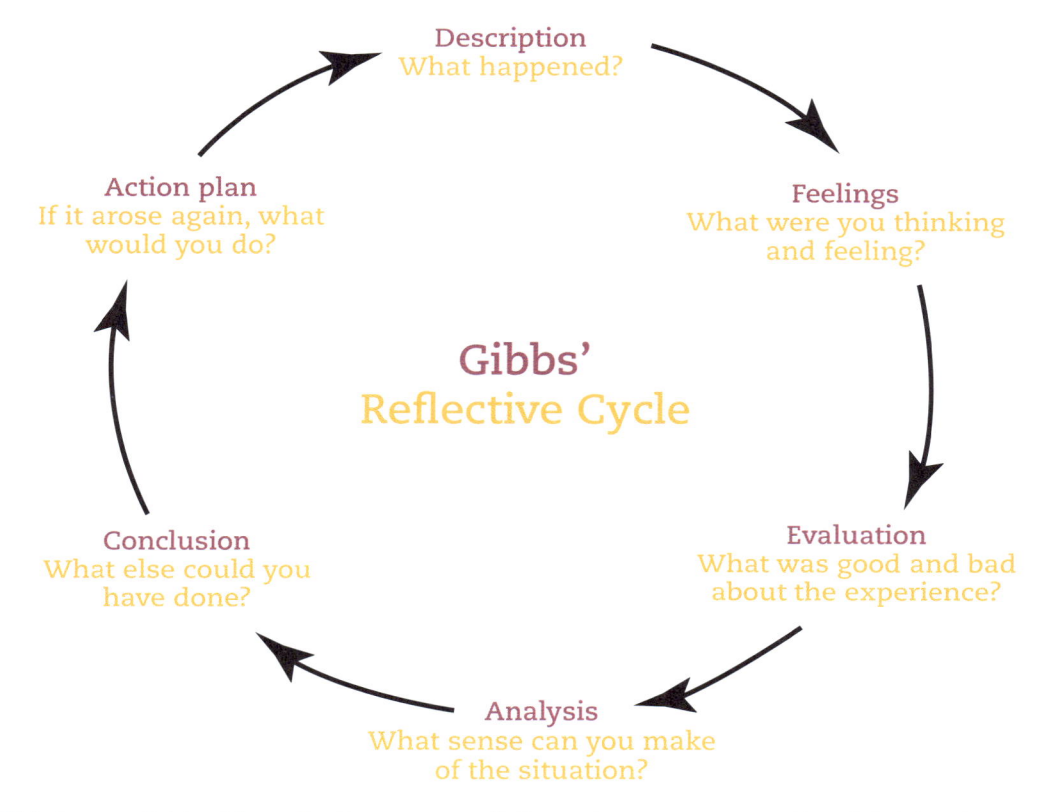

- Description: What happened?
- Feelings: What were you thinking and feeling?
- Evaluation: What was good and bad about the experience?
- Analysis: What sense can you make of the situation?
- Conclusion: What else could you have done?
- Action plan: If it arose again, what would you do?

This is a useful tool for reflecting on an activity such as a group meeting, job interview or oral presentation and learning from the experience. There are six stages to the cycle.

1. **Description:**
   What happened? What, where and when? Who did/said what, what did you do/read/see/hear? In what order did things happen? What were the circumstances? What were you responsible for?

2. **Feelings:**
   What were you thinking about? What did you feel before this situation took place? What did you feel while this situation took place? What do you think other people felt during this situation? What did you feel after the situation? What do you think about the situation now? What do you think other people feel about the situation now?

3. **Evaluation:**
   What was good or bad about the experience? What pleased, interested or was important to you? What made you unhappy? What difficulties were there? Who/what was unhelpful? Why? What needs improvement?

4. **Analysis:**
   What sense can you make of the situation? Compare theory and practice. What similarities or differences are there between this experience and other experiences? Think about what actually happened. What choices did you make and what effect did they have?

5. **Conclusion:**
   What else could you have done? What have you learned for the future?

6. **Action Plan:**
   What will you do next time? If a similar situation arose again, what would you do?

Appendix 3

QQI Level 5 Learning Outcomes and Relevant Chapters

Learning Outcome	Chapter(s)
1. Analyse a range of current issues in communications and information technology.	15, 16, 17
2. Summarise in practical terms the elements of legislation that must be observed in a personal and/or work context, to include health, safety and welfare at work and communications-related legislation.	18
3. Use appropriate nonverbal and visual communication in personal- and work-related settings, to include one-to-one, in a group/team, and in formal and informal interaction.	5, 6, 8 & 9
4. Demonstrate verbal skills appropriate to working under general direction, to include making a case and presenting a point of view in group discussion, formal meetings, interviews.	4, 5, 6, 7
5. Demonstrate listening skills appropriate to working under general direction, to include making eye contact, receiving and interpreting information, control of personal response.	3
6. Use reading techniques appropriate to a task, to include skimming, obtaining an overview, identifying key points, critical evaluation, in-depth analysis.	10
7. Critique information from a range of complex written material, to include technical/vocational, personal, literary, and written and visual media texts.	10, 11
8. Research a relevant vocational topic, to include use of primary and secondary sources, acknowledgement of sources, use of enquiry techniques and methods to establish validity and reliability.	14, 18
9. Use drafting, proofreading and editing skills to write a range of documents that follow the conventions of language usage (spelling, punctuation, syntax), to include creative writing, business proposals, correspondence, reports, memoranda, minutes, applications.	11, 12, 13, 14
10. Demonstrate communications styles and techniques relevant to different situations in work and leisure, to include one-to-one and group contexts in conversation, interview, oral presentation, question and answer session and for the purposes of persuading, advocacy and informing.	4, 5, 6, 7
11. Choose the appropriate communications technology to give and receive requests, instructions, suggestions, discussion and feedback in both work and leisure, to include a rationale for choosing one technology over another in different contexts and for different messages.	15, 16, 17

Bibliography

Aiken, M. (2016) *The Cyber Effect*. London: John Murray.

Barry, A. M. S. (1997) *Visual Intelligence. Perception, Image and Manipulation in Visual Communication*. Albany, NY: State University of New York Press.

Beck, A., Bennett, P. and Wall, P. (2004) *Communication Studies: The Essential Resource*. London and New York: Routledge.

Beddows, C. (1991) *Communication Pack*. Maidenhead: McGraw-Hill.

Briggs, B. (2013) *Introduction to Consensus*. Mexico: Morelos.

Bryson, B. (1990) *Mother Tongue: The English Language*. London: Penguin.

Chalker, S. and Weiner, E. (1994) *The Oxford Dictionary of English Grammar*. Oxford: Oxford University Press.

Cite This For Me. (2022) *Save Time and Improve your Marks with CiteThisForMe, The No. 1 Citation Tool*. Available at: https://www.citethisforme.com (Downloaded 26 February 2022).

Crystal, D. (2008) *Txtng, the gr8 db8*. Oxford: Oxford University Press.

Cuddy, A. (2022) *Your body language shapes who you are*. Available at https://www.ted.com/talks/amy_cuddy_your_body_language_may_shape_who_you_are (Downloaded 25 February 2022).

Daunt, S. (1996) *Communication Skills*. Dublin: Gill & Macmillan.

Dimbleby, R. and Burton, G. (1992) *More Than Words. An Introduction to Communication*. London: Routledge.

Forsyth, P. (1997) *30 Minutes before a Presentation*. London: Kogan Page.

Foy, G. (2001) *Text Production with Microsoft Word*, Dublin: Gill & Macmillan.

Gibbs, G. (1988) *Learning by Doing*. Available at: https://thoughtsmostlyaboutlearning.files.wordpress.com/2015/12/learning-by-doing-graham-gibbs.pdf (Downloaded 25 February 2022).

Harvard Referencing Style (2018). Dublin: UCD Library. Available at: https://www.nmhs.ucd.ie/sites/default/files/harvard_guide_november_2018.pdf (Downloaded 25 February 2022).

Hurst, B. (1996) *The Handbook of Communication Skills*. London: Kogan Page.

Irishstatutebook.ie (2022) *Harassment, Harmful Communications and Related Offences Act 2020*. Available at: https://www.irishstatutebook.ie/eli/2020/act/32/enacted/en/print (Downloaded 26 February 2022).

Janner, G. (1983) *Janner's Complete Letter Writer*. London: Business Books.

Keller, M. (2000) *Social Media and Interpersonal Communication*. Available at: https://www.socialworktoday.com/archive/051313p10.shtml (Downloaded 24 February 2022).

Lester, P. M. (2000) *Visual Communication: Images with Messages*. Belmont, California: Wadsworth/Thomson Learning.

McClave, H. (2001) *Communication for Business*. Dublin: Gill & Macmillan.

McCroskey, J. C. (2001) *An Introduction to Rhetorical Communication*. Massachusetts: Allyn and Bacon.

Molony, S. (2022) *Seven Things We Learned as Facebook Whistleblower Frances Haugen appeared before Oireachtas Committee*. Available at: https://www.independent.ie/irish-news/politics/seven-things-we-learned-as-facebook-whistleblower-frances-haugen-appeared-before-oireachtas-committee-41377728.html (Downloaded 22 February 2022).

Morgan, J. and Welton, P. (1986) *See What I Mean. An Introduction to Visual Communication*. London: Edward Arnold.

Morris, D. (1978) *Manwatching*. London: Triad.

Pinker, S. (1994) *The Language Instinct*. London: Penguin Books.

Purves, B. (1987) *Information Graphics*. Cheltenham: Stanley Thornes.

Raha, M. (1999) *Angel*. Available at: http://www.storybytes.com/view-stories/2000/angel.html (Downloaded 26 February 2022).

Richards, J. C. (2008) *Teaching Listening and Speaking, From Theory to Practice*. New York: Cambridge University Press.

Richardson, W. (2009) *Blogs, Wikis, Podcasts and Other Powerful Web Tools for Classrooms*. London: Sage.

Rosenberg, M. B. (2005) *Nonviolent Communication, A Language of Life*. Encinitas, California: Puddledancer Press.

Scher, A. and Verrall, C. (1975) *100 + Ideas for Drama*. Oxford: Heinemann Educational.

Scott, J. F. and Fox, C. (2005) *English & Communications for Business Studies*. Dublin: Gill & Macmillan.

Seely, J. (1977) *Dramakit*. Oxford: Oxford University Press.

Stanton, N. (1990) *Mastering Communication*. London: Macmillan.

Swann, A. (1989) *Communicating with Rough Visuals*. Oxford: Phaidon Press.

Tovey, H. and Share, P. (2003) *A Sociology of Ireland*. Dublin: Gill & Macmillan.

Truss, L. (2003) *Eats, Shoots & Leaves*. London: Profile.

Van Rooij, A. J. (2011) *Online Video Game Addiction. Exploring a new phenomenon*. PhD thesis. Rotterdam: Erasmus University.

Weiner, E. S. C. and Delahunty, A. (1994) *The Oxford Guide to English Usage*. Oxford: Oxford University Press.

Coffey, J. (2000) 'Nelson Mandela in Trinity', *Trinity Today*. (6), p. 17.

Winser, J. (ed.) (2000) *Future Talk. BT, Millenium Project. A Special Millennium Initiatve*. London: Forward Publishing.

Wood, J. T. (2000) *Communication in our Lives*. Stamford: Wadsworth, Thomson Learning.

Zuboff, S. (2019) *The Age of Surveillance Capitalism*. London: Profile Books.

Answers

Capital Letters, page 166

1. Paula, Robert and I are studying a course at Drumlinn College of Further Education.
2. It's an ETB-run college, the course is a QQI course and I'm on VTOS.
3. The college isn't far from Ballylinane and the M25.
4. Next summer we are going on a sponsored hike in the French Alps to raise money for Concern.
5. I do work experience at Setanta Designs every Tuesday, just behind the Customs House.
6. They dyed the Liffey green on St Patrick's Day.
7. The students aren't all Irish. One comes from Nigeria and another is Lithuanian.
8. Last Wednesday we watched *The Power of the Dog* starring Benedict Cumberbatch and Kirsten Dunst.
9. She said, 'Why don't you come in?'
10. Last year I went to Electric Picnic and this year I'm going to the Festival of the Fires.
11. We had our debs in the Royal Hotel last June and the DJ was rubbish.
12. There's a module in Customer Service, but we don't have to do German anymore.
13. I want to become a physiotherapist with Manchester United when I'm finished.

Subject/Verb Agreement, page 167

1. There are 450 students in the college.
2. Hector, together with his sister, Hattie, walks to school everyday.
3. She is one of those designers who like doing things their own way.
4. The wages they pay are very low.
5. The driver and passenger are happy.
6. That bunch of flowers has seen better days.
7. Which one of you two is the manager?
8. All four of them have a PhD.
9. Each of them was studying for years.
10. *Peaky Blinders* is my favourite TV programme.

Apostrophes, page 169

1. The swimmers' goggles
2. Shakespeare's plays
3. Rameses' tomb
4. The children's toys
5. The dog's bones
6. St Stephen's Green
7. The lambs' wool
8. St Thomas's Square

Apostrophes and Contractions, page 170

1. I couldn't eat another thing.
2. They're all we've got.
3. Don't you have your umbrella with you?
4. Who'll sit in the back with Sarah?
5. She's the best hope there is to win.
6. It's been raining.
7. Who'd have thought you had it in you?

Apostrophes and 's', page 171

1. We're tired of reading Shakespeare's plays. Can't we read some of Yeats' poetry?
2. The buses didn't stop at St Stephen's Green because the drivers' wage increase wasn't enough.
3. We're goin' to Donegal for a fortnight's holiday.
4. I'll get an hour's work done if Peter doesn't disturb me.
5. There's nothin' but rocks on Mars' surface.
6. If Goldilocks' hunger hadn't got the better of her, she'd have passed by the bears' house and none of this would've happened.
7. I've got to go to the doctor's 'cause my tonsils' swelling's got worse.
8. Here's Derek's jacket. It's covered in dogs' hairs.
9. The pub's windows look great but its doors' colours don't.
10. For heaven's sake if it's such a big deal we'll all go to Helen's.
11. The media's got to curtail its habit of prying into people's lives.

Six Hyphens and Seven Dashes, page 172

My sister-in-law came to stay for the weekend – she didn't even ring to warn us! Her husband – my brother Harry – is a long-legged evil-looking man – he even scares the dog. We watched the semi-final on television and then were about to have a big feed of pasta – my favourite – when we noticed the sell-by date on the packet – two weeks old!

Colon/Semi-colon, page 173

1. Out came the sun; off came the shirts.
2. We'll need the following: a hammer, nails, wood and paint.
3. To err is human; to forgive divine.
4. Here's the suspect's description: 6'2", brown hair, brown eyes and a moustache.
5. The speaker began: 'Good evening, Ladies and Gentlemen.'
6. Luxembourg is a small country; France is a large one.

Full Stop/Question Mark/Exclamation Mark, page 174

1. I don't know whether she's in or not.
2. Do we know if there is alien life in the Universe?
3. Help!
4. I wonder if I could borrow your hammer.
5. He told me why he was late.
6. Don't you dare!
7. How far do we have to travel?
8. What a great idea!

Commas, page 176

1. So Joe, do you think we have a chance of winning?
2. The doctor, a large friendly man, prescribed some pills.
3. Singing at the top of his voice, Steve prepared a splendid dinner.
4. Josephine, meanwhile, was reading the paper.
5. 'Don't you think,' she enquired, 'we should call the vet?'
6. The Delaneys live in number 46, and the Mulligans live in number 45.
7. The train, travelling at 120 mph, had 14 carriages.
8. Having finished their meal, the family took the last bus home.
9. I put on my coat, picked up my things, bade farewell and left the building.
10. It was, like, the worst book I've ever read.
11. I told you yesterday, we had to submit the assignment.
12. You're finished now, aren't you?

Inverted Commas/Quotation Marks, page 177

1. 'It's all right,' she said, 'everything will be better in the morning.'
2. 'What kind of a word is "bodacious" anyway?' he enquired.
3. He used to be a successful film producer, but now he's been 'cancelled'.
4. Give us your rendition of 'As Time Goes By'.
5. 'Teachers to Strike' yelled the headline across the front page.
6. In the words of Samuel Beckett: 'We are all born mad. Some remain so.'

Brackets, page 177

1. The ship (if you could call it that) will sail at 10.30 pm.
2. We sat in the shade (it was too hot to do anything else) drinking ice-cold water.
3. The people who are really stressed these days (not counting nurses) are senior management.
4. The books (both thrillers) lay on his desk gathering dust.
5. She shouted after him, '*Ich liebe dich* (I love you),' but it was too late. He was gone.
6. This steady increase in temperature (known as global warming) is set to get worse over the coming century.

Confusing Words, page 178

1. There is a group of men outside, and they're carrying umbrellas under their arms.
2. I've been at this bus stop for 45 minutes and I'm sick of being kept waiting.
3. We're all going to Donegal, which is where we were last year for our holidays.
4. There are two gunslingers coming to this town. That is two too many.
5. It's been a long time since the union got its way.

Two Words or One? Page 178

1. Is there a post office nearby?
2. Communications is easy, whereas Maths is hard.
3. She fell into his arms with a heavy sigh.
4. On the count of three, all together now.
5. When he found it in the river, the briefcase was still intact.
6. He slammed his fist on the table, thereby breaking his wrist.
7. We have to do a practical as well as a theoretical exam.
8. Who knows what's in store for us?
9. Don't you get a lot of ice with your drink?
10. In fact Ireland need three points to qualify.
11. Bring an umbrella in case it rains.

12. That holiday has left me deeply in debt.
13. It will be all right on the night.

More Confusing Words, page 179

1. We dropped into the off-licence to get some beer for the party.
2. Is this a licensed premises?
3. She decided to break off their relationship.
4. I have an awful pain in my back. I hope I don't have a slipped disc.
5. We saw a fantastic programme on television last night.
6. After all the Christmas eating and drinking, he was scared to weigh himself.
7. He called to say he'd be late due to a board meeting.
8. Police are investigating an incident in a city centre shopping mall.

Index

algorithms 240, 245, 247, 270
Alphabet (Google) 239
Amazon 239, 241, 242, 252
Anders, William (astronaut) 135
Angelou, Maya 48
Apollo 8 mission **135**
appearance 112–14
   clothes and 114
   club membership 113
   discussion about 113
   gender 113
   interests and tastes 113
   nationality 113
   occupation 112
   personality 112
   role 113
   sexual orientation 113
   status 113
appendix/appendices 216
Apple 103, 239, 240, 241, 242, 251
application forms 195–8
Arrien, Angeles 75
art 131
attention span 38, 245

baby signing 111
bibliography 216–17
Black Lives Matter 23, 121
blogs 243
Bohm, David, *On Dialogue* 5
Booth, Paul 156–7, 158–9
Bowman, Nicholas David 157–8, 159
business letters 204–6
   general guidelines 205
   layout 205
   letter of adjustment 206
   letter of complaint 206
   letter of enquiry 206
   reply to an enquiry 206
   sample business letter 204

Canva (design tool) 141, 210
carbon footprint 251–2
censorship 249
Chaplin, Charlie, *Great Dictator, The* 105
charts
   bar charts 143, **143**, 225, **225**
   flow charts 144, **144**
   organisation charts 144, **144**
   pie charts **225**, 226
Child Trafficking and Pornography Act (1998) 269
children
   facial expression and 114
   internet and 248, 249, 250
   mobile phones and 236
Chinese miming 132
cloud computing 239, 242, 252
CO_2 emissions 251
Coco's Law 269
coltan, mining of 251
communication
   context 10, 13
   definition 4–5
   guide to effective communication 13–14
   Homo Sapiens and 3
   intercultural 29–30
   media appropriateness 11–12
   the media of 10–11
   Neanderthals and 3
   nonverbal 2, 100
   one-way communication 10
   technology and 3–4
   two-way communication 10

communication needs and purposes 5–7
    (1) survival 5
    (2) co-operation 5
    (3) personal needs 5
    (4) relationships 6
    (5) persuasion 6
    (6) power 6
    (7) societal needs 6
    (8) economy 6
    (9) information 6
    (10) making sense of the world 7
    (11) decision-making 7
    (12) self-expression 7
communication process 8–10
    feedback 8, 9, 13
    interpret/decode 8, 9, 13
    message 8, 9, 13
    noise/interference 9
    receiver 8, 9, 13
    sender 8, 9, 13
communication technology (CT) 233–52
    activities 237–8, 252
    advantages 233
    business (E-commerce) and 241–2
    children and 250
    convergence 236
    disadvantages 233
    entertainment and 242
    environment and 251–2
    examples 233
    fake news 246–7
    impact on society 241–6
    news and information 243
    ownership and control 239–41
    privacy and security 248–50
    regulation 249–50
    safe surfing 248–9
    social media 243–6
    timeline 235–6
    videoconferencing 246
communications revolution 3–4
Constitution of Ireland 270
Copyright and Related Rights Act (2000) 271–2
Cordal, Isaac, art installation **139**
Covey, Stephen R. 34

COVID-19 pandemic 125, 241, 242, 246, 250
critical evaluation 160–1
culture 21–2
curriculum vitae (CV) 198–201
cyberbullying 157, 245, 250, 269
cybercriminals 248
CyberSafeKids 249, 250

dance 7, 131
data centres 251
data protection 267–9
Data Protection Acts (1988–2018) 267
Data Protection Commission 240, 268
DataReportal 244
Deepfake technology 247
Defamation Act (2009) 270–1
Democratic Republic of Congo 251
Digital Rights Ireland 249
Digital Safety Commissioner 270
Dimbleby, Richard, and Burton, Graeme, *More than Words* 5–7
discrimination 23, 26, 59, 67, 245
Donnie Darko (film) 189–90
DSM (Diagnostic and Statistical Manual of Mental Disorders) 158

e-commerce 239, 241–2
e-waste 251
echo chambers 245
Einstein, Albert 234
email 261–5
    activity 265
    business/formal email 263–4
    email etiquette 264
    phishing 265
    spam 264
    using 262–3
emojis 115, 141, 258
environment
    communication technology and 251–2
    nonverbal communication and 129–30
ethnicity 25
ethnocentrism 25
EU Digital Services Act (2022) 271
eye contact 116–17

Facebook Messenger 244, 257, 259
Facebook (Meta) 240, 244, 251
facial expression 114–15
fake news 246–7
family territory 122
fax 260
filter bubble 245, 252
focus group 220, 226
Frankenstein (film) 142
freedom of expression 249, 270, 271
Freedom of Information Act (2014) 270

Gaiman, Neil 105
gender 26
General Data Protection Regulation (GDPR) 240, 267, 268–9
gestures 117–19
Gibbs' Reflective Cycle 90, 106, 277–8
Google 239
grammar basics 165–8
  capital letters 165–6
  confusing words 178–9
  Latin terms 167
  numbers 168
  paragraph 168
  phrases 167
  sentence 165
  subject/verb agreement 167–8
groups 73–4
  effective communication in 76–7
  facilitation methods 87–9
  flying geese, lessons from 74–5
  group discussion 78–9, 90
  group influence 76
  reasons for joining 74–5
  synergy 77
  tips for effective discussions 90
  see also meetings
Guide to the Safety, Health and Welfare at Work (General Application) Regulations (2007) 274
Gyllenhaal, Jake 189–90

Harassment, Harmful Communications and Related Offences Act (2020) 269
Harvard Style of bibliography 216–17

Haugen, Frances 240
Hawking, Stephen 46
health and safety legislation 272–4
Heaney, Seamus, 'Digging' 186–7
Hiberno-English 22
Homo Sapiens 3
Hotline.ie 249

images 134–6
infographics 142–6
  bar charts 143, **143**, 225
  diagrams 145, **145**
  flow charts 144, **144**
  graphs 142, **142**
  histograms 143, **143**
  maps 146, **146**
  organisation charts 144, **144**
  pictograms 143, **143**
  pie charts 226
  tables 145, **145**
informed opinion 160, 161, 187
Instagram 217, 240, 244, 257
intercultural communication 29–30
  (1) resistance 29
  (2) tolerance 29
  (3) understanding 29
  (4) respect 29
  (5) participation 29–30
internet
  birth of 236
  children and 250
  e-commerce and 241
  entertainment and 242
  news/information and 243
  privacy and security 248
  regulation 249–50
  safe surfing 248–9
internet addiction 158
interpersonal communication, social media and 156–9
interviews 61–71
  formal interviews 65
  informal interviews 65
  preparation for 62–4
  questions, types of 65–7
  STAR interview method 67–70, **67**

structure 64–5
  tips for effective interviews 71
invoices 207–8
Irish culture 21–2

Kaepernick, Colin 121
Kearney, Richard (philosopher) 125
Keller, Maura, 'Social Media and Interpersonal Communication' 156–9, 161
Kennedy, John F. 105
Knightley, Keira 135–6, **136**

Le Guin, Ursula K. 2
leaflets/brochures 210–11
legislation 267–75
  copyright 271–2
  data protection 267–9
  defamation 270–1
  electronic communications regulations 269–70
  freedom of information (FOI) 270
  health and safety 272–4
  Prohibition of Incitement to Hatred Act (1989) 275
  Road Traffic Act (2006) 275
Leonardo da Vinci, *Last Supper, The* **138**
letters
  formal/business letters 204–6
  letter of application 202–3
  see also personal letters
LinkedIn 201, 244
listening 34–5
  active listening 39–40
  barriers to 37–8
  control of response 44
  informational listening 36
  interrupting 41
  listening activities 38–9, 42–3
  listening for pleasure 37
  listening to discriminate 37
  listening to interpret 37
  note-taking 41–2
  paraphrasing 40–1
  relational listening 36
  selective listening 39
  self-assessment 35

'Talking Stick' 39
  tips for effective listening 45
  types of 36–7
logos 140, **140**
Lott, Tim, Short Story Tweet 184

McGuinness, Martin **25**
Massachusetts Institute of Technology (MIT) 247
media appropriateness 11–12, 13
media of communication 10–11
  (1) written 10
  (2) spoken 10
  (3) visual 10
  (4) technological 10
  (5) mass media 10
meetings 79–90
  amendment 89
  chairperson, role of 80–1
  communication at 85–6
  conflict 86
  consensus 86–7
  decision-making 86–9
  documents for 81–4
  motion 86
  point of order 89
  purpose of meetings 80
  quorum 89
  roles/formal roles at 80–1
  seating arrangements **85**
  secretary, role of 81
  standing orders 89
  terminology 89
  tips for effective meetings 90
  treasurer, role of 81
  types of 80
  see also groups
memorandum (memo) 207
Meta (Facebook) 240
#MeToo 23
Microsoft 103, 221, 239, 240–1
Milano, Alyssa 23
mind map 95, **95**, 98
minority social communities 22, 24
mobile phones 259–60
  mobile etiquette 257–8

Road Traffic Act (2006) and 275
    safe use of 259, 275
music 7, 130–1

Neanderthals 3
negotiation skills 56–8
news, online 243
noise/noises 9, 38, 128
nonverbal communication (NVC) 2, 100, 110–32
    activities 112, 113–14, 115, 117, 118, 119, 123, 128–9, 130, 132
    advantages of 109
    appearance and 112–14
    art 131
    Chinese miming 132
    dance 131
    disadvantages of 109
    environment 129–30
    examples of 109
    eye contact 116–17
    facial expression 114–15
    gestures 117–19
    music 130–1
    orientation and 124
    paralanguage 127–9
    physical contact 124–7
    posture 119–21
    reactions to 132
    role-play 132
    signs and codes 131
    silence 129
    smell 131
    sounds 131
    territory 121–4
    time 130

Obama, Barack 105, 112, **112**, 247
Olympic Opening Ceremony Tokyo (2021) 120, **120**
one-way communication 10, 276
Online Safety and Media Regulation Bill 269
online surveillance 248
Open Space Technology 87–8

Paisley, Revd Ian 25, **25**
Panti Bliss' Noble Call speech 105
paralanguage 127–9
perception 16–19
    activities 17, 19
    iceberg analogy 20
    people perception 19, 20
    selection 18–19
    sensory variation 17–18
personal letters 190–3
    condolences 192
    congratulations 193
    layout 191–2
    sample letter 191
    thanks 192
personal opinion 161
personal space 122–4
personal territory 122–3
personal writing 181
    activities 182, 184–5, 193–4
    confusing words 193–4
    personal letters 190–3
    poetry 185–7
    preparation 181–2
    reviews 187–90
    short stories 182–5
    tip for choosing what to write 193
    writing as a response 180–1
phishing 265
physical contact 124–7
    functional 125
    handshake techniques 126
    intimate 125
    playful/supportive 125
    ritual 125
    types of 125
    variations 126
Pinterest 244
Pioneer spacecraft 147, **147**
podcasts 239, 243
poetry 185–7
    alliteration 186
    assonance 185
    metaphor 186
    onomatopoeia 186
    simile 186

Poetry Online (video) 187
political correctness 30
posters and flyers 141–2, 146
posture 100–1, 119–21
prejudice 20–1, 24
presentations 92–107
　audience 96
　delivery 100–1
　extended conversation 94
　handouts 104
　mind map 95, 98
　practising 99, 105
　preparation 95–6, 105–6
　public speaking, fear of 93–4
　questions, dealing with 104
　structure and organisation 96–9
　support material 102–4
　timeline of presentation 99
　tips for 106
　venue 101
　visual aids 102–4
　vocal warmup 105–6
　see also public speaking
press releases 209–10, 212, 227
primary research 220–6
Prohibition of Incitement to Hatred Act (1989) 275
public speaking
　eye contact 101
　facial expression 101
　fear of 93–4
　gestures 101
　nonverbal communication 100
　posture 100–1
　vocal warmup 105–6
　voice 100
　see also presentations; speaking
punctuation 168–79
　activities 169, 170, 171, 172, 173, 174, 177–9
　apostrophe (') 169–71
　brackets/parentheses () 177–8
　colon (:) 172–3
　comma (,) 174–6
　dash (–) 172
　ellipsis (...) 174
　exclamation mark (!) 174

full stop 173–4
hyphen (-) 171–2
inverted commas/quotation marks ('') ("") 176–7
question mark (?) 174
semi-colon (;) 173
Putin, Vladimir 112, **112**

qualitative research 220, 226
quantitative research 220–5
questionnaires 221–4
questions at interviews 65–7
　closed questions 65–6
　discriminatory questions 66–7
　hypothetical questions 66
　leading questions 66–7
　mirror questions 66
　probing questions 66
　STAR method questions 68–70
　summary questions 66
　see also interviews

race and ethnicity 25
Raha, Maria, 'Angel' 184–5
reading
　activites 152–3, 154, 156–9
　close reading 155
　critical evaluation 160–1
　informed opinion 161
　normal reading 153–4
　personal opinion 161
　purpose of 150–2
　re-reading 154
　reading self-check 151
　scanning 152–3
　skimming 153
　speeds of reading 151–2
　tips for a close reading 155
　types of 152–5
　writing a summary 159–60
reports 214–32
　activities 231–2
　components 215–17
　language and format 219
　long reports 215
　references 218

   research 219–28
   routine reports 214
   sample short structured report 228–30
   short reports 215–17, 228–30
   special reports 214–15
   tips for effective reports 231
   topic, choosing 219
   types of 214–15
research 219–28
   primary research 219, 220–6
   qualitative research 220, 226
   quantitative research 220–5
   secondary research 220, 227–8
reviews 187–90
   activity 189–90
   album review 188
   book review 188
   concert/gig review 188
   Donnie Darko (film) 189–90
   film review 187–8
   purpose of 187
Riverdance 131
Road Traffic Act (2006) 275
Robinson, Mary 105
Rowling, J.K. 150
Rumi, *Gates of Speech, The* 46

Safety, Health and Welfare at Work Act (2005) 272
SAR (Specific Absorption Rate) 259
Scott, Martin, *Donnie Darko* review 189–90
secondary research 220, 227–8
sectarianism 25–6
Seinfeld 124
sexism 26
sexting 269
sexual harassment 23, 125
short stories 182–5
   'Angel' (Raha) 184–5
   Short Story Tweet (Lott) 184
signs and codes, nonverbal 131
silence 129
smartphones 38, 246, 250, 252, 253, 254, 257
smell 131
SMS (Short Message Service) 259
Snapchat 244, 257

social communities 22–4
social media 236, 240, 243–6, 247, 257
   children and 250
   future of 158–9
   information overload 157–8
   interpersonal communication and 156–9
   privacy, protecting 158
   use in Ireland 244–5
   see also cyberbullying
Social Media Disorder 245
socialisation 26–8
sounds 131
space bubble 122, 123
spam 264
speaking 46–60
   advocacy 60
   benefits of 47
   conversation 52–3
   formal speaking 54
   informal speaking 54
   intent and consent 54–5
   language of speech 51–2
   negotiation skills 56–8
   persuasion 60
   presenting a point of view 59
   tongue-twisters 49–50
   voice 48–51, 100
   see also presentations; public speaking
speeches
   three-word speech 106
   viral/famous 105
STAR interview method 67–70, **67**
stereotyping 19
SurveyMonkey 221
surveys 220–1
SWOT analysis 230
symbols 139–40, **140**
synergy 77

Team Ireland **120**
telephone 253–60
   activities 255, 258, 260
   fax 260
   messages 255–6
   mobile etiquette 257–8
   smartphones 38, 246, 250, 252, 253, 254, 257

Index 295

telephone technique 254–6
text messaging 258–9
voicemail 256–7
territory
  proximity and 123–4
  types of 121–4
text messaging 258–9
Thunberg, Greta 105
TikTok 244, 250
time, nonverbal communication and 130
tongue-twisters 49–50, 106
tribal territory 121–2
Trump, Donald 44, 112, **112**, 240
TV streaming services 242
Twitter 23, 184, 236, 244, 247
two-way communication 10, 52

Universal Declaration of Human Rights 249

videoconferencing 246
viral speeches 105
visual communication 133–48
  activities 146–7
  advantages of 109
  disadvantages of 109, 136
  examples of 109
  images 134–6
  infographics 142–6
  posters and flyers 141–2
  visual interpretation 139–41
  visual language 136–9
  visual message, creating 147–8
  visual production 141
visual display units (VDUs) 273–4
visual interpretation 139–41
visual language 136–9
  basic elements of 136
  boundaries 138
  colour/light 137
  depth 137
  movement/direction 139
  perspective 138
  position 138
  size 137
  texture 137
visual message, creating 147–8

visual production 141
vocal qualities 127
vocal segregates 128
vocal warmup 105–6
vocalisations 128
voice
  articulation 49–50
  emphasis 49, 100
  expression 50–1
  oral presentation and 100
  pace/speed 49, 100
  pause 100
  pitch and tone 48–9, 100
  volume 49, 100
voicemail 256–7

websites
  factchecking 247
  GDPR and 268–9
  useful 201
Webwise 249
WhatsApp 163, 236, 240, 244, 257, 259
Wikipedia 243, 247
Wong, David 234
Wood, Julia, *Communication in Our Lives* 27
workplace documents 195–213
  activities 211–13
  application forms 195–8
  curriculum vitae 198–201
  formal/business letters 204–6
  invoices 207–8
  leaflets/brochures 210–11
  letter of application 202–3
  memorandum 207
  press releases 209–10
  tips for effective documents 211
World Café 88–9
World Wide Web 236
writer's block 182
writing 162–79
  academic writing 164
  activities 161, 162–3, 164, 166, 167–8
  advantages 149
  business writing 165
  creative writing 164
  critical evaluation 160–1

descriptive writing 163
disadvantages 149
examples 149
grammar basics 165–8
instructive writing 162–3
narrative writing 163
persuasive writing 163–4
punctuation 168–79
tips for 160, 179
types of 162–5
writing a summary 159–60
see also personal writing

xenophobia 25, 249

YouTube 124, 131, 187, 236, 239, 244, 247, 250, 252

Zoom 236, 246, 251
Zuboff, Shoshana 239, 245
Zuckerberg, Mark 236, 240